A PRACTICAL JOURNAL OF THE X WINDOW SYSTEM

THE X RESOURCE

ISSUE 1 • WINTER 1992   Y0-BWX-790

PROCEEDINGS

6TH ANNUAL X TECHNICAL CONFERENCE

SPONSORED BY THE MIT X CONSORTIUM

BOSTON, MASSACHUSETTS
JANUARY 13-15, 1992

O'Reilly & Associates, Inc.

A PRACTICAL JOURNAL OF THE X WINDOW SYSTEM

THE X RESOURCE

TABLE OF CONTENTS

ISSUE 1 • WINTER 1992

TABLE OF CONTENTS, *CONTINUED*

THE X RESOURCE: A PRACTICAL JOURNAL OF THE X WINDOW SYSTEM

O'Reilly & Associates, Inc.

The Official Publisher of the
MIT X Consortium Technical Conference Proceedings
and approved publisher of X Consortium public review specifications.

PUBLISHER

Tim O'Reilly

EDITOR

Adrian Nye
(O'Reilly and Associates, Inc.)

MANAGING EDITOR

Alain Hénon
(Usenix Association, O'Reilly and Associates, Inc.)

EDITORIAL ADVISORY BOARD

Jeff Barr (Visix Software, Inc.)
David Bealby (Sun Microsystems)
Todd Brunhoff (Tektronix Resource Labs)
Kevin Calhoun (Informix Software)
Ellis Cohen (Open Software Foundation)
Wayne Dyksen (Dept. of Computer Science, Purdue University)
Jim Fulton (Network Computing Devices, Inc.)
Ronald Hughes (CrossWind Technologies, Inc.)
Bob Joyce (Aspect, Inc.)
Phil Karlton (Silicon Graphics, Inc.)
John Koegel (University of Lowell)
Mark Linton (Silicon Graphics, Inc.)
Chris Peterson (Integrated Computer Solutions, Inc.)
Ralph Swick (Digital Equipment Corporation)
Bob Scheifler with the staff (MIT X Consortium) (acting as a single board member)

COVER AND INTERIOR FORMAT DESIGN

Edie Freedman

TYPESETTING

Interactive Composition Corporation

ILLUSTRATIONS

Chris Reilley

FROM THE EDITOR

The primary goal of *The X Resource* is to improve communication among programmers in the X community. This includes helping application developers understand software tools better, and also helping tool developers understand the needs and experiences of application developers. And we hope not to let anyone forget the end user!

The MIT X Consortium's Annual Technical Conference has traditionally been where the state of the art is discussed, and where future directions and trends are established. But relatively few people can attend the conference. That makes it difficult for the many thousands of programmers who cannot attend to stay up-to-date.

To help solve this problem, O'Reilly and Associates is publishing these proceedings in cooperation with the X Consortium, for the first time. Subscribers to *The X Resource* (a quarterly) will automatically be mailed these proceedings as their January issue. We also hope that ongoing publication of the proceedings will encourage the development of even more and even better papers for future Technical Conferences.

This journal will also publish the Public Review stage specifications of proposed X Consortium standards as special issues. We will provide conceptual introductions that will allow more people to comment knowledgeably on these documents. This allows you to get involved in developing X standards, or at least to get an advance look at proposed standards.

Each regular issue of the journal carries news from the X Consortium. In the premiere issue, published in November 1991, Bob Scheifler describes what's new in X Release 5 including some interpretation that's not found anywhere else.

We at ORA have noticed that standard X contains some undocumented nooks and crannies. For example, there is little documentation on how to use existing extensions such as Shape and the X Input Extension, nor on how to write extensions. There is also a lot of public domain and free software that's not adequately documented or publicized, so people reinvent the wheel. These topics are too small for books, or would be out of date by the time a book could be published. So in addition to columns and practical papers, *The X Resource* contains documentation to fill these holes. Our premier issue contains documentation for *editres* (the new resource editor application) and for some public domain widgets.

Last but not least, I want to emphasize that this journal is for X and for you. We value your input and feedback, since this journal is still just beginning. We need your writing to keep this journal going. If you would like to contribute to this journal, see the last five pages of this issue for basic information.

We would like to thank the USENIX Association for help in producing this issue, and the X Consortium for making it possible.

6TH ANNUAL X TECHNICAL CONFERENCE PROGRAM COMMITTEE

Larry Cable, *SunSoft, Inc.*

Stephen Gildea, *MIT X Consortium*

Sally Vander Heiden, *NCR Corporation*

Sam Leffler, *Silicon Graphics, Inc.*

Stu Lewin, *Lockheed Sanders, Inc.*

Mark Manasse, *Digital Equipment Corporation*

Tom Paquin, *Silicon Graphics, Inc.*

Randy Pausch, *University of Virginia*

Garry Paxinos, *Metro Link, Inc.*

Jeanne Smith, *International Business Machines Corporation*

Amanda Walker, *Visix Software, Inc.*

Can You Bet Your Life On X?

Using the X Window System
for Command and Control Displays

Jeff Malacarne

Abstract

Using the X Window System for life-critical applications requires special considerations for user interactivity, safety, and long system life-cycles. This paper addresses the key issues and approaches for using X for Command and Control displays in systems that direct the movement of real-world vehicles. Growth of the standard to incorporate critical enabling features for this class of applications is also discussed.

I. Introduction

Real-time Command and Control systems, such as air traffic control, vessel traffic, air defense, and Navy tactical systems, are increasingly based on a distributed computing environment with multiple workstations. Workstation operators interact with the system to monitor and/or direct the movement of numerous fast moving vehicles. These vehicles carry human life and frequently operate in densely populated airspaces and waterways. Workstations for these systems must provide operators with a form of multi-media capability by integrating a variety of types of information gathered from multiple data processing and sensor sources.

The X Window System provides a standard baseline for networked graphics that satisfies many commercial applications. Tapping the commercial momentum behind this standard offers several benefits for all distributed display systems. Real-time, life-critical Command and Control systems, however, demand several display capabilities that are not required by major commercial markets and are therefore not well supported by X. A discussion of issues and approaches for applying X to this class of applications is presented as follows:

Jeff Malacarne is a Sr. Staff Engineer at Hughes Aircraft Co.

Section II. Overview of Command and Control Applications: presents a brief description of typical systems in order to provide a frame of reference.

Section III. Integrated Display Requirements: presents several types of information displayed on Command and Control workstations.

Section IV. Applying X: discusses several Command and Control workstation characteristics with respect to benefits or problems posed by using the X Window System.

Section V. Summary/Conclusion: presents a summary of previous sections and discusses future directions.

II. Overview of Command and Control Applications

This section presents brief descriptions of air traffic control, vessel traffic, air defense, and Navy tactical display systems. The primary mission for each system is addressed in order to identify needs for critical display features discussed in later sections. Typical display scenarios are shown in Figure 1.

Air Traffic Control (ATC)

Air traffic control systems direct the flight of commercial and military transport aircraft around the world. The primary task involves constructing and following flight plans that maximize the distance between aircraft within designated air corridors. Control responsibilities are typically divided into three areas; terminal control, approach control, and en-route control.

Terminal control is performed in the airport tower and directs the movement of aircraft taxiing on the ground. Approach control operations direct aircraft during takeoff and landing. En-route control is normally performed at centralized facilities and directs flights as they travel toward destinations at higher altitudes. Controller responsibilities include tracking actual situations, comparing against flight plans, and updating plans as required. Two controllers often work as a team with one controller managing flight plans and the other directing the aircraft. Hand offs of flights are performed between the three control operations and between regional en-route centers. This operation involves voice communication and secure computer networking between remote facilities.

Workstations for terminal control involve standard high resolution monochrome and color monitors, but must provide a viewable display in bright sunlight. Modern approach and en-route control workstations almost exclusively utilize a 2kx2k color monitor. A large viewing area (20"x20"), square aspect ratio, and flat CRT surface are standard requirements. Displayed information includes data derived from external radar systems (tracks), and real-time interactivity must be maintained under all display load conditions. Multi-screen workstations often use additional lower resolution screens (1280x1024) to provide auxiliary output. Touch screens are used to provide input devices for soft switch panels displayed on the CRTs.

Common workstations are used for multiple controller tasks. Task allocation among controller personnel changes as the traffic load varies throughout each day, week, and season. For example, less traffic must be monitored during night hours and each controller can therefore be responsible for a larger area. Workstations must be

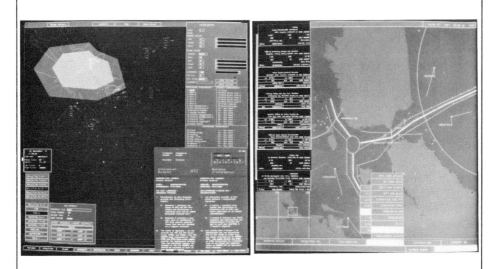

(a) Air Traffic Control   *(b) Vessel Traffic Services*

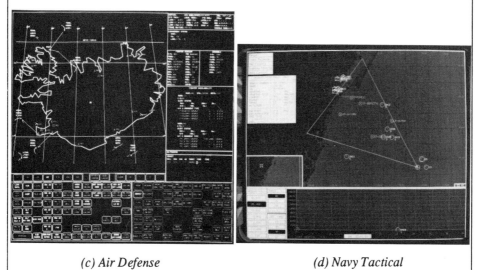

(c) Air Defense   *(d) Navy Tactical*

Figure 1: Command and Control display scenarios. Interaction using common GUI constructs (such as menus, dialogue boxes, and soft switches) must be supported concurrently with real-time display of externally sourced situation data.

dynamically reconfigurable to allow a single operator (with one keyboard and pointer) to use one, two, or three workstation displays to perform this range of tasks. This requirement dictates networked communication between workstations, and a flexible mechanical structure to allow adjacent workstation monitors to slide out and swivel to face the controller.

Vessel Traffic Services (VTS)

Systems that monitor and/or direct the movement of ships in and around harbors perform many of the same functions as air traffic control systems. One major difference is the speed and mobility of the crafts being controlled. For this class of applications, response times for display updates of radar derived data becomes less critical. Workstations for these systems, however, must meet the same criteria for interactivity and must also provide a large, flat color display surface.

Air Defense (AD)

Air defense systems monitor airspaces for unfriendly intrusion and direct the flight of intercept aircraft or the firing of surface-to-air missiles. This mission differs from air and vessel traffic control since many of the aircraft being tracked are uncooperative and are attempting to avoid detection. Instead of maximizing the space between flights, dynamic intercept plans are constructed to direct aircraft into the same airspace as unfriendly or unknown targets.

Since the aircraft involved are typically moving at very high speeds, the overall reaction time of the system is key to mission success. Workstations for these systems must meet strict real-time performance parameters to ensure that critical information is rapidly available to the operator.

Navy Tactical

Shipboard tactical systems combine air defense functions with surface (anti-ship) warfare and antisubmarine warfare (ASW) missions. A wide variety of friendly and unfriendly vehicles must be detected, tracked, and identified. Air, surface, and subsurface vehicles are monitored and directed. Each operator is responsible for a subset of the environment in terms of area and type of vehicles being tracked.

Workstations for these systems must also meet strict real-time response parameters while displaying a large variety of track and graphics information (including 3D presentation of radar coverage and doctrine zones). Militarized or ruggedized equipment is required and standard high resolution (1280x1024) color displays are used. Large screen displays are often used to allow all personnel in a command center to view a given situation. Control of offensive weapons also requires strict considerations for software reliability.

In addition to user interaction and tactical graphics output, the display of radar video and sonar returns is required. Additionally, TV video and image processing is being evaluated for flight deck observation, target classification, and bomb damage assessment.

III. Integrated Display Requirements

This section describes the general display requirements for an integrated workstation for Command and Control applications. Data sources, content, and display formats are discussed. Typical display formats are shown in Figure 2.

Real-Time User Interaction

Command and Control workstation user interfaces utilize many of the same graphics and window oriented capabilities provided by commercial workstations. Like mainstream commercial applications, these user interfaces involve text and simple graphics windows providing menus, soft switch panels, and system status information. The user interface for the embedded workstation application becomes a primary design issue because it is the controller's full-time job to operate this equipment. Long shifts on watch dictate special attention to factors contributing to operator fatigue such as interaction delays, uneven and non-responsive cursor motion, incorrect use of colors, and rendering flicker. Given the life and death consequences of operator fatigue, optimizing these factors becomes a primary design imperative.

General computer/human interface (CHI) issues regarding menus and soft switch panels arise due to the application specific nature of the workstation. Operator interfaces are limited to a well-defined set of interactions and application software is stable compared to most commercial software packages (eg. word processors). Operators undergo extensive training on the functions and capabilities of the workstation and the application software to become expert users. Graphical user interfaces that are highly menu driven provide several advantages for inexperienced users, but can be a hindrance for expert users. Application experts can interact more efficiently if more functions are available with a single action. Consequently, the first impression of a Command and Control display is often that of a myriad of buttons and switches, much like looking at an airplane cockpit for the first time.

Some systems employ arrays of on-screen push buttons while others utilize hard switch panels or programmable flat panel displays with touch input. Pop up approaches are also utilized to reduce clutter on the display, but static soft panel displays are also employed. Systems that use on-screen soft panels often have touch overlays on the CRT to allow operators to make switch actions rapidly without involving the X cursor. Hard panels offer benefits in terms of tactile feedback for switch actions and can be activated reliably without looking directly at the switch. Menus and soft panels provide more design flexibility but rely on visual feedback (such as highlighting) and require the operator to look directly at the action being performed.

Configuration options for user preferences allow each operator to customize the interface, but this flexibility is usually limited to the orientation of windows on the display. Operator interactions for window placement are restricted to configurations that ensure that critical data is not obscured.

Tactical Real-Time Graphics

Command and Control systems involve the display of radar derived real-world situation information. A typical situation display consists of a 2-dimensional view of

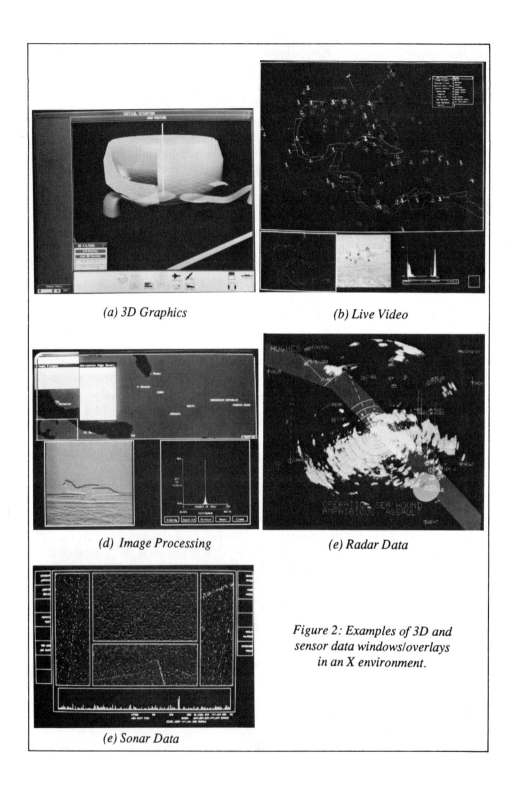

(a) 3D Graphics

(b) Live Video

(d) Image Processing

(e) Radar Data

Figure 2: Examples of 3D and sensor data windows/overlays in an X environment.

(e) Sonar Data

tracks, maps, latitude/longitude lines, radar coverage areas, and air corridors. Display information is received from the system via a LAN concurrently with operator interaction. This creates a second source of input data which must be displayed in real-time. System performance parameters require a maximum delay between radar detection and the display of information to the operator. Graphics performance requirements are strict since this overall time must be divided between radar signal processing, system application processing, workstation application processing, and display generation. Some systems require a worst case workstation response time of less than 150ms from LAN to CRT.

Tracks are graphical objects that represent real-world vehicles and are derived from radar data. Updates of track positions are received from system computers at fixed intervals due to the cyclic nature of radar antenna rotation. These updates must be displayed quickly and, unlike CAD or many other commercial graphics systems, responsiveness to user actions must be maintained in spite of heavy loading during updates. Map and other background data is normally modified in response to operator actions, instead of system requests. Much of the data must be category selectable to filter unnecessary information from the screen. Interactive capabilities for selecting on-screen graphics objects, including tracks, is also required.

Display loads typically include several hundred tracks, each with 5 or 6 history positions or associated radar plots. For some systems, the track load can be well in excess of one thousand. Each track consists of multiple overlaid symbols, multiple vectors, and multiple text strings (see Figure 3). Vectors are normally positioned with one end point at the center of the track position and the other end point at some scalable or non-scalable offset from the track center. Each track history or radar plot consists of a symbol or marker and can be displayed as a cyclic blinking sequence (marquee). The real-time update of tracks and plots creates a text/symbol intensive display load, since the data block of each track typically contains 20 characters.

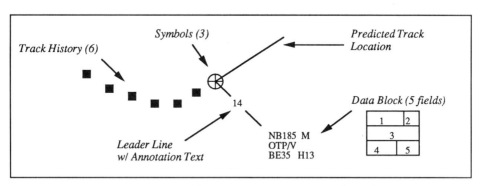

Figure 3: A Typical Graphical Representation of Track Data

Video/Image Processing

Movable and scalable video windows are used for the display of TV Video from cameras, tape, or disc. Uses for video windows include taxiway/flight deck monitoring, viewing remote locations, or interactive training and maintenance. Image processing accelerators provide additional capabilities for improving image quality and extracting information for image understanding. The different types of equipment used in a large system requires workstation support for a large variety of video formats and standards. Video LAN or cable TV type systems are being developed to provide common system distribution mechanisms.

Radar Data

Radar data represents the raw radar returns using a standard video signal format and is often overlaid with the synthetic, radar-derived situation display discussed previously. Instead of a horizontal raster, however, radar video creates a circular pattern. Each scan line spans from the center to circle's edge and represents the amplitude and distance of the return signal in a given direction. The angle of the line within the circle is incremented as the radar antenna rotates. A full rotation of the antenna is rendered as a full circle on the display.

Radar scan conversion for raster displays involves hardware accelerators to convert coordinates and perform image filtering at video data rates. Real-time image processing is required since the amount of radar data that maps to bit mapped image data differs with distance away from the antenna. Data from multiple radial scans are combined to define pixels near the antenna (center of the display) while pixels at the edge may involve interpolation of data between consecutive radar scan lines. Operator controllable artificial persistence (aging) is also provided to mimic older radar equipment and to aid in target tracking.

Sonar Data

Sonar data represents an acoustic depiction of the marine surface or subsurface environment in an area of interest. Active (transmit/listen) and passive (listen only) sonar systems collect, signal process, and packetize acoustic data which is periodically sent to the workstation. This data is normally transmitted via digital computer interface and involves specialized high speed image processing hardware. The workstation's function is to format the acoustic database for display, process operator requests for viewing manipulation, and manage the database as new data is received.

The acoustic formats consist of intensity modulated horizontal, vertical, and circular rasters (B-scan, PPI) and amplitude modulated line segments (A-scan). This data is overlaid with text and graphic support information. A typical acoustic display can contain 2 million bits of data which may require waterfall (scrolling) updates every .5 second.

IV. Applying X

This section presents several issues for Command and Control workstations and related benefits or problems associated with using the X Window System.

Robust GUI

Although the X Window System was developed for commercial workstations and terminals, several capabilities apply directly to Command and Control display systems. Graphical user interfaces (GUI) have resulted in improved computer/human interface (CHI) by tapping more of the human visual system for information transfer. Command and Control display systems can use X to realize these benefits.

Graphics Capabilities

The X Window System does not support several graphics capabilities required for Command and Control situation displays. Situation display support, without impact on user interaction, has been implemented as an X extension set called TREX (Tactical Real-time Extension to X). TREX utilizes X's networking capabilities to support remote client/server connections as well as high speed optimizations for internal workstation connections (see Figure 4). A high performance, multi-context 2D rendering engine is used to provide independent drawing paths for X and TREX simultaneously. TREX provides several PEX-like graphics capabilities as follows:

Track List Management/Display Lists

In a raster display system, several operations such as pan, scale, or window exposure may necessitate the redrawing of data on the screen. With a streaming interface like X, the application must manage a graphics database to retain what was on the screen in the event a redraw is required. Server-side display lists can retain the information required to regenerate the display and remove the need to retransmit large amounts of information across the client/server interface. Display lists can also be edited and/or filtered during display updates and for some systems, can be used directly as the workstation track database.

World Coordinate Transformations

Display data for maps, tracks, and plots are managed in a world coordinate system that is independent from the device coordinate system. Two dimensional transformation of data positions presents a floating-point compute intensive task. Performing these viewing transformations within the server supports world coordinate display lists, reduces the loop for pan/zoom operations, and reduces client/server interface traffic.

Integrated Track Graphics Primitive

The most significant component of a situation display is track data. Tracks that are constructed from independent primitives involve some overhead for processing each primitive independently. TREX provides an optimized

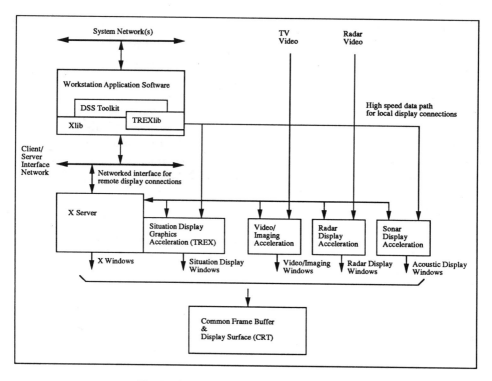

Figure 4: Integrated Workstation Architecture

primitive for tracks which incorporates multiple symbols, multiple vectors, and multiple annotation text strings into a single compact object. Updating track position requires only a single x/y position to be modified for each track in the display list. Track positions can also be copied directly into history symbol primitives within the server during updates.

Multiple Overlays With Double Buffering

High performance update capability can be optimized by separating data with different update requirements into transparent overlays. This reduces the amount of display regeneration required for a given update and therefore increases the workstation's ability to perform updates faster. TREX provides mechanisms for dividing the frame buffer into multiple overlays of programmable depth. Overlays involve more than simple plane masking during drawing to properly handle expose events and double-buffering. Independent double buffering for each overlay is provided. Typically, GUI features reside in an overlay without double buffering while the situation display window utilizes multiple overlays to separate map, track, and radar plot information. Overlays can also be used to provide manageable transparent X Windows.

Blink and Cyclic Plot Display

Several systems require a generalized blinking attribute. Air defense systems often utilize marquee (cyclic) blinking effects for radar plots or track histories. The X Window System provides no blinking capabilities and these features are often hardware dependent. TREX provides programmable blink rates, duty cycles, and blink colors. Cyclic plot display is supported within the server by specifying groups of display lists (containing plots) to be processed periodically. Repeated display list processing (to redraw the plots), combined with double-buffering (to erase the plots), create the desired marquee effect without application involvement.

Deterministic Real-Time Behavior

Command and Control displays, like any real-time system, require deterministic response to input from the system and user concurrently. Many X implementations are Unix-based, which introduces non-deterministic workstation behavior even if "real-time OS extensions" are provided. Independent of operating system behavior, X only provides a single, uninterruptable path to the display. This results in a system with unpredictable response and jerky cursor motion during drawing. Improvements can be made by implementing the server on a real-time operating system and providing multiple, concurrent execution paths for display processing.

X Server and Xlib ports to Wind River Systems' VxWorks operating system were implemented in mid-1989 and have demonstrated consistent behavior with negligible operating system overhead. However, support for real-time response with a single-threaded X Server required the addition of multiple data paths for graphics processing in the TREX extension. TREX provides a second process (and processor) for rendering track updates for situation displays. This approach frees the standard X Server to continue with user interaction tasks concurrently with situation display updates. TREX also provides prioritized, interruptable display lists and streaming interfaces to permit high priority data to be displayed immediately by interrupting other display processing.

Distributed Computing

The X Window System's support for distributed computing provides standard mechanisms for user access to multiple software programs on multiple networked computers. Command and Control systems typically utilize distributed processing and networking to connect multiple computer, sensor, and display resources. X utilizes a client/server model to provide network transparent access to a display from multiple application processes. The server controls client access to the display resources and user input. Client applications can be running locally on the same machine as the server, or remotely across a network on an entirely different type of machine. Multiple clients can utilize display resources with or without knowledge of each other.

One of the primary performance bottlenecks in the X Window System, however, is the client/server interface. Optimized shared-memory interfaces can be utilized for local workstation clients while maintaining full standard network capabilities for remote connections. Augmenting the server with display lists and cyclic plot functionality also reduces this bottleneck by reducing the amount of data transfer required between the client and server.

Popular commercial network protocols, such as TCP/IP and DECnet, are widely used for X. Many Command and Control systems utilize these standards as well, but several also use ISO/OSI or custom protocols. Implementing X using these protocols is achieved by porting at the socket layer or by providing compatible libraries using alternate protocols.

High Performance Sensor Data Display

Real-time display of data from camera, radar, and sonar sensors involves hardware data paths that must remain external to the X Window System. Control of hardware accelerators for video, imaging, radar, and sonar data can be provided via simple X extensions. Each sensor data type is implemented as a modular hardware and software option to support workstation configurations containing any combination of capabilities (see Figure 4).

Video and imaging extensions have been addressed by some X vendors, but the definition of Consortium approved standards has been slow. Simple custom extensions have therefore been developed to control video and imaging hardware to meet current Command and Control display requirements. These implementations will evolve towards standard extensions as they are defined.

Simple X extensions have also been defined to control radar scan conversion hardware. These functions are similar to those for normal video windows and provide basic controls for directing radar data into a window and defining color/intensity maps.

X extensions for sonar data combine TREX display list capabilities with image viewing functions. A server-side acoustic database is maintained and updated by the application. Specialized image viewing transformations are provided to support various acoustic display formats (A-scan, B-scan, and PPI).

Ada

Several, but not all, Command and Control system specifications require that system specific software be written in Ada. Providing Ada bindings for Xlib is therefore a necessity. The X Consortium has offered little formal support for the Ada language. However, public accessible binding source code and supported products by Ada compiler vendors have filled the need. Growing availability of Ada bindings for X toolkits such as Xt and Motif is allowing application software developers to take advantage of these products.

Display Support Software (DSS) was developed at Hughes to provide an Ada toolkit for Command and Control displays. DSS provides support for soft switch panels, tabular displays, and graphical situation displays. This software layer (see Figure 4) forms a configurable service shell that converts application specific objects (such as tracks) into graphics interface objects. DSS supports X-only or TREX platforms to allow application software to run without modification on commercial X platforms during development and TREX platforms for operational configurations.

Another issue exists regarding support for Ada tasking. Xlib must be re-entrant to properly support this capability, as well as to efficiently use the limited memory available in an embedded system. Implementing a re-entrant Xlib can be simplified by supporting re-entrancy only between different display connections. This requires each Ada task to open an independent display connection.

Commercial Software Development Tools

Although Command and Control systems typically involve embedded application software on specialized platforms, using the X Window System allows software development on widely available platforms and tools. Software development tasks from prototyping through program unit test can be performed using standard software development environments and workstations. Using standard environments offers the benefits of lower cost equipment, established training courses, and a common development and target environment. Application programs can execute on standard workstations and can output displays on these workstations or remotely on the target system. This supports early user interface prototyping and display on the actual target server. These benefits alone make X a worthy candidate for any application specific display equipment.

Availability/Reliability

An extremely high workstation availability (approaching 100%) is required for life critical systems. This is achieved by a system design that utilizes redundant workstations, LANS, and host computers. Hot backups are operational at all times to provide rapid recovery upon workstation failure. Fallback modes for degraded system operation are in place and typically run concurrently with the normal operational processing. This allows the backup systems to be continually validated and supports rapid switch-over upon system failure.

A modular, reconfigurable architecture must be in place throughout the system in order for this approach to be viable. X's client/server model supports reconfiguration by allowing remote access to the display by multiple application processing platforms.

Reliability is ensured for application software through the use of formal development processes, but the use of commercial-of-the-shelf (COTS) or public domain software such as the X sample implementation introduces unknowns. Several factors must therefore be examined before this type of software can be used for operational systems. These factors include known reliability statistics from the manufacturer and measured reliability during system development and test.

The cooperative public review of the X Consortium's sample implementation has established a baseline for reliable window system software. Workstation software undergoes years of system integration test in which failure data is collected. To date, workstations using the sample implementation on a real-time operating system have demonstrated acceptable reliability. Integration failures have been repeatable, traceable, and correctable. Ongoing validation with frozen software configurations will support planned operational system requirements and integration schedules beginning in the 4Q92/1Q93 time frame.

Fast Restart

A fast restart (20-40 seconds) upon reconfiguration or system failure is often required for adequate failure recovery. This poses a problem for most Unix operating system implementations but can be achieved using real-time operating systems. Executable images for embedded application programs can be pre-built with the operating system kernel and loaded rapidly from disk or EPROM. This limits the workstation software flexibility but is acceptable because the operational system will utilize a fixed application program.

Display Recording/Playback

Continuous recording of display output for playback is a requirement for several air traffic control systems. This capability allows the review of system and operator actions in the event of a system failure for analysis and identification of corrective actions. Recording of display output directly to tape is not currently possible due to the 2kx2k video format. Can mechanisms be provided within the workstation? This would involve large amounts of data and represent a significant load on the CPU. Capturing of application output can be performed at several interfaces such as the application calls to Xlib, the X protocol, or the hardware interface. Recording cursor motion can be performed by soliciting events, or within the server. The best approach for this capability is still under study.

Maintenance

Unlike typical commercial products, Command and Control systems involve long term (20 year) sustaining and maintenance. This presents configuration control and upgrade problems when commercial products are employed. Due to the expensive integration test cycles for most systems, upgrades of individual hardware or software components are not used unless they offer significant benefits. Standard commercial practice does not normally involve maintaining every released version of a product. This presents a difficulty when problems arise with a version of a component that is no longer supported. It is therefore essential that the system implementor freeze a maintainable version of all components used in the system. Source code and hardware designs are often purchased in order to place the entire system under configuration control. In-house design is often used even though similar products are available. This is due to the cost of design data and difficulties in establishing long term vendor relationships when purchase quantities are relatively small.

The fact that the X Window System sample implementation is in the public domain has allowed system integrators to rapidly develop products and capture the necessary design data. Long term maintenance is under the control of the system implementor and is therefore manageable.

Performance Benchmarking

Workstation performance characterization is critical early in the system design. Several primitive level benchmarks are available for X performance analysis and standard picture level benchmarks have also been defined. However, these levels of performance measurement remain inadequate to accurately determine the performance of a workstation in a real-time Command and Control system. Because the workstation is a component of a specific system solution, graphics performance parameters such as "X vectors per second" are somewhat irrelevant as a measure of fitness for use. For this reason, application level benchmarks must be used to evaluate workstation performance. In general, these benchmarks augment the picture level analysis with dynamic tasks which model the processing of the final application environment. Graphics performance and real-time user interaction are evaluated while LAN processing, data management, and other application tasks are contending for workstation resources.

Commercially available workstations have demonstrated rapidly improving graphics performance overall, but have failed to provide adequate interaction during display processing. Figure 5 shows application level benchmarking results for a commercial Unix workstation and an application specific workstation using TREX. Both platforms utilize 68030 processors and high performance graphics accelerators.

The first graph (Figure 5a) shows track processing performance and demonstrates the relative performance of text optimized rendering hardware versus high end graphics accelerators for CAD applications. Because text performance is critical to many commercial X applications, high performance text configurations for commercial workstations are becoming more common. Track update performance on X platforms is therefore improving rapidly as new products become available.

A more difficult problem for Command and Control applications using X is interactivity. The second graph (Figure 5b) shows the response time to selecting a track during track updates. User response through the single threaded X server and single workstation processor degrades linearly as the track update load increases. TREX, which implements separate data paths and processors for user interaction and track updates, demonstrates high performance deterministic interactivity that is independent of track update loading.

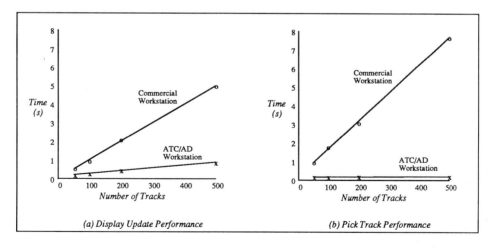

Figure 5: Command and Control Application Level Benchmark Data.

V. Summary/Conclusion

Table 1 shows a summary of Command and Control display characteristics, support provided by the X Window System, and approaches for implementing unsupported capabilities in an X-based environment.

Applying PEX

As discussed previously, display list and viewing capabilities have been implemented in the TREX extension set in order to support high performance updates for situation displays. PEX also provides these capabilities in a form consistent with the PHIGS standard. (TREX was originally developed with the intent of evolution towards PEX). Applying PEX as the graphics standard for drawing situation displays presents performance issues. In addition to PEX, a small extension set providing overlays, double-buffering, and blink capabilities is still required.

As the performance of commercial X Window Systems increase, an architectural tradeoff emerges between standardized graphics functions (PEX) and customized client-side functions (built on top of X only). Figure 6 illustrates this tradeoff. PEX provides standard features at a higher level and simplifies application software development. PEX also provides higher performance for remote display connections. For a given application running locally on the workstation, custom graphics processing in the application can provide higher performance on standard X platforms. This is true if most PEX capabilities are not used and PEX can be replaced with a simple application library. Assuming mature, high performance 2D PEX platforms exist in the near future, this tradeoff will need to be evaluated on a system by system basis.

PEX's primary goal is to provide 3D capabilities in an X environment. The application of 3D graphics for Command and Control displays is currently an active area of research, but high performance 2D is a firm requirement. PEX implementations must, therefore, provide 2D optimized configurations to be cost effective. As stated previously, raw graphic throughput is not the only performance concern. Interactivity during heavy graphics loading is made worse by the addition of PEX processing functions within a single process or thread.

Impact of Multi-threaded X/PEX

The Multi-Threaded X (MTX) development that is currently in progress represents a major step toward providing support for real-time applications. This server architecture allows processing for multiple client connections, device input, and device output to be performed by independent threads of execution. This capability can be utilized to prevent long processing sequences within the server to lock out all other processing.

The extension of the multi-threading effort to PEX is also important for Command and Control displays. The TREX extension in use today provides prioritized, interruptable display lists in a separate processing path from the basic X Server. Replacing this capability with PEX requires multi-threaded display list processing. In

Table 1: X Support Summary

Command and Control Display Characteristic	Issue	X and Commercial Product Support	Current Solution
Robust GUI	Operator productivity	Excellent	X and associated toolkits
Situation Graphics	Concurrent with user interaction	Poor - single thread, limited viewing/ overlay, no blink	TREX Extension
Deterministic Response	150ms application response	Poor - Unix (non-real-time) oriented	Use real-time OS and TREX extension
Distributed Computing	System resource utilization, reconfiguration	Good	X (port to ISO/OSI protocols)
Sensor Data Display	Video data rates	Poor - Std exten. mechanism provided	Extensions for hardware control
Ada	Sample implementation in C	Fair - No Consortium support	Ada bindings, re-entrant Xlib
Development Tools	Development/targ et commonality	Good	X on standard development workstations
Availability/ Reliability	Safety: continuous operation	Fair - software is widely reviewed and in use	Redundancy, fallback
Fast Restart	Safety: failure recovery	Poor - not a primary X market concern	fixed, embedded application software and OS
Recording/ Playback	Safety: failure analysis	No support	To be determined
Maintenance	System life-cycle longer than products	Fair - rapidly evolving but public domain	Capture and maintain public domain code
Benchmarking	Need early performance verification	Fair - primitive level benchmarks available	Application level benchmarking

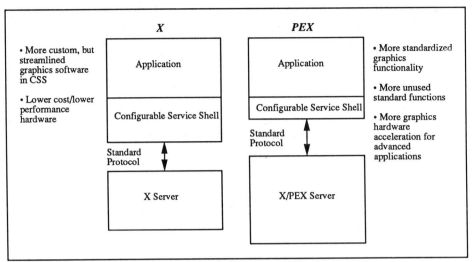

Figure 6: X Versus PEX

general, MTX/PEX will provide smooth cursor response and interactivity during drawing operations such as track updates.

Finale

The X Window System provides a solid basis for integrated Command and Control displays and is being used today in several life-critical systems under development worldwide. Within a few years, commercial airline flights over Canada and Europe will be directed by air traffic controllers using X displays. These systems are utilizing X's support for distributed processing, robust GUI, and public domain source code. The X Window System also offers several software development benefits such as abundant training courses and the ability to prototype application software using commercial platforms before moving to the embedded target. Extensions are currently required to support hardware acceleration of tactical graphics, video, imaging, radar, and sonar data. The development of multi-threaded X and PEX, as well as standard extension definitions for video and image processing, will reduce the amount of custom extensions required in the future.

References

Cooper, Bruce, & Malacarne, Jeff (1991). *Achieving Tactical Performance with the X Window System.* SID 91 DIGEST (18.3). Society for Information Display.

Malacarne, J., Matsutmoto, V., Pierce, C., & Rowberg, B. (1990). *TREX User's Manual.* Hughes Aircraft Co.

Nye, Adrian (1989). *Xlib Programming Manual.* O'Reilly & Associates, Inc.

Current specifications for several air traffic control, vessel traffic services, air defense, and navy programs. Specific programs not disclosed.

Author Information

Jeff Malacarne is a Sr. Staff Engineer for Hughes Aircraft Co., GSG, SSSD, Displays Laboratory. Jeff is the Graphics Technology IR&D Project Leader and is acting manager of the COPS ATC Workstation Development Group. He can be reached at (714) 732-0487 or "jmala@amd-1s.hac.com".

Integrating the GL into the X Environment

A High Performance Rendering Extension Working With and Not Against X

Phil Karlton

Abstract

Previous and current versions of SGI's Graphics Library work by talking directly to the rendering hardware. It also contained its own window system primitives. This made it difficult to define clean semantics when trying to present the system as a unified whole.

The future GL has been designed to be able to exist as an X extension. For performance reasons, it is still necessary to allow local rendering to have access to the graphics pipeline; but the semantics have been slightly tweaked in a few places to allow a clean model to be represented.

This paper discusses that model and how it is expected to be used.

The IRIS GL

The IRIS GL (for "Graphics Library") is a software interface to graphics hardware. The interface consists of a set of several hundred procedures and functions that allow a programmer to specify the objects and operations involved in producing high-quality graphical images, specifically color images of three-dimensional objects. It is convenient to view the IRIS GL as a state machine that controls a set of specific drawing operatons.

Previous versions of the GL, contained many routines not strictly needed for doing 3-D rendering. There were routines for manipulating a window system, e.g. creating and moving windows, manipulating the cursor, etc. Some of these are hard to deal with in an X environment. In particular, the GL colormap model is very different than that of X. (It assumes that there is either TrueColor or ColorIndex and that all

---

Phil Karlton is the engineering manager for the IRIS GL^{TM} project at Silicon Graphics

ColorIndex windows share a single hardware color map with no notion of colormap management.) There were also calls that effectively changed the Visual for a window on the fly. This would be X heresy, but was reasonable within the original GL. Windows were expensive and it was cheaper to recast them than to make new ones. This is because they consume a scarce hardware resource.

There were routines for controlling input devices such as keyboards and mice. There were also string handling routines that assumed an ASCII character encoding and even a menuing package all presented at the same level of abstraction.

For historical reasons, some of the routines were not very graceful about dealing with shared resources. They had originally been designed with the notion that only a single application could have access to the display at a time.

In the design of the new GL, many of the potential incompatibilities were resolved by the simple expedient of removing functionality. Of course, we took care to make sure that X included that functionality, or that it was reasonable for it to be made available as part of the GLX extension.

We view this version as being a "window system neutral" rendering library. (It is specifically intended that the IRIS GL also be used in other windowing systems.) There are a few routines that do not cause rendering, but they are used to either enable special modes in the state machine or to allow the client to read back state.

In the new GL, display lists have taken on additional importance. Because every application is now potentially running remotely, careful use of the facility can substantially reduce the network overhead. Display lists are no longer editable; this means that logical compilation of the display list is possible. For many cases, the highest performance will be achieved only by using display lists.

The GL and X Marriage

The IRIX 4.0 release has addressed most of the problems associated with making the GL behave as a good X citizen. The main capability that is missing is to allow a client to do both GL or X rendering to the same drawable. Part of the problem comes from the fact that the client-server model has been ignored through most of the previous development of the GL. GL applications ported to the new GL/X environment will have to consider where flushing or synchronization of the rendering stream has to be done.

Previous versions of the GL also had the shortcoming of not being able to do GL rendering to a Pixmap or to any kind of window backing store.

The GL specification is purposefully vague on how rendering contexts (the abstract GL state machine) come to be created and how they are associated with a drawing surface. The GL/X interface provides explicit routines to accomplish that. A rendering context can be used with multiple Drawables as long as those Drawables are conformable.

An application may use any rendering context it owns to render into any conforming

Window whether or not that application created the window. As is true in X in general, if you can name an object you can manipulate it. The result of this is that multiple applications can render into the same window, each using its own rendering context.

Each connection can have at most one current rendering context. A rendering context can be current for only a single connection at one time. This latter restriction is often needed by local rendering libraries to prevent race conditions without seriously degrading performance. See below.

X and the GL have different conventions for naming entry points and macros. The GL/X extension adopts those of the GL.

Only a limited amount state is shared between the GL and X: the pixels in frame buffers and pixmaps and potentially the notion of the front and back buffers. (If an X window is configured with more than two buffers, then an attempt to bind a glContext to that window will fail.) At the time that this paper is being written, the definition of the X multi-buffering extension is not quite adequate to support the GL/X needs. A proposal has been made, and if it is accepted, then that API will be made a part of the GL/X model.

For machines on which it makes sense, it is intended that there be a version of the client side library that is protected against multiple threads attempting to access the same connection. This should be accomplished by having appropriate definitions for LockDisplay and UnlockDisplay. Since there is some performance penalty for doing the locking, a non-safe version of the library will also be built. It is not permitted for interrupt routines to share a connection (and hence a rendering context) with the main thread. It will be possible for an application to be written as a set of co-operating processes.

Care must be taken since not all GL commands are available for all rendering contexts. A command that is inappropriate in a rendering context will raise the same error whether it is executed from a list or it is executed in immediate mode.

Sharing Display Lists

Most GL state is small and is fairly easily retrieved using the Get mechanisms. This is not true of GL display lists, which are commonly used for (among other things) potentially large models of some physical object. Since these lists can be large, and since there can be many of them, it is often desirable for multiple rendering contexts to share the display lists.

GL/X provides for this in a limited way; the lists can be shared only if the rendering contexts share a single address space (such as when the rendering contexts are both within a single X server). Via sharing of a display list, a single model can be used in both a double-buffered 4-bit deep visual and a single-buffered 8-bit deep visual. On low end systems, the extra color resolution can be used effectively when animation stops.

Dealing with Non-configurable Visuals

No new GL visual is created in this model. A major change from previous versions of the GL is that allocation of overlay planes and main planes for every GL window is no longer done. It is possible for a client to create Windows with both an overlay and main plane Visual and then to move them in concert to keep them them aligned. To accomplish what was done by a drawmode/gconfig pair in GL4, the GL5 client can use the following paradigm.

- Make the windows which are to share the same screen area children of a single window (that will never get written into). Make the children big enough that they always occlude their entire parent. When something has to be moved or resized, do the operation to the parent.

- Have the subwindows be background none so that the X server will not paint into the area when a restacking occurs.

- Select for device input events on the parent window, not on the children. If input events occur with the focus or cursor in a child, they will be inherited by the parent. Input dispatching will not have to worry about which of the children is on top.

Local Rendering and Atomicity

For performance reasons, it is desirable to allow a GL client that is rendering to a graphics engine directly connected to the executing CPU to avoid passing the "tokens" through the X server. This model specifically allows for that, but does not mandate that any implementation support it. It is important that semantic guarantees not be broken in the local case. When local rendering is happening, the address space of the renderer is that of the local process and not the X server. There will be a way for the client to force X server rendering for the GL calls. Some of the interface semantics were chosen with an eye on performance of high speed rendering in the local case.

The application can mix GL and X rendering calls to the same Window or Pixmap. Note that the two rendering streams are potentially independent, and there is no guarantee about the relative order of execution when mixing the rendering models. Synchronization between the two rendering streams is the responsibility of the application, and can be accomplished by using XSync and glFinsh. Some performance degradation may be experienced if much switching between GL and X rendering is done.

X has atomicity and sequentiality requirements that limit the amount of parallelism possible when interpreting the command stream. Because the local case has already introduced potential race conditions, the requirements on the implementation of the remote case have been relaxed; there is no benefit to having them stronger than the local case. In particular, since clients should be designed to behave correctly in both the local and remote cases, they cannot depend upon strict sequencing of rendering if X and GL are mixed into a single drawable. Maintaining this sequentiality would necessitate unacceptable performance costs for the local client. Synchronization is in the hands of the client can be maintained with moderate cost and the judicious use of the glFinish, glXWaitContext and XSync calls. Without explicit synchronization, the rendering can be done in parallel. This is true even when the rendering is being done by the X server.

Encoding on the X Byte Stream

For the remote case, it is important to minimize the overhead associated with interpreting the GL/X extension requests. For this reason all of the calls have been broken up into two categories.

X requests that hold a single extension request

Each of the glX functions is encoded by a separate X extension request. In addition there is a separate X extension request for each of the GL calls that can not be put into a display list. The two PixelStore commands (glPixelStorei and glPixelStoref) are treated exceptionally. Since they are used to describe information that is not necessarily shareable, they are never communicated to the X server. This information is maintained locally by the client side library. Some of this information is used to minimize the amount of information that needs to be transferred by commands such as glDrawPixel.

X requests that hold multiple GL commands

The rest of the GL calls are those that are eligible to be put into display lists. Multiple instances of these commands are grouped together into a single X extension request (glXRender) as shown in Figure 1.

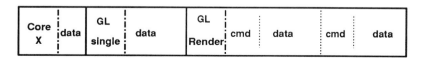

Figure 1: The GL/X byte stream.

This is done in order to minimize the amount of dispatching within the X server. The library will pack as many GL commands as possible single X requests (without breaking the maximum size limit). No GL command will be allowed to be split across multiple glXRender requests unless that GL command started at the beginning of the X requests. In other words, if the command is not at the beginning of an X request, it is completely represented within that X request.

It should be noted that it is legal to have a **glBgnPolygon** in one request, followed by **glVertex** calls, and the **glEndPolygon** in some subsequent request. A command is not the same as a primitive.

Wire representations and byte swapping

Unsigned and signed integers are represented just as they are in the core X protocol. Single and Double precision floating point numbers are sent in IEEE floating point format.

Byte swapping on the encapsulated GL byte stream is done by the server using the same rule as the core X protocol. Single precision floating point values are swapped in the same way that 32-bit integers are swapped. Double precision floating point values are potentially swapped across all 8 bytes.

Author Information

Phil Karlton received a B.A. in mathematics from the University of California at Santa Barbara in 1971. In 1978, he received a M.S. in Computer Science from Carnegie-Mellon University after passing all of his exams in the first two years and failing to write a thesis in the subsequent four and a half years. He joined the System Development Department at Xerox where he worked on Tajo, the tools and window system for the Mesa Development Environment. He was also a member of the Star User Interface Board while at Xerox. In 1984 he joined Digital Equipment Corporation in the Western Software Laboratory. While at WSL he was a member of the original design team for the X11 protocol and also a member of a team of four who produced the R1 sample server. Since 1989, he has been at Silicon Graphics where he contributed to the CASE effort there. Eventually he was given engineering responsibility for the IRIS GL software effort probably as punishment for helping convince SGI to make the GL available by license.

A PostScript X Server

William Raves

Abstract

An efficient, non-interactive technique for generating quality hardcopy output from X Window System clients which conform to a standard toolkit or X library interface is currently lacking. To compensate, an experimental X Window System server that produces PostScript code instead of driving a traditional video tube has been developed. This article discusses some of the implementation issues and explores limitations, outstanding problems, and areas for further work. The operation and performance of the server are contrasted with existing facilities for rendering client windows on a hardcopy device.

Introduction

The X Window System is a popular environment for the deployment of applications which exploit high resolution bitmapped displays, pointing devices, and graphical user interface components. The primary orientation of X development to this point, however, has been very much toward direct interaction with the end user. The production of printed multi-window images and reports has received little attention to date, in spite of the fact that printed output is a requirement for many applications. Printing can be used to capture and document some snapshot of a client's data or to generate pre-defined application-specific reports. This paper summarizes a development effort targeted toward the production of high-quality printed reports and window images within the X Window System environment. In this context, "high-quality" refers to output in the PostScript language which can be rendered on paper by a high-resolution printer. Applications which produce such reports should conform to the X application programmer's interface, rather than some other interface such as that

William Raves (bill@sunquest.com) is a software engineer at Sunquest Information Systems Inc. where he is currently engaged in the development of a clinical information system for hospital intensive care environments.

provided by Display PostScript or InterViews. The primary goal of this effort was "proof of concept" rather than the construction of release-quality software.

Existing Strategies

A variety of techniques can be utilized in the X world to satisfy the hardcopy requirement. This section explores some of these alternatives.

Window Dump

The easiest method is to perform a "dump" of a window or region of the screen. A typical UNIX pipeline to perform this task is:

xwd | xpr -device ps | lpr

The window dump program, **xwd**, produces a pixel-by-pixel **xwd**-specific representation of an arbitrary window on the display. It requires identification of a window to be dumped either by interactive selection or by a *window id* which can be obtained by executing the **xlswins** program. The **xpr** utility converts the window dump data to a variety of target formats. In the case above, the conversion is to PostScript code which consists primarily of an ASCII hexidecimal encoding of the bits of the window. These encodings are processed during PostScript interpretation by the PostScript *image* operator. Although this technique allows the user to guide an X client to an arbitrary internal state, several disadvantages can be identified:

- user interaction may be necessary

- an intermediate image file is produced which can be on the order of hundreds of thousands of bytes

- the output is restricted to what can be displayed on the screen

- the captured image is rasterized and this can result in jagged edges, especially noticeable on textual output.

In short, this multi-stage process is time and space consuming and cannot take advantage of the considerably higher resolutions of devices such as laser printers.

Application-specific Report Generators

An alternate strategy for hardcopy production is to include the report generation module within the application itself. One problem with this method is that the application must be suspended while the report is being generated. This can be a serious problem for complex, multipage reports. In addition, a sizable printing module must be duplicated in each application which supports a hardcopy report capability. If, on the other hand, report generation is handled by one or more separate dedicated printing applications, the invoking process can continue normal execution while the report is being produced but this method is not easily extensible — substantially different reports would require new printing applications.

Faced with performance constraints or a considerable coding effort, it may be decided to sacrifice elements associated with high quality printing such as multiple fonts and point sizes and graphical images. In addition, some of the techniques mentioned above cannot take advantage of components of the screen-based presentation (such as the unique appearance of an application-specific or toolkit-specific widget) without substantial code duplication or re-engineering.

Hardcopy Client Library

Another possible approach is the development of a library which multiplexes between X protocol output and hardcopy output. A possible implementation of such a library might function as a name-space replacement for the X library (**Xlib**) since this is the lowest level X protocol interface *both* for applications *and* for toolkits. The library interface would be the same as the existing Xlib interface — identical function names and function signatures. The drawing functions would direct an output request, based upon some external flag, either to the corresponding Xlib function or to a new hardcopy function. Xlib would exist in its current form except all of the drawing functions would be renamed. Unfortunately, this strategy involves a considerable software effort since the hardcopy portion of the library would have to duplicate a large portion of the functionality of the X server. This includes maintaining state information such as the window hierarchy, handling activities such as window clipping, and maintaining and managing other resources such as pixmaps, fonts, and so on.

In order to avoid some of the problems mentioned in this section, a different approach was taken which leveraged as much as possible from existing software. There is already a well-known and well-proven application in the X environment which can produce high-quality multi-window images. It supports all of the graphics primitives of the X library and, more importantly, at the final rendering stage. This application is the X server itself. The strategy discussed below involved modifying the device-dependent portion of a sample X server to produce PostScript code instead of driving a traditional graphics output device such as a high resolution display.

Implementation

The basis for our port was the sample monochrome frame buffer server which is part of X11 release 4 from the X Consortium. The monochrome version was chosen because of its relative simplicity and its close match to a monochrome laser printer. The configuration of the ported server was a stripped-down version of the sample server — no support for extensions, backing store, or save unders. In addition, as will be discussed later, most of the support for input devices was excised.

The following sections detail some of the issues which had to be dealt with during our port.

Client Connection

The basis for client-server connections in the X domain is the host name of the server, a display number, and a screen number. The syntax of this specification is

hostname:display_number:screen_number

The host name alone is obviously not sufficient to support two servers (one for the display, one for PostScript) running on the same host. The solution was to utilize the display number to distinguish the intended server. The prototype PostScript server uses display number one (1) as its unique identification. It is started with a command line such as

Xps :1 &

and a client would connect to it when given a display specification on the command line such as

-display *hostname***:1**

In an environment where multiple displays might be supported by a separate *display* server on the same host, some distinguished display number would have to be agreed upon. The screen number is not used in the current implementation of the PostScript X server.

There is currently no general mechanism for terminating a client and its connection to the prototype server without user interaction. This "interaction" consists of killing the client process which is suspended in its main event loop, waiting for input events which will never occur. This problem could be solved by developing "friendly" applications which close the connection after drawing or by utilizing a timeout in the server which would automatically sever a client connection that has been inactive for some time.

Server Output

The end result of pointing a client application at the PostScript X server would ordinarily be one or more printed pages. Since more than one client might be generating reports simultaneously, it is not possible to write PostScript directly to the printer. Instead, the server was modified to generate an ASCII file containing PostScript code. A possible strategy for keeping one client from interfering with another would be to start up and shut down an instance of the server for each client, distinguished by appropriate display or screen numbers. However, the solution adopted was to execute the server in the usual fashion, as a daemon, and to enhance the connection protocol of the server to create a unique file for each client. In order to ensure a degree of uniqueness in file names, the current time in seconds is utilized as a component of the file name. When this file is created, a configurable PostScript preamble is written to it initially. When a client connection is closed, a PostScript *showpage* directive is written to the end of the file.

Input Devices

A required step in porting a traditional X server is providing support for input devices. The PostScript server, however, has no need for input devices. Unfortunately, the sample server implementation insists upon at least one keyboard and one pointing device. It was necessary to supply and register dummy devices to satisfy this requirement. A similar requirement was encountered with respect to support for cursors. Again, dummy procedures were supplied and registered with the Screen data structure. Whenever it came to a choice between modifying device independent server code or adding some device dependent code, we chose the latter course.

Coordinate System

The PostScript coordinate system has its default origin at the lower left-hand corner of the page. The X coordinate system origin is at the upper left-hand corner of the display or window. In order to reconcile this difference of orientation, the PostScript output is globally translated to the top of the page with the following statement:

0 792 translate

This still is not sufficient since drawing along the positive y axis results in figures which move down the X display but up (and off) the PostScript page. To rectify this situation, the server negates all y-axis coordinates so that the drawing direction is oriented the same way as in the X world. The net result of global translation and y coordinate negation is to duplicate the X coordinate system model on the printed page. Note that, in our implementation, it is possible to supply a customized preamble to the server which can augment or override these global transformations, resulting in output which can be arbitrarily scaled, translated, or rotated.

Drawing Primitives

The final step of our port was the development of device-dependent drawing primitives that must be hooked into the graphics context and screen data structures of the server. The initial goal was to maximize the use of existing server code.

Drawing Functions

Recall that this port was based upon the monochrome frame buffer version of the sample server. This code assumes a memory-resident frame buffer whose dimensions match those of the display. The server relies upon the device-dependent layer (which may, in turn, rely upon the operating system) to see to it that the frame buffer representation is kept in sync with the state of the actual display hardware. All drawing is accomplished by setting and clearing bits in this region of memory. In fact, drawing can involve combining bits using any of the boolean-based functions taken from the following set:

Function	Definition
and	src AND dst
and-inverted	(NOT src) AND dst
and-reverse	src AND (NOT dst)
clear	0
copy	src
copy-inverted	NOT src
equiv	(NOT src) XOR dst
invert	NOT dst
nand	(NOT src) OR (NOT dst)
noop	dst
nor	(NOT src) AND (NOT dst)
or	src OR dst
or-inverted	(NOT src) OR dst
or-reverse	src OR (NOT dst)
set	1
xor	src XOR dst

Table 1: X drawing functions

Figure 1 illustrates the effects of applying these operations to a bitmap image and the tiled background of a window. The bitmap background color is white, the foreground color is black, and the window background is a 50% gray. Source and destination were combined using the **XCopyArea**() function.

The drawing primitives in the PostScript server, however, function somewhat differently. They do not manipulate bits in a memory buffer — they write PostScript code to a file. This underscores the most obvious short-coming of the PostScript X server. Since it does not retain what has already been drawn on the page, it cannot implement many of the drawing functions which combine bits of the source and destination. Figure 2 shows the results of the 16 logical drawing functions when processed by the PostScript X server. The functions *clear*, *copy*, *copy-inverted*, *noop*, and *set* present no problem because only source bits or *all* destination bits are affected. Also note that the functions *or* and *or-inverted* can be represented accurately since they follow the PostScript paint model of applying layers of opaque paint to the drawing surface through a mask.

The functions *and*, *and-inverted*, *and-reverse*, *equiv*, *invert*, *nand*, *nor*, *or-reverse*, and *xor* cannot be implemented by the PostScript X server. In practice, however, this does not seem to constitute a serious deficiency for the types of applications which we have in mind. For example, several of the unsupported functions are used in interactive contexts which are clearly beyond the scope of the intended problem domain. The

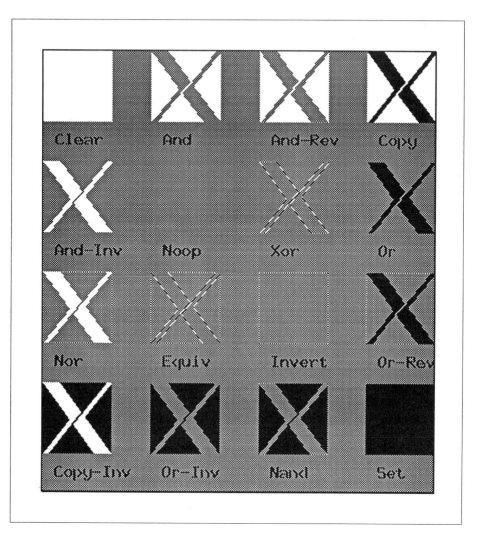

Figure 1: Sample server drawing functions

most commonly used functions in X applications are *copy*, *invert*, and *xor*. The latter two are used almost exclusively for feedback during user interaction. Furthermore, it should be pointed out that this short-coming does not apply to boolean functions between two drawables which are pixmaps when these pixmaps are filled using bitblock transfers (bitblts). Since these pixmaps are still represented in the server as memory regions, their bits can be combined as expected.

A similar limitation exists for *images* which can be regions of a window drawable.

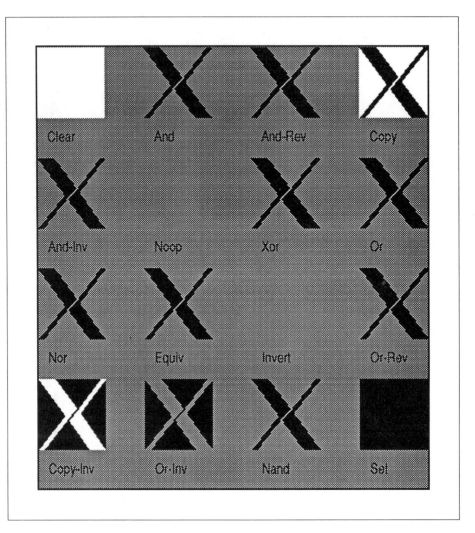

Figure 2: PostScript X server drawing functions

The relevant Xlib functions are **XGetImage** and **XGetSubImage** which can be used to retrieve rectangular regions of windows. Since windows do not have an in-memory version within the PostScript X server, these retrieval procedures are unavailable. Again, this restriction does not apply to images whose source is a pixmap as described above, nor does it apply to the output of images to the printed page. Images are not yet widely used in X applications and, when they are used to represent portions of windows, the context is usually an interactive one.

Pixmap Drawing

Drawing into pixmaps posed an additional problem for the implementation. Since both pixmaps and the frame buffer are areas of memory, the sample server makes no practical distinction regarding the drawing destination. Later, a pixmap which has been scribbled on can be copied to the frame buffer using a memory copy or simple assignments. For the PostScript server, it was necessary to encapsulate drawing to pixmaps in PostScript procedures. These procedures are saved as text in memory until the pixmap is copied to a window drawable or, in this case, to the page, at which time the procedure definition is written to the output file, along with an invocation of the procedure. A record is kept of the pixmap id and its corresponding (contrived) procedure name, so that a procedure invocation can be output whenever the pixmap is copied via bitblts to a window drawable.

A pixmap can be any size and can serve as the destination of an arbitrary amount of drawing. This might result in very large PostScript procedures which the printer may be ill-equipped to handle. The entire procedure must be placed on the printer's operand stack which relies upon limited internal memory. To solve this problem, pixmap drawing is decomposed within the server into a number of smaller procedures which are executed consecutively when appropriate. This decomposition is based upon an arbitrary line count.

Given that pixmap drawing is represented by PostScript code, there are limitations as to what can be done with pixmaps in this server. These limitations only apply to pixmaps which serve as the destination for drawing primitives such as lines and text. Basically, a client can only copy these types of pixmap to a window. They cannot be combined in any fashion with other pixmaps. Again, however, this has not yet proved to be a serious short-coming since most of the time, when a pixmap is drawn to, it is subsequently transferred to a window.

Window Positioning

Although an application connected to the PostScript X server is not subject to user interaction, repositioning of windows can occur as a parent window is in the process of dynamically laying out its child windows. In the sample server, window relocation is accomplished by copying regions of the frame buffer. During client startup, these regions generally only contain window backgrounds and borders since the client will not start drawing into a window until it has received an expose event. However, as was mentioned previously, the PostScript X server has no in-memory representation of these background and border bits — they are only represented by PostScript code already written to the output file. In these cases, the background and border regions of the window at its new destination have to be artificially regenerated by the server.

Area Filling

The monochrome frame buffer code of the sample server handles area filling by decomposing the region to be filled into horizontal spans. The pixels in each span are then turned on or off depending upon color and drawing operation. Although this strategy is not appropriate for PostScript which has its own filling commands based on arbitrarily-shaped regions, it was retained in our server in keeping with our development goals. As a quick, simple optimization, when it came time to generate the PostScript fill code, we coalesced contiguous spans with the same width and the same x coordinate and wrote out a fill sequence for this combined area.

Font selection

The X Window System is distributed with a library of fonts in an X-specific format known as "server normal font". The standard font set has grown over time and, as of Release 4, includes 75 and 100 dot-per-inch fonts from a variety of font vendors, as well as a collection of foreign language and miscellaneous fonts. Apart from the basic design or typeface, each font is distinguished by a set of font properties which includes slant, width, point size, and spacing. In contrast, PostScript fonts are described in a variety of ways including outlines to be filled, lines, or bitmaps. Each font describes a collection of 1 point characters which can be arbitrarily transformed by PostScript operators. The fonts themselves are stored in dictionaries which are resident in the printer. These are supplied by the printer manufacturer or have been otherwise downloaded to the printer.

Since X server normal fonts are unintelligible to a PostScript interpreter, the problem for the PostScript X server is to match the font specified by the X client to a font available on the printer. This problem is similar to font matching problems faced by X clients when they are given a font specification which is not supported by the display server. Either a default font must be selected or some heuristics must be employed to pick a close approximation. Information about X fonts has been standardized according to the "X Logical Font Description". This description includes the font name and typographic properties such as slant, width, point size, and spacing. The point size property can be utilized as is since the PostScript interpreter can scale a font to an arbitrary point size. The family, weight, and slant properties from the logical font description are used in font selection in the server. Rather than hardwire the selection mechanism into the server, a configuration file specifies a mapping between these properties and a font name known to the printer. Table 2 provides a representation of a portion of such a file.

family	weight	slant	printer font
Times	Bold		Times-Bold
Times		I	Times-Italic
Times	Bold	I	Times-BoldItalic
Times			Times-Roman

Table 2: Sample font mapping

Rotated text

Although it is possible to print text at any angle in PostScript, the X protocol does not support rotated text. To achieve this effect, text is usually written into a pixmap, the pixmap is rotated, and the result is then copied to a drawable. While this presents no problem for the PostScript X server, a byproduct of this procedure is the rasterization of the text. This introduces the jagged edges characteristic of the PostScript rendition of a window dump. It appears as though the only way to avoid this situation, for applications which utilize a great deal of rotated text, is with an X protocol extension and compatible clients.

Implementation Summary

The current implementation of the PostScript X server, although not complete, was successful in meeting our goal of proof-of-concept with minimal development effort in a short time frame. Only a few changes were necessary to device independent code. A function call has been added to **connection.c** in **os/4.2bsd** to handle output file creation and initialization. Some exposure handling code in **dix/window.c** was commented out in situations where windows are unmapped and the cursor display code in **ddx/mi/misprite.c** has also been deactivated. New device-specific function names have been plugged into the Screen and graphics contexts structures in **ddx/mfb**. In addition, a few lines of code were added to **mfbwindow.c** to regenerate the borders and backgrounds of repositioned windows. Finally, a PostScript-specific output library was developed. This library consists of about 5500 lines of C code, much of which is very similar to the monochrome frame buffer source code.

Comparative Analysis

This section presents some comparative time and space statistics for window dumps and output of the PostScript X server on a SPARCstation 1+. The first table summarizes the production and print times using the prototype server (Xps) and the traditional method of printing X windows (xwd). Three client applications were used in this analysis:

- the **bitmap** program from the X11R4 release tape, using the calculator bitmap from the same tape

- the **periodic** program from the Motif demonstration suite, which displays a large window full of various Motif widgets

- a custom spreadsheet-like application which displays a 900x600 window containing a table of figures, a graph, and several Motif scrollbar and button widgets.

The following command lines were used to produce a PostScript version of the window dumps:

> **xwd**: xwd -nobdrs -xy >*file*.xwd
> **xpr**: xpr -device ps -portrait -output *file*.ps <*file*.xwd

Actual PostScript printing times were calculated by adding code to the PostScript files which computed these values. Printing was done on a QMS-PS 810 laser printer through a 9600 baud serial interface.

	bitmap		periodic		spreadsheet	
	xwd	Xps	xwd	Xps	xwd	Xps
xwd	6		20		6	
xpr	46		112		128	
print	89	32	212	137	160	28
total	141	32	344	137	294	28

Table 3: Production and print times in seconds

The following table summarizes the file sizes involved. Although the window dump steps can be connected with pipes, these figures still give some indication of the size of data being processed.

	bitmap		periodic		spreadsheet	
	xwd	Xps	xwd	Xps	xwd	Xps
xwd	312,786		798,765		601,704	
ps	79,003	23,142	198,965	110,863	149,905	33,629
total	391,789	23,142	997,730	110,863	751,609	33,629

Table 4: File sizes in bytes

It is important to emphasize that, apart from favorable economies in print times and intermediate file sizes, one can achieve great improvements in image quality using the PostScript X server compared to a rasterized window dump. Figure 3 demonstrates this difference using a portion of the output from the **periodic** client.

Other Issues, Problems, Directions

A usable PostScript X server is currently operational in our environment. However, the current implementation is based upon the goal of evaluating feasibility within a short time frame. As such, little attention has been paid to date to robustness and optimization.

There are currently no applications which take advantage of the resolution of the PostScript printer. The prototype server was tested using clients which assume a device coordinate system of roughly 1024x1024 and the resulting images were scaled to fill as much of a page as possible. Applications would need to be modified to

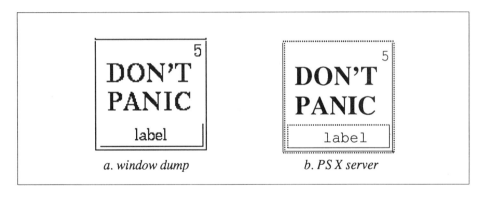

Figure 3: Image quality comparison

assume a much larger world/device coordinate system in order to take full advantage of the printer resolution.

Although none of the clients which were used to test the PostScript X server were changed in any way, other client-side modifications would be necessary in a hardcopy report environment to produce multi-page reports, to compose the output of multiple applications on a single page, or to omit the display of interaction widgets such as buttons and scrollbars.

Clients may engage (usually) indirectly with a window manager as a normal consequence of their initialization. This presents no problem when a client specifies a connection to the PostScript X server since there is no window manager connected to this server. Window manager specific requests are ignored. Clients are not adorned with the usual window manager decorations but this is desirable in the intended application.

Near-term development efforts will be directed toward the production of application-specific reports. These reports will require customizable page decorations and may span multiple pages. It is not yet clear how the implementation burden will be partitioned among the report clients, the server, and perhaps an intermediate page manager client, analogous to a traditional window manager. There is an evident need for client-specific configuration files for the PostScript preamble and font mapping — currently this information is supplied only when the server is invoked. Finally, although the initial development effort has focused on monochrome output, it should be relatively straight-forward to extend this effort to the sample color frame buffer.

Conclusion

The solution presented here to the hardcopy problem in the X environment is not an entirely general solution. For example, not all drawing functions can be supported; there are limitations concerning what can be done with certain classes of pixmaps; the resolution of some problems, such as the rasterization of rotated text, would require extensions to the X protocol; output is currently restricted to PostScript; and applications would require some modification to take advantage of higher resolutions and to produce page-specific, rather than display-specific, images.

Furthermore, the PostScript X server discussed here is also not intended to serve as a window dump replacement. It cannot reproduce a full screen multi-client image nor can it be used to generate hardcopy output after one has interactively navigated a client display to some arbitrary state without additional client engineering.

Nevertheless, it seems that the development of an X server for a PostScript output device is a feasible alternative for document production. Such a server is capable of producing documents at printer resolution in a timely fashion. A sufficiently critical subset of functionality can be supported in an X server which produces PostScript output to satisfy a wide class of high quality printed reports combining text and graphics.

Acknowledgements

The design and implementation of the PostScript X server was the work of the author as a member of the IntelliCare project design team at Sunquest. The idea for modifying the X server to emit PostScript originated with Bill Mitchell and was elaborated in conjunction with Mark McCourt and the author. These individuals, along with group members Mike Slocum and Wendy Debray, also provided valuable feedback on the content of this article.

References

1. Adobe Systems Inc., **An Overview of the Display PostScript System**, Adobe Systems Document, March 25, 1988

2. Adobe Systems Inc., **PostScript Language Reference Manual**, Addison-Wesley, 1989

3. Adobe Systems Inc., **PostScript Language Tutorial and Cookbook**, Addison-Wesley, 1989

4. Angebrannt, Susan, Raymond Drewry, Philip Karlton, Todd Newman, *Definition of the Porting Layer for the X v11 Sample Server*, **X11 Release 4 Document**, March 1988

5. Angebrannt, Susan, Raymond Drewry, Philip Karlton, Todd Newman, *Strategies for Porting the X v11 Sample Server*, **X11 Release 4 Document**, March 1988

6. Kent, Christopher A., *XDPS: A Display PostScript System Extension for DECwindows*, **Digital Technical Journal**, 2:3, Summer 1990

7. Linton, Mark A., Paul R. Calder, *The Design and Implementation of InterViews*, **USENIX C++ Papers**, 1987

8. MIT X Consortium, *X Logical Font Description Conventions Version 1.3*, **X11 Release 4 Document**, 1988

9. Nye, Adrian, **Xlib Programming Manual for Version 11**, O'Reilly & Associates, 1988

10. Reichard, Kevin, Eric F. Johnson, *Trying to Get What You See in X*, **UNIX Review**, 9:5, May 1991

11. Scheifler, Robert W., James Gettys, Ron Newman, **X Window System C Library and Protocol Reference**, Digital Press, 1988

How Not to Implement Overlays in X

Todd Newman

Overlay planes have been supported in non-windowing graphics systems for many years, but they are not generally available in X. In presenting a description of overlays for those not familiar with it, we set the stage for seeing how overlays might work in a window system. Then we discuss details of how to match overlay semantics with X semantics. We then explain how overlays are implemented in our servers and what is good and bad with the approach we took. We then mention problems with the implementation: things the implementation does not do and things it does not do well enough. We tried to add overlays by only making changes within the DDX layer. We have come to the conclusion that it is not possible to achieve adequate performance and a minimal number of exposures in an implementation of overlays in X without modifying the DIX layer.

What Are Overlay Planes?

Overlay planes are just a segregated set of bitplanes. Graphics hardware can display either the set of overlay planes, the set of normal bit planes, or both[1]. We'll refer to these sets of planes as *layers*. On some hardware, it is possible to determine on a per pixel basis whether the overlay or normal layer will be displayed. Displaying both layers is only interesting if there is a way for the normal planes to be seen through the overlay planes. This is done by designating some pixel value in the overlay layer to be transparent. When the overlay layer is enabled and contains the transparent pixel, the normal layer will be seen. When the overlay layer is enabled and contains other pixel values, those will be seen. If the overlay layer is not enabled, the normal layer will be seen.

Todd Newman is a member of the technical staff at Silicon Graphics, Inc.
[1] Some Tektronix workstations can blend overlay and normal planes. Our work does not support this feature. Tektronix is working on an extension to support it.

Overlay planes are a performance hack. When an application takes a long time to create an image, we may want to display some data on the screen temporarily without forcing the application to redraw its image when the temporary data has gone away. By drawing the temporary data in the overlay layer, the other normal layer can be left undisturbed. For example, let us image an application designed to annotate satellite photographs (similar to what's done on the television weather forecast). Suppose these photographs have been converted into 24 bit images. These images may take several seconds to pull off a disk. It would be very annoying if every time we used a drop down menu over such images, we had to wait a few seconds for the image to be redrawn. By putting the drop down in the overlay planes, we can avoid changing the pixel values in the normal planes.

In the same example, suppose we wanted to draw some lines over our image, but did not want to alter the image permanently. Perhaps we want to plot several possible trajectories for a storm. Again, we would not want to have to redraw the underlaying image as we considered the possibilities. If we enabled the overlay layer and filled it with a transparent pixel, we'd see our original map. We could draw trajectories in the overlay planes with an opaque pixel, and erase them by clearing the overlay back to the transparent pixel value.

When we introduce windowing to this discussion we find two more reasons why we might want to use overlay planes. The first is similar to the first point raised above, another application might create windows that would interfere with our laboriously created scene. But if those windows were in the overlay planes, they wouldn't. Even if our scene did not take a long time to render, we still might not want other application windows clipping ours. Many hardware platforms pay a performance penalty when the window is clipped by too many others. While we can still render many frames per second, if we clip a scene by too many other windows, our frame rate will go down.

Hardware Support for Overlay Planes

Overlay plane support has been provided by hardware vendors for many years, more years, in fact, than window systems have been. The result is that the typical hardware model is designed to support efficiently one overlay window, presumably running over one application. The framebuffer has a set of pixel planes reserved for overlays. These planes are treated as if they were in a PseudoColor visual. If there are n planes, then the colormap has 2^n entries. A special pixel value, usually either 0 or 2^n-1, is reserved for the transparent pixel. Regardless of the value loaded into the colormap for this entry, the hardware will display whatever is in the normal planes here.

More sophisticated hardware may provided a mechanism to disable the display of overlay planes for a given area of the screen, to treat these extra planes as underlay planes (that is, planes that are only displayed if the normal planes contain a transparent pixel), or even to enable multiple banks of overlay planes. This control can be provided either as a set of extra bits in each pixel, or a separate display mode table. For example, on an SGI 4D35G, the same bits that control how overlay planes are displayed also control the depth of a pixel and what sort of colormap, TrueColor or PseudoColor, is used to interpret the pixel. In other words, these are the bits that do the work of providing different visuals.

Matching Overlays with X Semantics

Given the functionality we wish to provide for handling overlays, a very straightforward model presents itself: overlays are drawings in windows with a special kind of visual. Overlay windows follow the same stacking rules as any other kind of window. Colormaps created for overlay visuals will have one fewer entry writable by the user, if the workstation provides a transparent pixel. A special property can be added to the root window that lets applications that wish to know about overlays find out which visuals are overlay visuals and what the special properties of the overlay colormaps for those visuals are. Exposure and visibility events for overlay windows must be calculated differently, but this should not be exposed to the client. This model lets us extend the functionality of X without extending or changing the fundamental objects and functions.

Since most hardware puts the overlay layer on top of the normal layer, it is tempting to insist that overlay windows should always be on top of normal windows. We[2] considered implementing overlays this way, as it makes things considerably easier. If overlay windows can only be overlapped by other overlay windows, handling exposures becomes much easier. Unfortunately, the window tree that results does not match a user's intuition of how window systems work. Windows appear to have the wrong parent; transparent pixels reveal unrelated pixels below them. A brief examination of what happens when two top level windows with children in the overlay planes overlap should make it clear why overlay windows have to follow regular X stacking rules.

Figure 1. Not what the user expected

Imagine a top level window A that has an overlay window A1 as a child. If the application writes transparent pixels in A1, the user expects to see pixels from A appear. In a system without overlays, nothing comes between a parent window and its children. Now imagine a second application with top level window B. Let window B

---

[2] Our implementation team consisted of Todd Newman, Jeff Weinstein, and Peter Daifuku. We received considerable technical advice from Tom Paquin and Phil Karlton

partially overlap A. Since A1 is above all normal plane windows, B does not overlap A1. In other words, the parent window A is clipped by window B, but the child window A1 is not clipped. So the transparent pixels in A1 will now show either pixels from window A or pixels from window B. Clearly, this is not what the user would expect.

The problem in the previous approach was that not every normal plane window had a child in the overlay planes. Consider a scenario where every top level window had an associated overlay window which is assumed to be filled with transparent pixels. Then window B would have a child B1. When window B overlapped window A, window B1 would overlap window A1 in a similar way. Then the pixels of A1 that were a problem before would already be obscured by (transparent) pixels from window B1. This scheme doubles the number of window tree manipulations which is an unacceptable performance hit. That's particularly bad since most of the applications would never use these shadow overlay windows. Also, input distribution in this scheme is a nightmare.

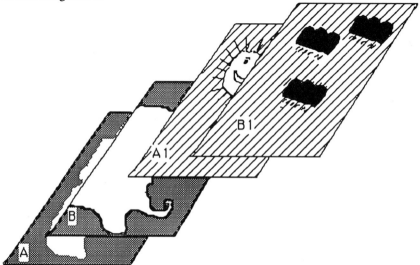

Figure 2. Still not right

We do not consider it appropriate to hide the existence of transparent pixels from application writers. On the other hand, most existing applications have no mechanism using transparency or need to use it. These applications should work unmodified on a system supporting overlays. Our answer was to preallocate one colormap entry in colormaps for overlay visuals. If the preallocated entry were in the highest cell in the hardware map, we could present the user with a colormap that had 2^n-1 entries and we could make the colormap static or dynamic. Silicon Graphics workstations are hardwired to use pixel value 0 as the transparent pixel, so we must steal the first colormap entry. It cannot be written to, since the hardware will ignore whatever values are written there. It cannot be read, since we don't guarantee what value will be read back. This matches the situation of using a dynamic colormap in which another user has privately allocated the first entry. So on our implementation, an AllocAll request on an overlay colormap will always fail.

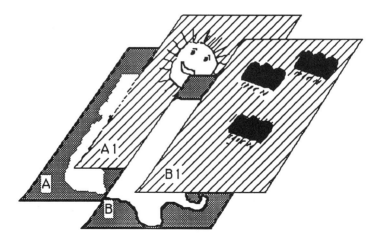

Figure 3. How it should work

There are other ways for hardware to handle transparency. Some hardware does allocate the last entry in colormap for the transparent pixel. Some workstations actually use a color value rather than a pixel value for transparency. (This is similar to the blue screen techniques used in video.) On these workstations, one could preallocate a colormap entry and load it with this transparent color. If some hardware did not provide a transparent pixel -- one could always disable the overlay planes for that pixel, after all -- then it would not be necessary to steal an entry in that colormap.

Most of this work has been to hide the implementation of overlays from old applications and new ones that do not need to know about overlays. Overlay windows look just like other windows. And overlay visuals look just like regular visuals. Of course, window managers and user applications which wish to know about overlays need a way to find the overlay visuals. Our server communicates the necessary information by hanging a property, SERVER_OVERLAY_VISUALS, off the root window. That property contains a list of structures that identify an overlay visual, what kind of transparent pixel it supports, what the transparent pixel value is, and the visual's layer. (See below for an explanation of layers).

Treating overlays in the manner described above produces some expected and some unexpected changes in the production of events. Remember that our purpose in implementing overlays was to reduce the number of exposure events on normal plane windows, and our design achieves that result. But to make overlays conform to users' expectations, we have to force normal plane windows to obscure overlay plane windows. Since the hardware doesn't provide for this, we have to fill the obscured part of overlay plane windows with transparent pixels. If the normal plane window is now moved, we have to generate an Expose event to restore the bits in the overlay plane. It may seem like we have not gained anything, only traded one expose event in the normal planes for another in the overlay planes. However, it turns out that windows in the overlay planes are usually much easier to regenerate; they contain mostly text and simple drawings. Anything complicated could always be put in another window in the normal planes. Overlay plane windows are often transients that never get obscured at all.

Transparent pixels make Visibility events much more perplexing. If an overlay plane window gets mapped over a normal plane window of the same size and origin, should we generate a Visibility event, and if so, which one? If the overlay window contains no transparent pixels, the normal window is complete obscured. If the overlay plane window contains only transparent pixels, we really don't need to send any Visibility event. It really did not seem reasonable to have to determine visibility status as each pixel was being drawn. We decided that for Visibility events, we would treat overlay window as any other window and ignore transparent pixels. It is possible that an application may receive a VisibilityObscured event for a window some pixels of which may actually be visible. On reflection, it would be better to send a PartiallyObscured event in this case.

The Two Clip Lists: Rendering Clip And Visibility Clip

The goal of minimizing exposure events impels us to make a distinction between a window being clipped for rendering and its being clipped for visibility. That is, if a normal plane window is partially overlapped by an overlay plane window, the application program should continue to render into the whole normal plane window. Otherwise, when the overlay plane window went away, we'd have to generate an Expose event to repair the window, and we might as well have put the overlay plane window in the normal planes. Worse yet, while the overlay planes were up the normal planes would be stagnant. So the normal plane window is not clipped for rendering. We need one clip list to know where to render and another to know what parts of the window can be seen by the user.

Clip Computation

The window code in the DIX layer assumes that a window can only be clipped by its siblings or by something that clips its parent. With overlays, the window can be clipped by any descendent of the root window. For example, a window in the overlay planes may be a grandchild of its top-level window. (In practice, the Motif toolkit often produces window stacks seven or eight layers deep.) A dialog box in the overlay planes will be created as a child of the root window. The dialog box will change the rendering clip of the overlay window, but will only change the visibility of the top level window. With overlays, a window may be clipped by almost any descendent of the root window.

The simplifying assumption made by the DIX window code means that it does not have to tell the DDX layer about most changes to the window tree. The DDX layer is informed about Map and Unmap events when they happen and about almost everything else at validate time. Even for Map events, we don't get enough information. By the time `ValidateTree` is called, the DIX layer has gracefully covered up all the evidence that would allow implementors to figure out what was going on.

We could, of course, solve this by walking the entire widow tree in front to back order, calculating what layer every window was in and whether it was clipped for rendering or just for visibility. This is, of course, prohibitively slow, so we do not do this. Almost all the difficulty in implementing overlays has come from trying to find an acceptably fast alternative to a complete tree walk that still gives us the information we need to compute correctly the clip lists, or at least come to an acceptably close approximation to the correct clip lists. A complete solution probably requires a complete redesign of this code.

Colormaps

It might seem that colormaps should not need to be discussed at length in a paper on overlay planes -- but they do. On the Personal Iris workstations, we have 4 bitplanes for overlays. These bitplanes are used to index into a 15 entry colormap. Entry 0 is reserved for the transparent pixel.   So we're all set to support 4 bit deep overlay windows.

This is not what our software developers want. They would much rather see those four bit planes divided into two sets of two planes each. One set would be used as overlay planes belonging to applications to be used for non-permanent drawing over complex scenes. The other set would be used for popping up transient system windows, such as drop down windows and dialog boxes. This split predates our support of overlays in X, and was part of an attempt to provide similar functions.

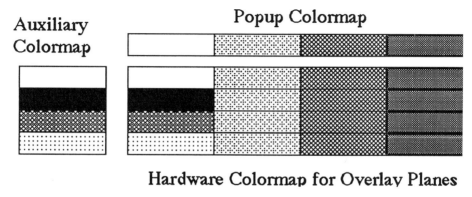

Figure 3. Combining two logical colormaps into one hardware colormap

It is not hard to adjust planemasks appropriately so that windows in popup layer only write one pair of pixels and windows in the overlay layer only write the other pair. The problem is what to do about colormap lookups. Remember that the hardware always looks up all four bits at once. Suppose we put the popup bits in the low order two bits of the overlay planes and the other two bits (call them 'auxiliary' bits) in the high order. How can we arrange the 16 entries in the hardware colormap so that we see the correct colors for each layer? The answer is: we can't. Entry 0 will be the transparent entry, since that's how the hardware works. This is somewhat convenient, as if both the overlay and popup layers have a 0, we should have transparency. To go further, if either layer has a transparent pixel, it's easy to figure out how to load the colormap. So the first four entries in the colormap have been assigned; these make up the values for the popup colormap. And the fifth, ninth, and thirteenth entries, which have the two low order bits set to zero, are loaded with the second, third, and fourth values from the auxiliary layer colormap. What about the rest of the entries? These are the cases when both layers have a non-zero value? We decided that in such cases, the popup layer would win. So if there's a popup window on top of an auxiliary window, we will see the colors of the popup window. When the popup window goes away, we'll zero out those two bits, and the auxiliary plane window will become visible.

Of course, if we put an auxiliary plane window on top of a popup window, we've got a problem. We've set up the colormap so that we'll see the popup plane pixel. The only solution is to zero out the popup plane underneath the auxiliary plane window. When the auxiliary plane window moves, we'll have to generate an Expose event on the popup window.

Interference

Notice how similar this is to the problem when we put a normal plane window over an overlay plane window. Again we have to zero out the overlay plane window to see the window that is logically on top of it. Again, we have to generate an Expose event to restore the underlaying window. In both these cases, we may say that the window on top interferes with the window below it. *Interference* is a property shared by all windows in a given layer. That is, all windows in the normal plane layer interfere with windows in the popup and auxiliary layer. Windows in the auxiliary layer interfere with windows in the popup layer. The relation is not symmetric. Windows in the popup layer do not interfere with windows in the auxiliary layer. Windows in the popup and auxiliary layer do not interfere with windows in the normal layer. (That's why we started all this, after all.) Interference is reflexive: all layers interfere with themselves.

Much of our design is based on the two notions of layers and of interference. We thought that by clever use of regions that aggregated all the windows in a layer we could perform fewer region calculations and simplify the layer code. We thought that by generalizing the concept of interference, we would not make the normal planes a privileged layer and could make any layer the default. While we still believe that these two concepts are useful, neither of those plans worked out in practice.

Layers

In writing our version of `ValidateTree`, which was designed to support overlays, we emulated the design of the standard code found in `miValidateTree`. To minimize the number of regions against which a window must be clipped, the code maintains a clipping universe that is the only possible area where a window might be visible. A window's *universe* is the visible area of its parent, less any area already allocated to the window's previous siblings. Any space not within the universe need not be considered. (A region might have a hole in it, of course. That space is not within the region, though it is surrounded by it.) A child's universe is a proper subset of its parent's universe.

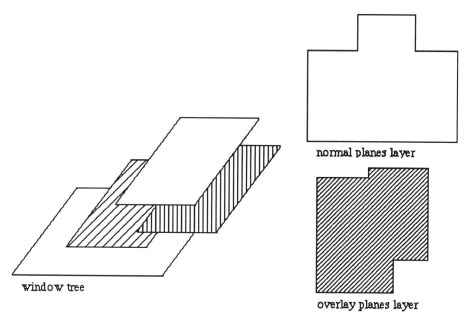

normal planes layer

overlay planes layer

window tree

Figure 4. A window tree and related layers

Our implementation also used universes, but we had many more of them. First, we had universes for every layer. Originally, windows only had to clip against other windows in the same layer. When we realized that layers could interfere with each other, we had to change things. Rather than make windows clip against all layers, we tried to subtract space from the layer's universe when a window was created that interfered with that layer. Unfortunately, when we collect the regions for all the windows in a layer into one region, we lose information about the stacking order of those windows. Then when we map a window that interferes with that layer, it is no longer possible to tell which windows in the interfered layer are on top of the new window and can ignore it and which are below it and must clip against it.

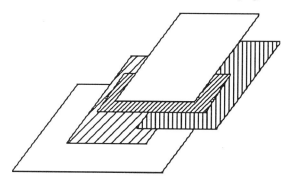

Figure 5. Adding another overlay window

In Figure 4 above, the striped windows in the window tree are in the overlay planes, the hollow windows are in the normal planes. The window tree shows the stacking order. The two regions on the right show the normal layer and the overlay layer. Note how they show the total area used in each layer, but given no idea about stacking order. When, in Figure 5, we introduce a new overlay window into the tree, how do we decide which part of the overlay window is clipped to the normal region and which part is logically above all normal plane windows and should not be clipped? The regions give no hint as to which part of the area came from which window. We never found a heuristic that correctly computed all cases.

We also needed a universe to compute visibility. We only needed one universe for visibility. Keeping a visibility universe, which got progressively smaller as we moved down the window tree, allowed us to speed up the visibility computations as much as possible. The visibility universe is exactly the same as the MI code's universe.

Despite several weeks spent optimizing the code, our ValidateTree was many times slower than the one in the MI code. As this made many window intensive applications, xmh in particular, unacceptable slow, I had to come up with a work-around. Every window keeps track of the number of children it has in the overlay planes. If the highest relevant window does not have any children in the overlay planes and we know that nothing has been unmapped recently ValidateTree calls a special QuickValidateTree routine. QuickValidateTree and its helper QuickComputeClips look just like the routines in mivaltree.c, except that they compute new values for the rendering clip list and then copy that region to the visibility clip list.

We have to keep both lists up to date because we cannot predict when a user will start up an application that uses overlays. Once overlays are involved the contents of the two clip lists starts to diverge, so we cannot use two pointers to the same clip region. It is no doubt possible to keep enough bookkeeping information around to allow us to maintain only one list most of the time, but the added code complexity and implementation time precluded me from considering this more deeply.

SlideAndSizeWindow Knows Less Than It Thinks It Does

Along with the problem of DIX code that did not pass enough information into the DDX layer, we also had the problem of DIX code that thought it knew better than the DDX layer. SlideAndSizeWindow calls ValidateTree and should trust it to have generated the correct exposures. But it does not. It recomputes all the exposures for the children. It seems that the goal was to minimize the number of expose events sent to clients by coalescing several small exposures into one larger one. These exposures would be correct in the absence of overlay planes. As it is, they generate more exposures and they are sometimes incorrect. We have devised a work-around for this, but it is not aesthetically appealing.

Backing Store Missing

We never got backing store to work on the system. The problem is that the MI backing store code assumed that we only had to back up as many bits as the deepest window on the screen. We need to change to code understand that the screen may be deeper than that. This is not conceptually hard to do, but it will require a substantial rewrite of the existing code. We did not have time to fix this.

No Support for Multiple Use Layers

Another shortcoming was that our layer model doesn't describe the alpha/overlay planes on the Silicon Graphics VGX workstation. These planes could be used either as the Alpha buffer of a 3D window, or as an 8 bit overlay layer. The problem was that if an application created a window in the alpha/overlay planes, there was nothing to prevent it from trying to move that window. In particular, it could be moved on top of a 3D window that was using its alpha buffer. We couldn't use the same bits for both windows, and there was no mechanism for generating an exposure on the alpha plane of the overlapped window. We solved this by disallowing the use of these planes as overlay planes. Notice how this differs from our handling of the interference between the pup and auxiliary layers. The difference is that we had a mechanism for telling an X window that it needed to generate an exposure. We didn't have a way to do this for GL windows.

Cannot Put Default Visual in the Overlay Layers

It was a design goal that the default visual could be in any layer. Many users would like to make the root window be in the popup layer. That would eliminate exposures on complex images caused by random applications like clocks, mail readers, and terminal emulators. Unfortunately, a widespread bug in our code implicitly assumed that popup windows, like dialog boxes, which obscured normal plane windows were in a different layer than their parents. This is true for the general case; and always true when the root window is in the normal planes. But when the root window was in the popup layer and the dialog box was in the popup layer, we were not filling with transparent bits when the dialog box went away.

Exposures Due To Popup/Overlay Interference

In theory, we should not need to generate an Expose event when a popup layer window ceases to obscure an auxiliary layer window, we should just fill the popup pixels with transparent pixels (See the above discussion on colormaps to see why.) This would be true if `ValidateTree` had enough information to tell what kind of window had moved or been unmapped to expose the auxiliary layer window. This information is available to the DIX layer window code, but not to us down in the DDX trenches. To avoid having to examine the entire window tree, we make the following simplifying assumption: if a window is in a layer that can be interfered with, and it gets exposed, we will assume that it has been interfered with. This is trivially true for layers that can never be interfered with, such as normal layers, and for layers that are always interfered with, like the popup layer. It is often true for the auxiliary layer. Fixing the server not to generate exposures in the cases where they really are not needed will require a complete redesign of this code.

So Now What?

A proper solution will require changing the DIX layer window code and it will involve a new design not based on layered universes. Should the window code in the DIX layer know about overlays? Probably not, because not all systems have overlay hardware, but then DDX layer must have enough information. The current design hides too much information. We can figure out what a window overlaps, but not what was overlapping it. Either the DIX layer should know about overlay planes, so that it does the right bookkeeping, or we can broaden the interface between DDX and DIX so that DDX gets informed of every change to the window tree. For most changes on most windows, the DDX layer would do nothing. When overlay plane windows were present, we could figure out what windows are overlapped and mark them. Then when we get to `ValidateTree`, we'll have a fighting chance of figuring out what to do.

Collapsing layers into regions loses critical information about the window stack that is needed to compute clip lists properly. Whatever approach is used the next time, it will need a way to combine rapidly stacking information and layering information. Perhaps the regions could be extended to include that stacking information or the window tree could be extended to include layering information.

Our implementation was moderately successful. The system gets much slower when overlays are in use. The system still has some bugs (mostly unnecessary exposures) that will be impossible to fix in the current design. But we added overlays without having to mangle the basic concepts of X. We preserved the user's and application writer's view of the window tree, exposures, and colormaps. Furthermore, we did this without significantly slowing down the server when overlays are not being used. If we did not solve the overlay problem to our own satisfaction, we did make a good first approximation in terms of function, usability, and performance.

Todd Newman graduated from Harvard with an AB in Philosophy in 1981 and joined Microsoft where he worked on applications, laptop computers, and compilers. After a brief stint at Aion Corporation working on expert system software, he moved to the Digital Equipment Corporation. He was part of a team of four that implemented the first X11 sample server for MIT. He ported the X server to the DECstation 3100 and DECstation 5000/200 PXG. He worked on the protocol encoding for PEX and helped implement PEX on the VAXstation 3540. In April 1991, he joined Silicon Graphics, where he is again working on X servers.

NFB, an X Server Porting Layer

Jeff Weinstein

NFB is a porting layer for the X server that is intended to provide better support than the current MI for displays with graphics accelerators. The design goals of the NFB include quick server bringup with good initial performance, machine independent support for such advanced hardware features as multiple hardware colormaps and overlays, machine independent rendering optimizations, and the ability to easily track MIT changes. The NFB code can be broken down into several areas: DDX rendering, windowing, and advanced hardware support.

Jeff Weinstein is a Member of the Technical Staff at Silicon Graphics Computer Systems.

This paper assumes some knowledge of such X constructs as visuals, colormaps, pixmaps, etc. It also assumes some understanding of internal workings of the X server sample implementation. For more information about the internals of the X server see Angebranndt[1].

NFB Genealogy

NFB is a third generation porting layer. It descends from the X11 Sample Server's MI layer, and IBM's PPC. MI was originally implemented as part of the Sample Server efforts by Todd Newman and Raymond Drewry of Digital's Workstation Systems Engineering. The intent of MI was to provide a least common denominator porting layer that provided a full DDX rendering implementation. MI reduced all X primitives to lists of spans, which resulted in poor performance for many important primitives such as text, rectangle fills, line drawing, scrolling, etc.

The second generation was PPC, which was created in the summer of 1986 by Tom Paquin, Jeff Weinstein, and Paul Shupak, then of IBM's ACIS Palo Alto development group. We needed to support a handful of 8-bit color graphics boards, none of which had direct mapped framebuffers. At the time CFB was inadequate due to our lack of a mapped frame buffer, and its lack of performance. PPC's major goal was to support quick bringup and performance tuning of 8-bit accelerated X servers. It met these goals very well, being the basis for a half-dozen DDX implementations. The quickest PPC server bringup took less than three hours. PPC was however limited to 8-bits per pixel, and would have required a major overhaul to support multiple depths and visuals.

DDX rendering

MI takes the approach of reducing all DDX rendering operations into operations on lists of spans. This gives very poor performance for many X primitives, such as area fills, characters, lines, copies, etc. The NFB approach is to define a small set of higher level primitives upon which to build the DDX rendering. There are several layers of primitives that allow quick incremental optimization by someone who is unfamiliar with the internals of the X server. As they become more familiar with the internals of the server they can go on to higher levels of optimization for primitives that require the performance gain. While the NFB rendering routines do give reasonably good performance and a quick bringup, to get competitive product performance it is really necessary to implement critical primitives by writing hardware specific code directly to the DDX interface.

NFB WinOps Layer

NFB, with some help from MI, provides a full DDX rendering implementation on top of the WinOps layer. The NFB drawing routines decompose their primitives into lists of rectangles or points, and will replicate stipple patterns. Tile replication is done in the TileRects() primitive, while stipple replication must be done by the NFB routines that call `DrawMonoImage()` and `DrawOpaqueMonoImage()`. Tiling was considered more important due to the larger amount of data required and because windowing operations require tiling. This layer requires little or no X server internals experience to implement. The routines in this layer are expected to apply the ALU function, planemask, and possibly foreground and background colors that they are passed as explicit parameters. These attributes are passed in as arguments, rather than as part of a GC to simplify the interface as much as possible for the implementor not familiar with X. These routines do not have to perform clipping or window coordinate translation.

The only X server data structures exposed to this layer are `DDXPoint`, `BoxPtr`, and `WindowPtr`. The window pointer can initially be treated as an opaque data type, and ignored by the implementor. It may be used later to get at the `ScreenPtr`, or to determine what visual or depth should be used for the drawing operation being performed.

At the lowest level NFB expects the following set of primitives:

- `CopyRect()` - perform screen to screen copy of specified rectangle. Must deal with all orientations.
- `DrawSolidRects()` - fill solid rectangles.
- `TileRects()` - fill rectangles with the given tile pattern.
- `DrawImage()` - draw a rectangular image.
- `ReadImage()` - read a rectangular image.
- `DrawMonoImage()` - draw a rectangular bitmap, color expanding foreground pixels.
- `DrawOpaqueMonoImage` - draw a rectangular bitmap, color expanding foreground and background pixels.
- `DrawPoints()` - draw multiple points.

Several of the above routines take either a bitmap or a full depth image. Bitmaps are represented by a pointer to the bitmap data, a pixel offset from the beginning of the byte pointed to, width, height, and stride. Images are represented by a pointer to the first byte of image data, width, height, and stride.

The image pointer parameter points to the first byte of the sub-image being displayed. Since the first pixel to be displayed does not have to be word aligned, all of these routines must deal correctly with unaligned pointers. The stride parameter is the number of bytes to increment the image pointer when moving it from one scanline of the image to the next. The stride parameter should not be used for width by the drawing routines. Its only use is in incrementing the image pointer, and it may be zero for one pixel high images. Figure 1 illustrates an example of drawing a subset of an 8-bit image.

`DrawMonoImage()` and `DrawOpaqueMonoImage()` are each passed a bitmap. The bitmap pointer is not guaranteed to be word aligned. The bitmap pointer plus pixel offset may point to a bit that is not in the same word as the pointer. In practice these routines

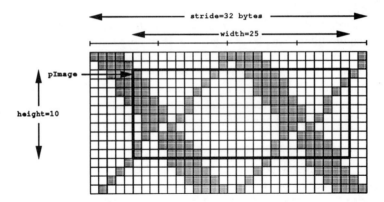

Figure 1 - image example

require the most code, since there are several cases of alignment and padding that can be easily optimized, and the general case is relatively slow. Figure 2 illustrates an example bitmap that would be used when drawing a clipped character.

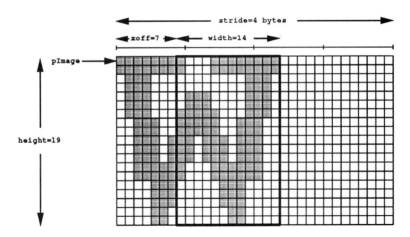

Figure 2 - bitmap example

These primitives were selected because they provide enough functionality to create a reasonably performing DDX rendering implementation, and will easily support the required window operations.

An initial implementation need only provide `DrawImage()` and `ReadImage()` to get full function X rendering. A sample implementation of the other routines, called GEN that is based on `DrawImage()` is provided. The GEN package also provides templates for the other pieces necessary to bring up the server, including colormap, cursor, and initialization routines. The code that actually writes to the graphics hardware can simply be dropped into these function templates.

GC Validation

NFB provides a generalized `ValidateGC()` routine that does the machine independent portions of GC validation. If the drawable being validated is a pixmap, then `cfbValidateGC()` is called. For pixmaps deeper than 8 bits per pixel, we use a variant of the cfb code that supports 16 or 32 bits per pixel. If the drawable is a window, then `nfbValidateGC()` computes the GC composite clip, calls a routine to compute the reduced rasterop(see *NFB Futures* below), and then calls a machine dependent routine to compute the `GCOps` structure and perform any other necessary validation.

Windowing Support

NFB provides a complete implementation of DDX windowing routines, which includes `CreateWindow()`, `DestroyWindow()`, `PositionWindow()`, `ChangeWindowAttributes()`, `RealizeWindow()`, `UnrealizeWindow()`, `ValidateTree()`, `WindowExposures()`, `PaintWindowBackground()`, `PaintWindowBorder()`, and `CopyWindow()`. Most of the windowing code is there to deal with Display IDs, colormaps, and overlays, as described below.

Advanced Hardware Support

NFB includes support for advanced hardware features such as multiple hardware colormaps and overlays. Most of the code supporting these features is machine independent and table driven.

Visual devPrivates

The MIT sample server implementation does not provide a devPrivate field as part of the `VisualRec`. Since some of the information needed to manage Display IDs and colormaps is per-visual we added a devPrivate structure to each visual. The `nfbVisualPriv` specifies a default Display ID for windows of that visual, the colormap group for that visual, and another devPrivate for machine dependent information.

Display IDs

Multiple colormaps, multiple visuals, overlays, and multibuffering are all related in that they all require some mechanism to tell the hardware what colormap or visual class (TrueColor or PseudoColor for example) a particular pixel in the frame buffer should be displayed with. NFB maintains a Display ID (DID) for each window. The DID is a machine dependent opaque identifier that is used by the DDX and the hardware to ensure that a pixel is displayed on the screen with the correct colormap, visual, and buffer (for the multibuffer extension). `nfbValidateTree()` calculates the areas of the screen that are displayed with each DID, and calls a machine dependent routine to effect any changes in the hardware.

There is no dependence in NFB upon the hardware representation of DIDs. SGI graphics hardware currently uses two dramatically different schemes. The first uses extra frame-buffer bitplanes to determine the DID of each pixel. Thus each pixel has several extra bits to specify one of 2^n DIDs. To update the DIDs you simply draw a set of rectangles to the DID planes with the "foreground color" being the DID value. The second scheme uses a run length encoded table of DID transitions, which is traversed by the video backend hardware during each video scan. To update the DID table a new set of transitions must be calculated based on the regions passed in by NFB, then the table is copied into the hardware DID memory. The NFB interface should also support other types of DID hardware.

When a window is created its DID is determined based on either the colormap or visual of the window. When a window's colormap is installed in the hardware, the window is displayed with the DID of the hardware colormap. When the window's colormap is not installed, the window is displayed with the DID of the visual, which will probably result in incorrect colors, but the pixels will be displayed with the correct visual class. Colormap changes or installations may cause the DID of a window to change after it is created.

Colormaps

The NFB has two data structures for managing multiple hardware colormaps. They are the nfbHWCmap, and the nfbCmapGroup structures. The nfbHWCmap structure represents a physical hardware colormap. The nfbCmapGroup structure represents a Colormap Group, which is a set of hardware colormaps that can be treated as interchangeable. Each visual specifies a Colormap Group that will be used by colormaps of that visual.

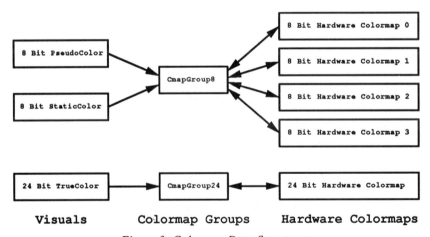

Figure 3- Colormap Data Structures

The colormap group structure contains a list of the hardware colormaps that are part of that group, and function pointers to routines that do the machine dependent parts of

`InstallColormap()` and `StoreColors()`. The hardware colormap structure contains a pointer to the X colormap currently installed in the given hardware colormap, a list of hardware colormaps that this one conflicts with, the DID to use for windows using this colormap, and a set of flags. Two colormaps conflict when installing one causes the other to be uninstalled. For example, an 8-bit colormap and a 12-bit colormap may share the same 4096 entry hardware lookup table.

The NFB code does all the machine independent parts of colormap installation which includes the following:

- select a hardware colormap from the appropriate colormap group.
- find any colormaps that this one "conflicts" with, and uninstall them.
- generate colormap notify events for all conflicting colormaps, and the X colormap that previously occupied the selected hardware colormap.
- call the machine dependent InstallColormap() routine to actually write the colors to the hardware.
- generate colormap notify events for the colormap just installed.
- call machine dependent routines to update DID information for any window that is using the installed colormap.

In addition to `InstallColormap()`, NFB provides a complete implementation of the other DDX colormap routines, `CreateColormap()`, `DestroyColormap()`, `UninstallColormap()`, `ListInstalledColormaps()`, `StoreColors()`, and `ResolveColor()`.

The DDX implementor needs to provide routines to install the colors of an X colormap into each type of hardware colormap, and routines to store colors into each type of hardware colormap. The `nfbHWCmap` and `nfbCmapGroup` data structures need to be created and initialized statically at compile time or during DDX startup.

Overlays

Overlay planes are simply an alternate set of frame buffer bitplanes, that are generally used to display transient data "over" more permanent or difficult to redraw data. Several systems provide overlay functionality outside of the window system. Either the window system doesn't know about the overlays, or they are managed using a window tree that is separate from the "main" window tree. The NFB implements overlay planes as a first class window system citizen, preserving the window tree hierarchy and window stacking order.

NFB based X servers on machines that provide overlay planes export one or more visuals that correspond to the various sets of overlay bitplanes. Windows are simply created with one of the overlay visuals. Depending on the underlying hardware, overlay windows might have a transparent pixel, which when drawn will cause the contents of the non-overlay window directly below to show through.

The NFB uses a general notion of frame buffer layers to implement overlay support. Each set of independent bitplanes is a layer. The NFB implementation of `ValidateTree()` computes the clipping of windows in different, non-interfering layers separately, so a window in the overlays on top of a window in the non-overlay planes would not clip the non-overlay window. To determine the layer of a window the NFB uses a simple table that maps DIDs to layers. Adding overlay support for a new device requires the creation of this table and possibly addition of some code to the machine dependent routine that updates DID information in the hardware.

A more detailed description of the NFB overlay implementation and its strengths and weaknesses can be found in Newman[2].

NFB Futures

There are several enhancements planned for NFB in the near future. Some of the framework needed for these new features is already in place since we anticipated the need early in the design.

Rasterop, Tile, and Stipple Reduction

It was always our intention to implement rasterop reduction in the NFB. Rasterop reduction involves combining foreground, planemask, and alu components of the GC in a way that produces a "simpler" alu operation. For example, for fill style FillSolid an ALU of GXor could be reduced to GXset by ANDing the bits of foreground into the planemask. Typically the most gain would be achieved when a read-modify-write operation is transformed into a simple write operation.

The NFB GC devPrivate structure contains the fields necessary to implement rasterop reduction. There are two copies of the foreground, background, alu, and planemask. The first copy, the rRop, is intended to contain reduced copies of the GC components. The second copy, the hwRop, is a simple copy of the GC components. During GC validation the NFB validate code would fill in these fields with the information from the main GC, performing any reductions. The device dependent validation routine is then free to manipulate values in the rRop or hwRop to match the hardware, perhaps shifting bits around or performing other hardware dependent transformations.

The hwRop is intended to provide copies of the common GC components that have had the hardware dependent transformation performed on them for those operations that cannot use the reduced rasterop, such as image text.

Tiles that contain only two colors can be transformed into stipples. Tiles or stipples that contain only one color can be transformed into solid fills. The rRop and hwRop structures contain a stipple pointer and a fillstyle field, both currently unused, which are intended to be used to implement tile and stipple reduction. To keep GC validation efficient, some limit will have to be placed on the size of tiles and stipples that will be examined for possible reduction, since the entire contents of the pixmap must be examined.

Large Colormap Segmentation

All SGI machines with 24 or more bitplanes have a single 12-bit hardware colormap. Currently all colormaps for 8-bit visuals use the lower 256 entries of the 4096 entry colormap. This results in the same colormap flashing that is seen on 8-bit only systems when two or more colormaps are in use simultaneously. We could use the extra bitplanes and colormap entries to simulate sixteen 8-bit hardware colormaps, and reduce colormap flashing dramatically. The 8-bit hardware colormaps would conflict with the 12-bit hardware colormap, and vice versa. The top 4 bits of the 12-bit pixel values would be used as secondary DID planes, to select which part of the 12-bit colormap to use for a particular window.

Colormap Collision Detection

If only 8-bit colormaps are being used, then the above scheme would work well, but if a 12-bit colormap is also being used, then the possibility of significant colormap flashing still exists, even if the 12-bit colormap is only partially allocated.

The colormap segmentation technique described above could be improved by modifying the colormap conflict detection code to detect conflicts between parts of colormaps, rather than entire colormaps. When a 12-bit colormap is installed in the hardware, and then an attempt is made to install an 8-bit map, the server could search the 12-bit colormap for 256 contiguous entries that are not used, then use that portion of the 12-bit colormap to simultaneously install the 8-bit colormap.

This scheme does have some added cost. The colormap conflict calculation becomes more expensive, since colormap cell allocation has to be checked. Also, the conflict calculation has to be done for StoreColors() operations. This technique needs to be examined to determine whether it is worth this added cost to provide simultaneously installed 12-bit and 8-bit colormaps.

Dynamic Colormap Allocation

Future graphics hardware will have even larger color lookup tables that will be able to be split into multiple hardware colormaps of arbitrary size. Rather than impose a static allocation of 12, 8, and 4 bit colormaps, the space should be dynamically allocated on demand.

Multibuffering

The current sample implementation of the Multibuffer Extension is not well suited to support of multibuffering hardware. The sample implementation has embedded in its design the fact that the non-displayed buffers are pixmaps. An implementation of Multibuffer that supports hardware multibuffering with minimal DDX rendering changes is needed. The same mechanisms used to draw to different sets of bitplanes(overlays) or to display different visuals, can be used to draw to and display multiple buffers.

Dynamic DID Allocation

The current NFB implementation only provides for DIDs that are pre-allocated for visuals and hardware colormaps. Multibuffered windows will frequently change buffers, which under the current implementation would require changing the DID of that window. If a window that was performing multibuffering was assigned its own unique DID, then depending on underlying hardware, swapping buffers could be as simple as changing a bit in a hardware mode table. Some systems also support this form of multibuffering by syncing buffer changes to video vertical retrace. By dynamically allocating DIDs we can reduce the number of preallocated DIDs that may not be used, and allow multibuffered windows to allocate unique DIDs to facilitate efficient buffer swapping.

Dynamic DID allocation is also a prerequisite for dynamic colormap allocation, since the server would not know what DIDs to allocate until colormaps had been allocated.

The SGI X server already supports dynamic DID allocation as part of its support for the Iris GL 3D graphics library. This support needs to be extended to the DIDs that X uses and the code needs to be brought into NFB.

Object Caching in Hardware

It is often desirable to cache server objects in the graphics hardware. Some things worth caching are font glyphs, GCs, and pixmaps. A generalized external memory allocator can be provided to support DDX caching of these objects. Also hooks can be added to notify the DDX cache manager of a change to any cached object.

Returning Memory to the Operating System

Due to the way that unix memory allocation is typically implemented, once a process has asked the operating system for more memory, it never returns it. This results in X servers that grow, but never shrink. Typical culprits are large pixmaps and fonts. The X server could detect when a large pixmap is being created, or a large font is being loaded, and rather than calling malloc(), it could map a file using mmap(). When the resource is no longer needed, the file could be removed and unmapped, returning the memory to the operating system, rather than free()'ing it, which simply returns it to the process' heap of available memory.

Conclusions

The NFB has been very successful in supporting both quick server bringup and advanced hardware features. The X server for the IRIS Indigo was running two days after the raster engine chip came back from the fab. The video controller hadn't come back yet, so we had to use xwd and xwud to look at what was on the screen!

There are currently eight NFB based DDXs on SGI machines ranging from the fast 2D raster engine of the Iris Indigo, to the 3D graphics pipeline of the VGX. All of these machines use NFB support for rendering, colormaps, overlays, and DID management. SCO will be shipping an NFB based X server for VGA and other PC graphics boards as part of their next(X11R4) release of Open Desktop. SCO will also be releasing an NFB based server porting kit for independent graphics board vendors.

The goals of the NFB have been met without requiring changes to DIX code, thus allowing easy tracking of MIT changes. Recently Keith Packard and I upgraded the SGI server to X11R5 in just a few hours.

While the NFB rendering layers are a good tool for quick server bringup, they are not always suitable for a production X server. To get truly high performance from many of the common X graphics requests it is still necessary to implement hardware specific routines directly to the DDX layer.

Acknowledgments

Paul Shupak and Tom Paquin provided early feedback on the NFB design and fixed several bugs. Dave Spalding and Spencer Murray implemented the GEN routines and several of the NFB drawing routines. Todd Newman and Peter Daifuku made overlays work and fixed other NFB bugs. Thanks to Tom Paquin for creating an environment where we could do it right.

References

1. Susan Angebranndt, Raymond Drewry, Philip Karlton, Todd Newman, Bob Scheifler, Keith Packard, "Definition of the Porting Layer for the X v11 Sample Server", *X11 Release 5 documentation*, April 22, 1991.

2. Todd Newman, "How Not to Implement Overlays in X", *Proceedings of the 6th Annual Technical Conference on the X Window System*, January 1992.

The Multi-Threaded
X Server

John Allen Smith

Abstract

The current (R5) version of the MIT X server provides only single-threaded support of X client requests, event processing, and device input. Each request and event is processed one at a time to the exclusion of all other processing. This approach leads to a non-interactive server. With applications such as 3D graphics, video, and multimedia, the performance and usability of the current server is severely degraded.

This paper discusses design issues related to an X server with multi-threaded concurrent support, and shows how applications generating long duration protocol requests, such as multimedia and PEX, can take advantage of the gains in interactivity. We describe how the contention of server objects can be expressed more clearly with the object-oriented paradigm and how the client/server model uses concurrency to define the mechanisms embodied in a threaded implementation of the X server.

A design for the multi-threaded X server is discussed in which the ideas of objects and concurrency are seen as essential to solving the interactivity problem.

John Smith is a Senior Software Engineer at Data General Corp.,Research Triangle Park, NC

Introduction

The X Window System^{TM} [SG90] is based on the client-server model of process interaction. This paradigm is the basis of most network communication, and is followed in X to give users the appearance of seamless applications concurrently using distributed resources. In actuality, this model permits independent applications to display data and communicate over a local-area network by means of a well-defined client/server protocol.

Limitations of the X server

The R5 server processes one client protocol request at a time. If there are multiple clients in the client queue that are simultaneously sending requests to the server, the server will process requests using a round-robin scheduling policy. Each client can have up to ten requests processed before the server preempts that client and starts working on the next client. Although the current server is implemented with a single-thread of control, it tries to give the appearance of concurrency by switching between clients after each block of requests. The issue then is that the R5 server multiplexes rather than batches the client requests.

The R5 Server creates problems for client requests that require a large amount of execution time. For instance, if a client executing Phigs/Phigs+ Extension to X (PEX) requests were to generate a structure traversal, the server would walk the entire structure tree, and depending on the size of the structures and the type of traversal, this walk could take several hours to complete. While the server is walking the structure tree, all other pending requests and input events are queued. All client activity, including the window manager, and mouse motion is frozen. This policy supports serve-to-completion rather than any type of preemption.

For multi-processor platforms, it is highly inefficient, in terms of processor utilization, to execute the current server without some form of multi-tasking. The server could benefit by partitioning requests across the processors so that they are executing in parallel.

To solve this problem, the multi-threaded X (MTX) server will allow a greater degree of concurrency than is possible in the R5 X server. The MTX server will execute on a kernel supporting user level threads and will conform to the POSIX 1003.4a pthreads calling standard.

For a more detailed discussion of the rationale for developing a multi-threaded X server, see [Smi91].

Objectives

The primary goals of the MTX server are:

- Conform to the existing server protocol.

- Increase server interactivity.

- Efficiently use multi-processor workstation platforms.

The secondary goals of the MTX server are:

- Do not significantly degrade server performance from the R5 levels.

- Design the product with a CASE toolkit that supports the object-oriented (OO) paradigm [Int90]. We feel this design approach is a natural consequence of the client/server model as embodied in the X Window System and will result in a cleaner implementation. A beneficial side-effect of using a structured methodology is automatic documentation of the MTX server as the product is developed.

Object Oriented Design

After the limitations of the current X server were identified, it was realized that a new design was required for a concurrent implementation. Since the Multi-Threaded X (MTX) server will require the implementation of concurrent programming ideas, we were motivated to consider Object Oriented Structured Design (OOSD) techniques [HSE90] in the project life-cycle. Software through Pictures^{TM} (StP) [Int90], from Interactive Development Environments, Inc., is one such tool that provides a variant of the OOSD design process.

At the heart of OOSD, is the object-oriented (OO) paradigm [KM90]. The OO paradigm focuses on objects and emphasizes the relationship between those objects as fundamental to the system architecture.

Objects are treated as the basic run-time entities in this design approach. In the X server, these objects include the window, screen, region, drawable, pixmap, device, font, cursor, colormap, ClientResourceTable, selection, property, atom, client, and others. Each of these objects work at different layers of the server. For example, the region object is active at the machine independent (MI) layer and not the device independent (DIX) layer while the window is primarily a DIX object.

Objects are pieces of the design that are conceptually grouped into classes. Each class defines a set of permissible objects that are eventually implemented as user defined types. Hence, a class becomes an implementation of an Abstract Data Type (ADT). Further, a good design will result in the encapsulation of the ADT and all access to that ADT through a monitor.

Objects and classes are the first two facets of OOSD. Inheritance, polymorphism, and dynamic binding are the others. Inheritance allows the reuse of objects and other software entities such as modules. The current X server defines the Window and Pixmap as Drawables. The Window and Pixmap classes are derived from the more common class of drawables. Code to render to a drawable can be used for both a window object as well as a pixmap object because *render* is a polymorphic operation on the class *drawable*. Lastly, the function pointers defined in the routing of protocol requests is an example of using dynamic binding.

The Entity-Relationship diagram (ERD) in Figure 1 summarizes the information of the data object design. This ERD follows the methodology used by StP.

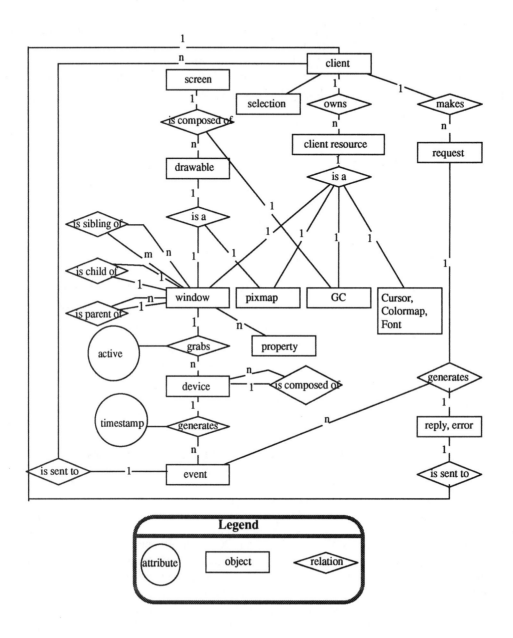

Figure 1: Entity-Relationship Diagram

Concurrency Mechanisms

Object-oriented techniques promote program modularity through the need for data abstraction. Concurrency is also concerned with data abstraction since this concept allows for the efficient management of resources in an environment requiring resource sharing and distributed problem solving. Data abstraction in turn leads to a development based on the concept of objects. Hence, we discover that concurrency is a natural consequence of the OO paradigm.

Solving problems using concurrency can be divided into three types [Agh90], pipeline, divide and conquer, and cooperative. The cooperative problem solving technique is very close to the description of how the client/server model operates. Since the MTX server is based on the client/server paradigm, we concluded that the cooperative technique is our best choice for the MTX server.

Since the application of cooperative problem solving involves the sharing and synchronization of resources among objects, we will manage those resources through the use of mutexes and condition variables. These synchronization tools are necessary in order to avoid deadlock and starvation.

In a concurrent environment such as OSF/1, access to shared data must be arbitrated by some access control policy [Kel89]. **Mutual exclusion** is one such policy that prevents two concurrent activities from accessing the same shared resources at the same time. These shared resources may include data as well as code segments called **regions**.

Mutual exclusion prevents activities from colliding over regions. If we want to prevent an activity from continuing until some general condition is met, then we must **synchronize** that activity with the condition. Hence, synchronization is a generalization of mutual exclusion. The use of conditions implies a causal dependence on the execution of activities. For instance, reading the drawables associated with a window object depends on the condition that the window object exist. If the create activity has not completed access to the window object, then the read activity will conditionally wait for synchronization from the create.

Read and write access to data structures that must be shared by many activities can be effectively managed using the Hoare monitor synchronization mechanism [Fin88]. This programming construct encapsulates the shared data object in a protective wrapper. The wrapper enforces mutual exclusion by allowing only one activity access to the shared data object. The monitor is a global object that advertises all of the public access routines of the object to the current set of activities.

The Hoare monitor is a poor performer, however, when there are many more reader than writer activities. We would like to allow multiple reads to occur concurrently while allowing only one write access at a time. This solution to the reader-writer problem is handled nicely by the crowd monitor. The crowd monitor has guard procedures that decide when each activity may enter or leave a reader or writer access group. These guard procedures arbitrate access to the protected data object. The crowd monitor determines which group currently has access permission, and queues those activities that must wait.

Also, activities should be able to exclusively lock multiple data objects before execution proceeds. For example, a ReparentWindow request will require that particular window objects be exclusively locked before a window is moved in the window hierarchy. This situation is similar to the readers/writers problem. Also, there are event queues that will be filled by input device activities and drained by activities that report the events to the appropriate clients. This is the producer/consumer problem.

These concurrency requirements convinced us to use crowd monitors in most cases. This assumes that we have access to mutex and condition primitives since crowd monitors can be built from these pieces. As we will see in the next section, our choice on how to thread the server will require that this concurrency mechanism be accessible in the threads package or, at least, allow its construction using primitives in the threads package.

Threaded X

The previous sections discussed how the MTX server is based on the client/server model and how this model is best expressed using an object-oriented methodology. In turn, this server model was shown to require concurrent activities that are best managed using concurrent programming constructs such as crowd monitors. This section will discuss how the OO paradigm and concurrency can be implemented with threads.

A thread is a sequential flow of control. There may be more than one thread executing within a process. Each thread shares the address space of the process with all other threads that are created in the process. A thread has its own execution stack, errno, and thread id. The benefits to using threads are that disjoint sets of code may be executed in parallel while sharing a common code and data address space. Using threads increases the concurrency and interactivity of a process, and allows for more efficient use of multiprocessor architectures.

In order to profit from kernels that support threads and multiprocessors, the MTX server will be targeted to run only on operating systems that conform to the POSIX 1003.4a standard. This standard supports

- the creation, control, and termination of threads

- the use of synchronization primitives by threads in a common, shared address space

Those users of the X Window System who can not or do not want to use the MTX server will continue to have access to the X11R5 server.

There are several issues to consider when threading the X server. These issues include

- what are the implementation constraints

- what level of granularity is needed to enforce resource locking

- what mechanism should be used to pass information between threads

- what is the impact of reentrancy

Constraints

The design of the MTX server will generate a list of objects and their related functions. The server must be designed so that those functions that do not collide over data objects execute in parallel, and those functions that are related are given fair access to data and are synchronized when required. There are several constraints that will affect the implementation of the server functionality.

Protocol Conformance

The MTX server must continue to conform with the existing X11 core protocol [SG90]. The X11 core protocol treats the service given to any one client as separate from all other clients. Hence, the protocol requests from each client must be treated as atomic and serial.

The MTX server must simulate the atomic behavior by not allowing different threads to collide over the same data object. In this way, the server executes each client request as if it were the only one being serviced.

The protocol demands that requests from the same client be executed in serial order. The effect of this requirement is that the MTX server should concurrently execute requests from the same client only if the *appearance* to the user is one of ordered changes. So, a client that generates a request for a font load and also a request to install a new colormap can expect the server to execute these requests concurrently since the font and colormap resources are distinct. Requests to change window attributes and reparent window must occur in serial order since these requests may access the same window resource.

System Resource Usage

The primary goal of the MTX server is to increase interactivity but not at the expense of the R5 server level of performance. Thread design and granularity of resource access must consider how server performance is impacted. Excessive context switching of threads and untuned resource locking strategies can both degrade performance. Related to performance is memory usage. A server that uses great amounts of memory or generates excessive paging will not be acceptable. Partitioning the server data and code into logical pieces should keep memory requirements at an acceptable level.

Implementation Tools

Implementation requires support tools such as debuggers and kernel monitors. Although not strictly a design constraint, lack of a multi-threaded debugger can affect the ability to test and debug multi-threaded code. The server implementor must either test and debug using an alternative to threads, such as co-routines, or strategically place printf/fflush pairs in the questionable code. Since thread execution can be non-deterministic, bugs may not always be reproducible. If the developer does not have support for multi-threaded debugging, he may be tempted to design his code to make less than efficient use of threads. If the code cannot be assured then it remains suspect.

Another useful tool for multiprocessor based servers is a kernel monitor. The kernel monitor allows the developer to determine how thread partitioning of the server functionality and OS thread scheduling affects the performance of the server. Monitoring kernel-level behavior is essential for discovering performance bottlenecks in the multi-threaded OS.

Resource Locking

Use of sharable data objects pervades the MTX server. The concurrency paradigm refers to these as sharable objects as *resources* and suggests that access to the resources be synchronized between multiple contending threads. The MTX server wants to avoid having two clients change the same window at the same time, for example.

In the OO design of the MTX server, we will generate an object hierarchy and a description of how the objects should be accessed. Part of the process of building the list of objects is discovering the locking requirements on those objects. Objects may theoretically be accessed in any of the read and write mode combinations, but practically, we want to impose resource locks to insure mutual exclusion while ensuring maximum concurrency. Locks on shared objects will be enforced by either Hoare monitors or crowd monitors. Event related objects will be protected by the Event Monitor, and the Client/Resource Table Monitor will protect the Client/Resource Table.

Another issue is the lock granularity. Lock granularity can be defined in terms of the size of the resource to be locked and the length of time that a resource is protected from mutual access (i.e from lock to unlock). Granularity is either fine or coarse grained. In fine grained locking, a small resource is locked frequently for very short periods of time. In coarse grained locking, a large resource is locked for long periods of time, but much more infrequently. Determining the lock granularity of each object will be dependent on the expected use of that object and the read/write access level required. The granularity will be coded in the object access routines.

Choosing the correct level of lock granularity for each resource will be important in maximizing performance and interactivity. For instance, if multiple threads reading trackball input were to lock around each read while updating the device record, then more time would be spent in locking/unlocking than if the thread were to execute a lock, multiple reads, and then an unlock. Since there is overhead in locking and unlocking, fine grained locking will consume many system resources but provide quick access to objects. Generally, coarse grained locking will consume fewer system resources but result in a higher probability of contention of threads. Fine grained locking increases interactivity at the expense of performance and memory usage while coarse grained locking increases performance at the expense of interactivity.

In order to increase the interactivity of the server but not degrade performance, the lock granularity for each object must be carefully considered with the above trade-offs in mind. An OO design will help to flesh out the expected usage patterns for each object in relation to each protocol request.

Reentrancy

Since threads share code and global data, the procedures that are callable from within threads must be reentrant or within a critical region. Requiring reentrancy means that most of the current server code can not be reused as is, even at the MI layer. To make the existing DIX code usable for example, all functions that access shared objects must be made to use a global locking strategy.

Alternatively, the MTX server could be divided into non-reentrant and reentrant pieces. The non-reentrant piece would be able to use existing server code and the reentrant code would be redesigned based on threads. This hybrid alternative is not practical since the OO redesign of the reentrant parts would not be compatible with the existing server and would make maintenance difficult.

Prototype Platforms

Prototyping, proof of concept, and benchmarking work can be completed using kernels that support threads. This includes Mach from Carnegie-Mellon University and OSF/1^{TM}. Mach is a distributed systems kernel [R+87] that uses Cthreads [CD88], and OSF/1, a derivative of Mach, supports POSIX 1003.4a standard pthreads.

The Cthreads library provides a high level C programming interface to the low level Mach kernel thread primitives. Cthreads supports multiple threads of control for concurrency and parallelism through shared variables, mutual exclusion of critical regions, and condition variables for thread synchronization.

Because Mach provides this user level view of threads, we decided to use Mach for our initial timing tests to determine if Mach threads would be capable of supporting the MTX server functionality. These tests proved positive and a prototype server using Mach was developed. A second prototype is under development to test the design of the resource locking strategy.

MTX Threads

The functionality of the MTX server will be approximately the same as that defined by the current R5 server. Although the functionality is equivalent, the implementation is not. The MTX server will be implemented with threads and concurrency support whereas the R5 server has a single thread of control. The current X server looks for client requests, input events, and new client connections within the *dispatch* code. By combining these three unrelated functions into one serial loop, the performance of the server suffers. Using threads, we can divide these functions into separate flows of control [T+87].

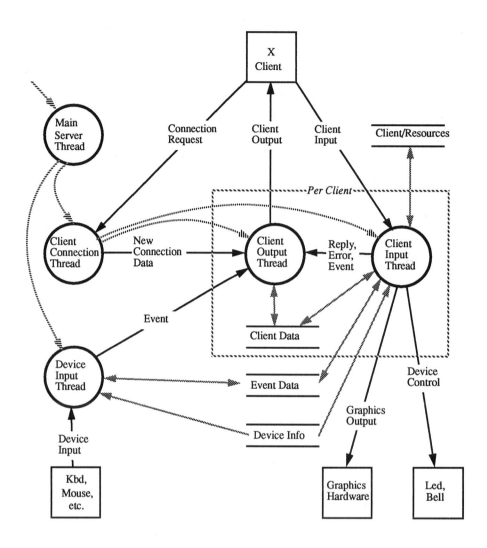

Figure 2: MTX Server Threads

A sample implementation of the use of threads in the MTX server is described below and is shown in Figure 2. In the diagram, circles indicate threads, boxes indicate external objects, dark directed lines indicate inter-thread data flow, grey directed lines indicate data object access, dashed directed lines indicate thread creation, and two horizontal lines enclose data objects.

A final implementation will not be realized until after the detailed design and prototype evaluations are complete.

Main Server Thread

The Main Server Thread (MST) manages the global MTX server environment. This thread initializes the MTX server and the input devices, and creates the Device Input Thread. It also creates the Client Connection Thread so that X Clients can establish communications with the server. If the MST receives a wakeup signal, it cleans up the global MTX server environment and checks to see if the server should reset or terminate. If it should reset, the MST reinitializes the environment and starts the MTX setup over again.

The functionality of the Main Server Thread is similar to that found in *main* in *main.c*. In the R5 implementation, the *dispatch* exists so that new client connections, new protocol requests, and new device input can be arbitrated fairly by the server. In the MTX server, however, these functions are broken into independent flows of control. Therefore, the *dispatch* loop has been removed from the MTX server.

Client Connection Thread(s)

New client connections are processed by at a Client Connection Thread (CCT). There will be a separate CCT to handle the different network transport types. For example, there will be a CCT to handle the shared-memory transport and another CCT to handle either TCP/ IP or DECnet.

When a new client connection is detected, the target CCT will accept the connection and create a new Client Input Thread. In this way, we push the validation of the client out of the CCT so that the CCT does not block during the validation handshake.

Client Input Thread(s)

Upon creation, the Client Input Thread (CIT) validates the client connection. The CIT determines byte order, accepts the client connection, sends server information to the client, adds the client information for this client to the client database, and creates the Client Output Thread to route events, replies, and errors back to the X Client.

If the X Client makes a successful connection to the MTX server, the CIT creates a Client object and a new entry in the Client Resource Table. The Client object is built from information gathered when the connection is established, and from default information in the server.

There exists a Client Input Thread for each client connected to the MTX server. After initialization, this thread processes requests for its assigned client while adhering to the atomicity and serial constraints described above. Once this thread is created, it will block until there is a client request. This thread also handles the byte ordering of the OS connection to the client. The request is processed similar to the function pointer mechanism used in the *dispatch* loop for *(* client-requestVector[MAJOROP])(client)*.

All Client Input Threads will be able to process any protocol request. Since each protocol request accesses both shared and private objects, locking policies will be invoked to protect multiple Client Input Threads from stepping on the same resources. Resources in the Client/Resource Table are considered to be shared objects. Access to these shared objects will be through the Client/Resource Table Monitor.

If a Client Input Thread wishes to gain access to event related objects (such as the event mask, GrabRec, or DeviceIntRec), the Client Input Thread will request access through the Event Monitor. The Event Monitor will insure exclusive access to the event related objects and block other requesting threads to enforce serial access to the event related objects. The Event Monitor will return control to the requesting Client Input Thread when the monitor finishes.

All events that originate in the Client Input Thread will be processed by the Event Monitor before routing to the X Client. Errors and replies that originate in the Client Input Thread will be sent directly to the corresponding Client Output Thread.

The Client Input Thread will also handle client shutdown activities. When a client dies or is killed, the appropriate Client Input Thread will free resources from the Client/Resource Table and cleanup local data structures. If the CIT represents the last client connected to the MTX server, then it will acquire a lock to insure that no new connections are made to the server while it notifies the Main Server Thread to wakeup and reset the server. The CIT will kill its COT mate and then exit.

If there is output to be sent to any devices, this thread will manage that activity through the DDX layer. This includes writing to the graphics output device and generating feedback for the feedback devices (i.e. led and bell). Writing to the graphics output devices is a frequent operation and could generate an unacceptable number of thread context switches if this functionality were placed in a thread other than the Client Input Thread.

The MTX server localizes the processing of client requests to a CIT. Therefore, some of the client connection masks that are found in R5's *connection.c* file can be removed. The CIT does a blocking read on the client's request socket; thus removing the dependence on the slow *select* call. Once the CIT detects a request, it does not have to use or manipulate any complicated masks to determine the client record or the client id. The CIT can immediately jump to validation of the request.

Only one input buffer exists per CIT rather than a pool of buffers as currently exists in the R5 server. This approach allows us to localize the input buffer processing to individual CITs and do away with possibly having to use a *select*.

Client Output Thread

There will be an equivalent Client Output Thread for each Client Input Thread. This thread is created by the Client Connection Thread coincident with the creation of the Client Input Thread.

The Client Input Thread and Device Input Thread (producer threads) will send events, replies, and errors to the Client Output Thread via an output buffer. The Client Output Thread will flush data from the output buffer to a client's socket. If the socket is full, the thread will block.

If the first output buffer is in use and a producer thread has data to give to the Client Output Thread, the Client Input Thread will use a second buffer until it also fills. Then, the producer thread will have to wait until some data is flushed to the socket before continuing.

Access to the COT output buffers is protected by event counters and a sequencer that dispenses "tickets". Each element in the output buffer is tagged with the ticket held by the producer thread. When the producer thread has finished generating output elements (such as events, replies, and errors), the COT will be notified. The COT will process output elements in ticket order, and only flush to the client those output elements tagged to the current available ticket.

An implementation of the COT requires that changes be made to the *WriteToClient* and *FlushAllOutput* modules. These modules will now write to the output buffers of the COT instead of directly to the network buffers.

Device Input Thread

The Device Input Thread (DIT) waits for device input and routes device events to selected Client Output Threads.

There will be at least one Device Input Thread to handle all device input to the server. Device input from the mouse, keyboard, trackball, etc. is currently placed in the *ProcessInputEvents* function. This function has device independent and device dependent code based on the type of device. The Device Input Thread will accept input from all registered devices. This thread would process the device input and format the correct events.

MTX Monitors

Read and write access to data structures that must be shared by many threads can be effectively managed using the Hoare monitor. This programming construct encapsulates the shared data object in a protective wrapper. The wrapper enforces mutual exclusion by allowing only one thread access to the shared data object at any one moment. The monitor is a global object that advertises all of the public access routines of the object to the current set of threads.

The Hoare monitor is acceptable if the object requires exclusive access. But, it is a poor performer when there are many more readers than writers. Typically, we would like to allow multiple reads to occur concurrently while allowing only one write access at a time.

This solution to the reader-writer problem is handled nicely by the crowd monitor. The crowd monitor has guard procedures that decide when each thread may enter or leave a reader or writer access group. These guard procedures arbitrate access to the protected data object. The crowd monitor determines which group currently has access permission, and queues those threads that must wait.

A Hoare monitor will be used to control access to the Event Object. A Hoare monitor will be used to control access to each client's Client Resource Table. Once the resource has been found, either a Hoare monitor or Crowd monitor will be used to access the details of the resource. For example, window record fields can be grouped by geometry, hierarchy, event propagation, and configuration. Access to event propagation fields is via a Hoare Monitor while the other groups are through separate Crowd Monitors.

Event Object Monitor

The Event Object Monitor (EOM) will arbitrate access to the event related data objects. These objects include the window event mask, the window optional donotpropagate mask, the grab record, the deviceint record, and others.

If a Client Input Thread or Device Input Thread needs to access one of these objects, the Event Monitor will check on the access mode requested. If the access mode is read only, and there are no threads accessing with write mode, then the reading thread is allowed to proceed. If there is a thread accessing with write mode, then all other requesting threads are blocked until the writing thread exits the monitor.

For a thread to successfully access the monitor with write mode, there must not be any threads currently accessing the monitor. If there are threads only reading via the monitor, then any new reading or writing threads are blocked, the current set of reading threads is allowed to complete, and the first writing thread is then allowed to gain access.

Client Resource Table Monitor

All resources such as windows, pixmaps, GCs, colormaps, etc. are kept in the Client/ Resource Table. When a client creates a resource, the client id is used as a unique index into the table. For each client, there is a hash table of resources where the resource id is used to hash into a table of buckets that contain a list of resources owned by that client. Each entry in the list in turn points to the actual resource object.

The resource-id is the unique identifier that is both understood by the Xlib and the MTX server sides of the client/server model. Since the X protocol must be preserved and the format of this resource-id is tied to the protocol, we must preserve this table in the MTX server.

The Client/Resource Table Monitor will maintain this table by processing add, read, and free requests from threads that manipulate these shared resources. The Client Input Threads and the Event Monitor are currently identified as those program elements manipulating shared resources and will use the Client/Resource Monitor.

Multimedia applications and X

One of the original driving problems for the design of a multi-threaded X server was the efficient use of PEX. Multiple PEX applications severely degrade the interactivity of the current X server as each 3D image is rendered. An application that uses all of the PEX graphics features, such as lighting, shading, and depth cueing, can make the other day-to-day applications unusable.

We can also envision that other proposed media extensions to X will compete in a similar way for server bandwidth.

The Video Extension (VEX) [Bru90] was proposed as an extension to X to provide a standard interface to video operations. These operations include video input and output, manipulating a video picture on the screen, acquiring digitized pixels from video frames, cutting portions of the screen for video recording devices, and control of external video devices. Full television resolution video processing is not yet a feasible application because video signal rates are still high compared to disk storage rates. But, applications that require lower video rates such as video post-production, simulation, video teleconferencing, and image processing could benefit from the use of VEX. Although the VEX proposal is yet to be approved by the MIT X Consortium, we must keep VEX in mind as we continue to list those applications that could benefit from a multi-threaded X server.

The X Image Extension (XIE) [Web91] is motivated by the growth in applications requiring efficient image rendition, document image management, and interactive continuous tone color enhancement and analysis. Cartographic and Geographic Information Services (GIS) applications would benefit mostly from the XIE standard.

By integrating PEX, VEX, and XIE applications with those requiring audio and graphic capabilities, the X server will be able to support a full range of multimedia services. This paper has demonstrated that the current X server does not give PEX users, let alone VEX and XIE applications, the performance and interactivity that they should expect. The MTX server attempts to address this problem by providing a server that can take advantage of threaded capabilities on platforms designed to support multimedia services.

A multi-threaded X server will allow users to manipulate multimedia applications while simultaneously reading mail or news, and editing a emacs document. Users can expect that highly interactive applications can coexist in an environment with reasonable performance if the server providing these services is designed from the beginning to solve these problems of concurrency.

Summary

This paper has shown how the current X server is incapable of adequately supporting long duration X extension services. The reason for this breakdown in service is due to the single-threaded, one request at a time, implementation of the current X server.

We have shown that in order to provide sufficient services in a client/server environment, the server must be designed with concurrency mechanisms in place to take advantage of SMP and multiprocessor operating systems. These concurrency mechanisms are best implemented after an object-oriented approach uncovers the objects and their inter-object relationships in the server.

The multi-threaded X server is being engineered with concurrency mechanisms to solve the problems of interactivity and performance that can be expected from high demand applications such as PEX.

No project of this complexity can proceed without proper tools. A CASE toolkit was chosen to automate design and implementation. In addition, Mach was chosen for its object-oriented approach to concurrency and distributed applications as well as its support of threads through the cthreads library.

Acknowledgments

This project is being developed in association with the MIT X Consortium. Thanks go to Keith Packard and Bob Scheifler of the MIT X Consortium, and Mike Haynes and Paul Layne of Data General for their continuing ideas and discussions.

Trademarks

X Window System^{TM} is a trademark of The Massachusetts Institute of Technology

Software through Pictures^{TM} is a registered trademark of Interactive Development Environments, Inc.

OSF/1^{TM} is a registered trademark of Open Software Foundation, Inc.

UNIX^{TM} is a registered trademark of Unix Systems Laboratories, Inc.

References

[Agh90] Gul Agha. *Concurrent object-oriented programming*. Commun. ACM, 33(9):125-141, September 1990.

[Bru90] Todd Brunhoff. *Vex Your Hardware VEX Version 5.6*. In Xhibition 90 Conference Proceedings, San Jose, CA, May 1990

[CD88] E.Cooper and R.Draves. *C threads*. Technical Report CMU-CS-88-154, School of Computer Science, Carnegie Mellon University, February 1988

[Fin88] R. Finkel. *An Operating Systems VADE MECUM*, chapter 8. Prentice Hall, Englewood Cliffs, NJ, 1988

[HSE90] B. Henderson-Sellers and J. Edwards. *The object-oriented systems life cycle*. Commun. ACM, 33(9):142-159, September 1990

[Int90] Interactive Development Environments, San Francisco, CA 94105. *Software through Pictures User Manual*, March 1990

[Kel89] M. Kelly. *Multiprocessor Aspects of the DG/UX Kernel*. Proceedings of the Winter 1989 USENIC Conference, pages 85-99. The USENIX Association, Berkely, CA., 1989

[KM90] T. Korson and J. McGregor. *Understanding object-oriented: A unifying paradigm*. Commun. ACM, 33(9):40-60, September 1990.

[R$^+$87] R. Rashid et al. *Machine-independent virtual memory management for paged uniprocessor and multiprocessor architectures*. Technical Report CMU-CS-87-140, School of Computer Science, Carnegie Mellon University, July 1987.

[SG90] R. Scheifler and J. Gettys. *X WIndow System: The Complete Reference to Xlib, X Protocol, ICCCM, XLFD*. Digital Press, 1990.

[Smi91] J. Smith. *Engineering a Multi-Threaded X Server*. In Xhibition Technical Conference, pages 17-27, 1991.

[T$^+$87] A. Tevanian et al. *Mach Threads and the UNIX Kernel: The Battle for Control*. In USENIX Summer Conf. Proc., 1987.

[Web91] John Weber. *XIE, a Proposed Standard Extension to the X11 Window System*. In 5th Annual X Technical Conference Technical Papers, Boston, MA, Jan 1991.

The author may be contacted at Data General Corporation, 62 T.W. Alexander Drive, Research Triangle Park, NC 27709; e-mail smithj@dg-rtp.dg.com

Prototyping MT-Safe Xt and XView Libraries

Bart Smaalders
Brian Warkentine
Kevin Clarke

Abstract

The use of multiple threads in X Windows applications promises substantial increases in usability and interactivity. Existing toolkits cannot be safely used in multi-threaded applications without considerable effort by the applications programmer, however. This paper describes progress to date on an effort to develop multi-thread-safe Xt and XView libraries. Particular attention is given to the internal design of the toolkits as it hinders supporting concurrency. A technique is described that makes the toolkits MT-safe with minimal changes to their design, and the prototyping efforts are described.

The authors are part of the Windows Performance Technologies group at Sun Soft, Inc.

Introduction

The increasing availability of application-visible threads promises to have a great impact on X Windows applications. In contrast to the usual scenario of busy applications hanging and sometimes blocking the window server, we will have the ability to construct GUI applications that can always respond to user input, regardless of whatever else they are doing. This will greatly simplify the task of writing distributed and computationally intensive windowing applications.

Threads represent a major paradigm shift for applications developers and some effort is required to convert existing applications and libraries. X window systems toolkits are no exception - most were not designed to be used in a multi-threaded (MT) environment, and will require modifications to work successfully. The eventual goal is to develop a window system toolkit that intrinsically supports threads, and provides all the benefits of a multi-threaded programming environment. A rational intermediate step is to make it possible to use the existing toolkits from a MT program, albeit not at full efficiency or concurrency.

This document describes some approaches to making the Xt and XView toolkits usable from an MT program, e.g. making those toolkits *MT-safe*. In this effort, we have maintained the existing APIs; in some cases, some performance advantages might be realized if some additional routines were made available.

Problem description

The problems experienced trying to use window system toolkits in an MT environment are a result of violating certain implicit assumptions made by the toolkit designer while writing the code. These assumptions are typically:

- There is only a single thread of control active in the toolkit.
- The flow of control is normal; e.g. no "long jumps", co-routines, etc.
- The overall control of the application is the task of the toolkit's event dispatching loop.

We have two basic approaches to solving this problem:

- Rewrite the code so as to relax these constraints; e.g. remove the implicit assumptions. This would permit us to have many threads inside the toolkit at once; the toolkit would be fully re-entrant.
- Protect the existing code using thread synchronization primitives such as mutexes so that the assumptions are not violated. In this case we protect the critical sections of the code with locks to prevent multiple threads from interfering with each other.

The first technique is considered the most desirable, since it permits the maximum amount of parallelism. However, for large libraries, this can be a formidable task, and it is often impossible to achieve complete success since there are large numbers of shared data structures essential to the function of the library. For example, in both Xt and XView large amounts of data indicating the position, color and size of a hierarchy of graphical objects are maintained and referenced in order to perform updates and modifications to any one of these objects. As a result, the data structure must not be changed during operations to these objects.

The usual technique is to use a combination of the two approaches, re-writing where possible and using locks where shared data structures need protection from un-coordinated access. Using locks is not a panacea, however; implementing locking for data structure access can be very difficult. In particular:

- The successful use of locking requires that the number of places a particular shared data structure is referenced is limited. Otherwise, the level of contention for the lock can be very high, and the effective concurrency is greatly reduced. Reader/writer locks can help this somewhat, but achieving useful parallelism would still require that any common operation hold only reader locks for widely referenced data structures.

- In order to prevent deadlock, all the locks acquired by threads must be obtained in the same order. This is difficult to implement in existing toolkits, since the toolkits traverse the data structures in different ways. In the case of XView, for example, an object may process the attribute list first, or have its superclass process the list first - the order is implementation dependent. Xt has a similar indeterminate propagation of calls in the case of resize events.

- One cannot avoid recursive acquisition of locks with out rewriting large amounts of the library - hence special locking mechanisms are required. For example, in XView the entry points are used extensively inside the toolkit, so any code inserted into the entry points will be executed multiple times. In addition, callback routines specified by the application writer will call toolkit routines.

In addition to the problems listed above, both Xt and XView provide event dispatching loops that are used to control single-threaded applications. Both toolkits provide support for events on user-supplied file descriptors, and XView provides wrappers for signals and wait calls. In order to maintain the existing APIs, we need to make sure that this event dispatching model is maintained.

Problem solution

After reviewing the structure and nature of the toolkits, it became clear that modifying the code to be completely reentrant would require a complete rethink of the toolkit architectures and data structures. The most likely effect of even successfully implementing fine-grained locking on the existing data structures would be to effectively enforce serial access by the various threads due to the amount of data sharing. In addition, locking the Xt internal data structures would also require managing those locks in external widget sets, since these widgets generally directly reference their superclass' data. Further impediments to complete concurrency are the requirement that X protocol requests be atomic and the design of the event handling in Xlib.

To avoid these problems, we decided to attempt to maintain the assumptions made by the toolkit designers while still supporting access by multiple threads, namely:

- There is only a single thread of control active in the toolkit at one time. The toolkit is not affected by the calls coming from different stacks as long as the one at a time restriction is maintained.

- The flow of control is normal; e.g. it follows the static call graphs, but some of those calls may take place in different threads. We end up emulating the traditional flow of control seen in single threaded applications, but having that flow consist of the synchronized actions of multiple threads.

A method of maintaining these invariants is to use a token to control access to the toolkit. Before any call can be made into the toolkit, the caller must hold the token. The default holder of the token is the event dispatch loop. Other threads wishing to acquire the token must signal their interest to the event dispatch loop and await the receipt of the token, which the event loop does as part of a dispatch operation. When the client thread completes the toolkit call, it releases the token. The event dispatch loop waits to reacquire the token before continuing.

What does this achieve? First, it allows only one thread to access the toolkit data structures at a time. Second, it prevents the event loop from contending with other threads for input from server connections while an application is communicating synchronously with the server, since the event loop is waiting to reacquire the token whenever another thread is accessing the display connection. Third, use of the token insures that the aggregate sum of toolkit accesses by all threads mimics the flow of control that one would see in a (admittedly complex) single-threaded application.

The advantage of the token approach is that no changes need be made to the toolkits except those required to add calls to the public entry points to acquire and release the token, and some minor additions to the event loop. The principle drawback is that we haven't achieved any parallelism inside the toolkit, so that toolkit access effectively serializes the threads. Fortunately most toolkit operations are of short enough duration so the serialization of access is not a problem in terms of interactivity. If this assumption is violated, the proposed approach loses much of its usefulness.

Token implementation

The implementation of the token system has undergone some evolution as required features were identified. This section discusses some of the implementation issues and their resolution.

Supporting recursion.

As mentioned before, the toolkits tend to call themselves extensively, often through the public interfaces. Since we have added calls to the public entry points to acquire and release the token, either one must arrange for the token to "count" the number of times it has been re-acquired (similar to a mutex that supports recursion), or one must insure that the public entry points are not used inside the toolkit, by providing alternate entry points that do not use the token routines.

An alternate method uses macros to rename calls to the protected entry points. This "renaming" method has the potential of minimizing the impact on performance, since it avoids any additional overhead except at entry points. However, it is not simple to make this robust, since the user will pass pointers to functions that call protected entry points for the toolkit to execute as callbacks.

Our initial implementation uses a counting token scheme; combining it with renamed non-public interfaces is probably a worthwhile performance enhancement and maintaining the counting model will take care of any recursive token acquisition due to callbacks.

Preventing starvation and "hogging" of the token.

The standard synchronization primitives in the Posix thread library as currently implemented do not impose any ordering on waiting threads. This feature avoids burdening applications that do not require the overhead that strict ordering would imply. In those situations where some number of threads may always be waiting on a mutex, there exists a possibility of starving one of the threads; e.g. one thread may not run at all, or more likely, a thread that only briefly releases the lock may prevent any other thread from acquiring the lock at all.

Since it is not difficult to devise situations (admittedly somewhat artificial) where several threads are continuously contending for the token, the token mechanism must impose ordering (typically FIFO) on the waiting threads. Without some ordering, some threads may be starved of token access, or the thread running the event loop dispatcher may not be able to reacquire the token and hence cause interactivity problems.

Token system details.

The following are the salient features of the token mechanism as currently implemented:

- The token implements strict ordering of waiting threads. This is achieved by providing a protected queue. Threads wishing to acquire the token acquire it immediately if it is not held. Otherwise, the thread adds itself to the queue of threads waiting to acquire the token, and goes to sleep on its own condition variable, which is accessible via the queue. As a thread releases the token, the token release routine signals the next thread waiting on the queue.

- The token also supplies an internal counting mechanism so that the token may be acquired recursively. If on attempting to acquire the token the thread determines that it already holds the token, an internal count is incremented. The same procedure is performed on releasing the token, with the actual release not performed until the recursion count reaches zero.

- In order to maintain acceptable interactivity, the token facility provides a routine to allow urgent threads (the event loop in practice) to jump to the head of the queue of threads waiting to acquire the token. This is required in the case of a large number of threads all trying to perform many drawing routines. In this case, the event loop would spend most of the time waiting to acquire the token, and would only run intermittently, damaging the perceived performance.

- A provision in the token request routine for calling a user-supplied notification function before blocking pending receipt of token is provided to allow client threads to notify the event loop dispatcher that another thread wishes to acquire the token. This is implemented in the token routine to prevent a race condition.

- Since the event dispatch loop is sitting in a select or poll call, a pipe is used to communicate requests for the token to the event dispatch loop.

Using Xlib calls from MT applications.

MIT has provided locking calls in the source for Xlib; these are implemented as macros and are normally defined as empty. Applications using only Xlib (no other toolkits) can simply supply the appropriate simple locking routines and re-compile Xlib. Applications using higher-level toolkits need to use the same token routines to protect Xlib calls that are used for the rest of the toolkit. This is required to prevent competition between the event loop and the synchronous toolkit calls in reading events from the display connection. This can be done simply by providing the appropriate locking routines for Xlib in the higher level toolkit library in such a way that they are always included. By placing the locking routines for pure Xlib applications in a separate object in the Xlib library we have automatic overloading of the locking routines as needed so long as the user doesn't attempt to use two high-level toolkits in the same executable.

It may be possible to make asynchronous Xlib calls just using the simple lock on the display provided by Xlib; this would require that synchronous calls have different locking routines than the asynchronous routines and hence require either changing Xlib or providing a special version for use with MT-safe higher level toolkits. For example, a drawing routine such as XDrawLine need only insert its data into the connection buffer atomically; routines such as XGetImage that perform an explicit round trip to the server are synchronous and must be the only routine attempting to access the server connection for the duration of the round trip. As a result, callers of these synchronous routines need to hold the token.

Performance aspects.

There are a couple of performance impacts with the token system, one of which can seriously affect performance in extreme situations. First, as mentioned above, the current implementation calls the token routines in each entry point. This adds two simple function calls to each traversal of an entry point by any thread, whether from inside the toolkit or not. The renaming scheme discussed above will reduce this substantially, and this doesn't seem to be a major problem in any case.

The more intractable and serious problem occurs when separate threads wish to make large numbers of toolkit calls (say many Xlib operations). The problem is that the event loop and client threads end up exchanging the token each time a toolkit or Xlib call is made. In the case where the client threads wish to make hundreds of separate toolkit calls, a considerable amount of time will be spent exchanging the token between the client and the event loop threads. In severe cases almost all of the time is spent in thrashing between the event loop and client threads.

There are several solutions:

- In some cases, the client code making the large number of calls can be made into a toolkit component (e.g. widget or object) and protected by the standard mechanisms. This is a good technique and is good programming practice, but is not always applicable.

- We can arrange for the routines that make heavy use of the toolkits to be called as part of the event loop thread, either as work procedures in Xt or as client event routines in XView. This can make application development less straightforward, but eliminates the performance problem.

- The calls to get and release the token could be exported for use by the sophisticated programmer. This violates our resolve not to change the API, but may be the highest performance solution.

- Arrange for the event loop to delay re-acquiring the token for enough milliseconds to prevent severe thrashing. This is clearly a stop-gap solution, but may be sufficient to reduce the amount of thrashing to acceptable levels.

We are continuing to experiment with alternative solutions.

Prototype Implementation

This section discusses some of the details of the prototype implementation. This work was performed using SunOS 5.0, X11R4 and Open Windows 3.0. Both Xt and XView libraries were converted, and some testing has been performed. Most of the following discussion covers Xt, both because it is of wider interest and because the implementation was more difficult than the XView version.

Token interface.

Four functions provide the Xt token interface: *XtInitializeToken*, *XtGetToken*, *XtReleaseToken*, and *_XtTokenDispatch*. The token is initialized with *XtInitializeToken*, which performs the following steps:

- Creates a process local Unix pipe.

- Registers the pipe with the Intrinsics via XtAppAddInput.

- Initializes the fifo queue and the mutex that protects access to the fifo queue.

- Acquires the token.

XtInitializeToken is called from the standard Intrinsics initialization routines such as XtToolkitInitialize. Because some toolkits such as OLIT layer this entry point behind their own initialization functions, *XtInitializeToken* only initializes the token the first time it is called.

XtInitializeToken should be called towards the end of toolkit initialization, so that the necessary data structures for XtAppAddInput are set up, such as the default application context.

The thread calling *XtInitializeToken* holds the token after initialization. The input event notification procedure registered with XtAppAddInput is responsible for handing off the token to other threads. This means the token will not be transferred until the event dispatcher (e.g. XtAppMainLoop, XtAppNextEvent) is invoked.

XtGetToken performs the following steps:

- Checks if the calling thread already holds the token. If so, it increments a counter for the number of times *XtGetToken* has been called and returns. This counter avoids attempts to reacquire the token if it is already held by the current thread, and indicates when it should be released.

- Calls the fifo routine fifo_signal_enter, which puts the calling thread at the end of the list of threads waiting for the token, and writes a short message on the pipe.

- At this point, *XtGetToken* blocks by going to sleep on its own condition variable.

- Another thread will call *XtReleaseToken*, which will unblock this thread.

- Set the counter for the number of times *XtGetToken* has been called to 1.

- Reads the data from the pipe and discards it.

- Returns, holding the token.

XtReleaseToken does the following:

- Checks the count of the number of times *XtGetToken* has been called for this thread, and decrements it.

- If the count is zero, then all the calls to *XtGetToken* have been matched and the token can be released. It does so by awakening the first thread on the fifo queue and passing the token to that thread.

The input notification procedure registered with XtAppAddInput is used to do token dispatching. Just before a thread blocks on *XtGetToken*, it writes a small message on the pipe. The contents of the message is meaningless, but the I/O acts as a signal to the thread running XtAppNextEvent that another thread needs the token. XtAppNextEvent will in turn awaken from the select call that it wraps and will invoke *_XtTokenDispatch*.

Writing the small message to the pipe has a useful side effect. XtAppNextEvent calls select, which usually blocks awaiting input from the server. Because the pipe's file descriptor is registered, it is also passed to select by XtAppNextEvent. The I/O will unblock the select so that the token can be dispatched without delay and regardless of server activity.

When XtAppNextEvent calls _XtTokenDispatch_ it holds the token. Ideally, it should call _XtReleaseToken_ to pass the token to other threads, and call _XtGetToken_ to reacquire the token when the other threads are done. This solution is not feasible because XtAppNextEvent may be called from deeply nested functions. For example, XtAppNextEvent is usually called by XtAppMainLoop. The nesting level is two in this case. Furthermore, XtAppNextEvent is a public entry point so it is not possible to predict the level of nesting it will be called from. For example, an application may invoke XtAppNextEvent from a callback, in this case the nesting count will be at least three (from XtCallCallbacks, XtDispatchEvent, and XtAppMainLoop).

Unfortunately, _XtReleaseToken_ is equivalent to stepping only one level at a time and releases the token only when the count drops to zero. A mechanism to circumvent the counting is implemented with the function _fifo_yield_. The following code shows how it is used in _XtTokenDispatch_ to pass the token to a waiting thread:

```
void
_XtTokenDispatch(XtPointer client_data, int *source, XtInputId *id)
{
    fifo_t * fifo = & ((token_t *)client_data)->fifo;
    int loops = 0;

    do {
        fifo_yield(fifo);
        loops++;
    } while(fifo_num_waiters(fifo) && (loops < 5));
}
```

This function is invoked from the protected event dispatch loop, so it has the token when it is called. Releasing the token is done by _fifo_yield_, which unblocks the first thread on the fifo list, puts itself at the head of the fifo, sets the count to zero, and blocks itself. At this point, the waiting thread executes. When this thread releases the token _fifo_yield_ unblocks holding the token. At that point, it restores the count to the previous value and returns to the caller.

The function _fifo_num_waiters_ is used to detect when there are threads remaining on the fifo list and the loops variable is used to allow control to return to the event dispatch loop occasionally so that interactive performance does not suffer. This is why _fifo_yield_ places the caller at the head of the queue rather than the tail - else if a large number of threads are waiting to acquire the token, interactive performance would suffer while the queue is drained.

Protecting entry points.

There are two possible methods of protecting entry points with the _XtGetToken_ and _XtReleaseToken_ calls. The first method is to modify the library source so that entry points acquire the token on entry and release the token before returning. The following code shows how *XtGetToken* and *XtReleaseToken* have been added to XtCreateManagedWidget:

```
Widget XtCreateManagedWidget(name, widget_class, parent, args, num_args)
    String name;
    WidgetClass widget_class;
    Widget parent;
    ArgList args;
    Cardinal num_args;
{
    register Widget widget;

    XtGetToken();
    widget = XtCreateWidget(name, widget_class, parent, args, num_args);
    XtManageChild(widget);
    XtReleaseToken();
    return widget;
}
```

This entry point is a simple case and the changes are fairly innocuous. There are three potential pitfalls in using this technique:

- First, initialization of local variables at declaration (before *XtGetToken*) should be treated with care. Some initialization, such as simple constant assignments, are okay. Assignments that invoke functions can be a little more difficult to analyze. When in doubt, it is best to move all initializations to the protected section.

- Second, some functions have multiple return points, each must be preceded by *XtReleaseToken* or reorganized to have a single exit point.

- Third, return values cannot be computed in the return statement. To insure protection, they must be assigned to a temporary variable before *XtReleaseToken* is called, and returned immediately following.

A second method to protect the toolkit is to provide wrappers for all the entry points. In this scheme, the C preprocessor is used to redefine the names of otherwise unprotected functions to protected functions. The wrappers will acquire the token, make the call to the unprotected function, release the token, and return. For example, protecting a typical entry point such as XtGetValues involves the following changes:

- In XtMtDefs.h, function names are wrapped.

```
...
#define XtGetValues XtGetValuesR
#define XtSetValues XtSetValuesR
...
```

These definitions in have the effect of redirecting all references, including function prototypes in Intrinsic.h, to the wrapper function. It is important that these macros are declared without arguments, this allows the functions to be referenced by address.

- XtMtFuncs.c[1] contains the body of the wrapper functions.

---

1. Some compilers may insist on seeing a prototype declaration for the wrapper. For clarity, this declaration is not shown.

```
#include <X11/Intrinsic.h>
...
void
XtGetValuesR(widget, args, num_args)
    Widget widget;
    ArgList args;
    int num_args;
{
    XtGetToken();
    XtGetValues(widget, args, num_args);
    XtReleaseToken();
}

void
XtSetValuesR(widget, args, num_args)
    Widget widget;
    ArgList args;
    int num_args;
{
    XtGetToken();
    XtSetValues(widget, args, num_args);
    XtReleaseToken();
}
...
```

A threaded application makes use of the wrapper entry points by including <X11/XtMtDefs.h> before <X11/Intrinsic.h>. By doing so, toolkit calls from the application threads refer to wrappers instead of unprotected entry points.

The redefinition method has some advantages:

- Nested calls to other entry points from within the toolkit incur no penalty for acquiring the token. This avoids two function calls and two tests (in *XtGetToken* and *XtReleaseToken*) for each nested toolkit entry.

- The structure of wrapper functions guarantees that all exit points of functions will be covered with *XtReleaseToken*.

- The wrapper functions are separate from the remainder of the toolkit, and can be collected together in one file.

- Single threaded applications can link with the same shared library and are unaffected because they do not refer to the protected entry points.

It is not possible to protect every entry point this way. For example, functions that use variable numbers of arguments (i.e. the XtVa* set of functions) cannot be wrapped because variable argument lists cannot be passed between functions using portable techniques. Also, application writers must be careful to include the function name redefinition file in each source file that references Xt Intrinsics functions. This problem could be eased by incorporating the following lines near the beginning of X11/Intrinsic.h:

```
#ifdef MT_SAFE
#include <X11/XtMtDefs.h>
#endif
```

Application code would make use of this by defining MT_SAFE as part of the compile line in the makefile.

Macro "entry points" (e.g. XtIsWidget) can't be fixed with either method. Fortunately, most of these macros are simply used for translating arguments to otherwise protected entry points. Some macros, such as those declared in IntrinsicP.h, directly dereference widget data structures and are intended for use by widget developers only. These are a problem if applications use them.

For the current MT-safe Intrinsics prototype, the redefinition scheme was employed for approximately 200 entry points that are declared in <X11/Intrinsic.h>. This provided the quickest way of getting coverage for most of the entry points. Functions declared in other include files and vararg functions have not been fixed at the time of this writing.

Global Data

In general, global data is a problem because it is impossible to synchronize access to it. LibXt.a has 56 global data symbols. Additionally, applications add data that is referenced throughout the Intrinsics. Resource declarations, resource names, and translations are examples. The 56 data symbols in libXt.a can be categorized into three groups:

- 25 Widget class record structures and widget class pointers (e.g. compositeClassRec, shellWidgetClass, etc.)

- 23 XrmQuarks (e.g. XtQAtom and XtQWindow)

- 8 miscellaneous

The 25 Widget class and the 23 XrmQuarks data symbols are considered read only. Three of the eight miscellaneous data symbols (colorConvertArgs, screenConvertArg, and visualConvertArgs) are read only constants, and one (XtCXtToolkitError) is a constant string for internal use only.

Three of the remaining miscellaneous symbols, _XtAppDestroyCount, _XtDpyDestroyCount, and _XtperDisplayList are not public interfaces. The last symbol, _XtInheritTranslations, is only accessed during widget class initialization, a protected operation.

An application that sets any of these miscellaneous data is errant regardless of concurrency.

Applications add data that is referenced throughout the Intrinsics. Resource declarations, resource names, and translations are examples. These types of data structures are generally modified only once during initialization, and read only later. Access to this type of data is serialized because it is modified only from within the toolkit.

As this analysis shows, the Intrinsics are fairly clean of exposed data. Where data is exposed, the references are read only or not for external use.

Implications For Application Developers.

Developers of multi-threaded applications should be aware of several issues:

• Multi-threaded applications will have additional synchronization issues.

A classic example is when multiple threads simultaneously access a common widget (perhaps with XtSetValues). If the application does not properly synchronize access, the widget's state at any time is indeterminate. For example, when two threads simultaneously set the same resource on the same widget, the calls are serialized and the first change is overwritten. The effect in this example may be innocuous and may go unnoticed by the application user, but variations on this problem can be serious.

In the following example, two threads have critical regions of code that are protected by a mutex. Thread 1 sets a resource on a widget and thread 2 executes a callback procedure:

thread 1:

```
{
    mutex_enter(...);
    /* in critical section, do something */
    XtSetValues(...);
    ...
    mutex_exit(...);
}
```

thread 2 executes the following callback:

```
callback_procedure1(...)
{
    mutex_enter(...);
    /* in critical section, do something */
    mutex_exit(...);
}
```

This code can deadlock under the following sequence of events:

```
thread 1              thread 2
--------              --------
mutex_enter(...);
                      [callback is invoked from thread
                      that has token, usually via XtDispatchEvent]

                      mutex_enter(...); <---Blocks on the mutex

XtSetValues(...); <-- Blocks on token
```

1. Thread 1 enters the critical region and acquires the mutex.

2. Thread 2 invokes callback_procedure1 from the dispatch loop. Because it is called by the dispatch loop, thread 2 already holds the token.

3. Thread 2 attempts to enter its critical region. It is blocked because thread 1 holds this mutex.

4. Thread 1 calls XtSetValues(). It is blocked because thread 2 holds the token.

Deadlock occurs because each thread is blocked on a primitive that the other thread holds.

There are several ways of solving this deadlock situation. First, the *XtGetToken* and *XtReleaseToken* could be used in place of the mutex to provide serialization. This is an obvious solution, but goes against the philosophy that the synchronization primitives should not be visible to applications.

A second approach is to employ the Intrinsics' callback mechanisms, such as a registering a WorkProc or directly calling a Callback, to ensure serialization. Using this technique the code for thread1 changes only slightly:

```
thread 1:
    {
        ...
        XtCallCallbacks( ... callback_procedure2 ...);
        ...
    }
    callback_procedure2(...)
    {
        ...
        XtSetValues(...);
        ...
    }
```

In this case, the application need not use a separate mutex. The callback_procedure2 is invoked from a protected function, XtCallCallbacks, so it implicitly holds the token and will not be interleaved with any other toolkit function. This effectively prohibits thread 2 from executing callback_procedure1 at the same time.

* Applications should not depend on the ordering of event callbacks.

An application expresses interest in an event by registering a callback procedure. These callback procedures are then invoked when the event dispatch loop is executing. In an MT application, execution of the event loop is interleaved with execution of other threads, and events may be dispatched to functions immediately after they are registered. This is only true if registration is executed from a thread that does not hold the token before and after registration.

For example, some single threaded applications register a work procedure from their callback procedures to get notification when all callbacks for an event have been completed. These applications depend on the fact that the work procedure will be invoked after all input dispatching is complete. This behavior in a threaded application may not be the same, depending on the situation at the time of registration.

* Threaded applications have alternatives on the use of toolkit features.

Some algorithms are more convenient to express using thread constructs rather than using the Intrinsic's facilities. Also, performance improvements can be expected on multiprocessor hardware. There are several examples that come to mind:

A thread that alternatively sleeps and processes provides the functional equivalent of the time-out facilities.

A thread that executes a long running algorithm can do so without explicitly dispatching events or using work procedures.

A thread may block on I/O without the intervention of the toolkit.

- Thread switching may hamper performance.

The technique of using an input event callback for dispatching the token has some performance drawbacks. Because threads are started and stopped when passing the token around, switching context between threads is common. For example, up to three context switches occur when passing the token from the event dispatcher to another thread. Although this ratio decreases as the number of threads waiting for the token increases, this may still be an unacceptable performance hit.

The obvious way to avoid this problem is to bracket intensive sections of toolkit calls with *XtGetToken* and *XtReleaseToken*. As mentioned previously, this is not recommended because it exposes the synchronization primitives to the application.

A second approach is to use the toolkit facilities to achieve the same thing. For example, the OpenLook Intrinsics Toolkit has a *Stub* widget so that applications can plug their own behavior into a widget. Plugging into the toolkit at this level avoids thrashing on thread switching because widget functions are invoked from protected entry points. The token is already held by the thread making the call to the widget function. Similar mechanisms, such as the XtCallCallbacks function, can achieve the same result.

- Signal Handling

The Xt Intrinsics do not provide any special provision for signal handling; this is left to the applications developer. In contrast, the XView notifier supplies a set of functions to be used to register signal handling routines for the client application. The use of the system supplied signal handler registration functions will cause notifier and application misbehavior. The notifier assumes that it alone will handle signals. Once the signal handler is registered it will be called by the notifier when a signal is posted to the process. This is guaranteed in single threaded programs.

However, with multiple threads running in the client application there is no longer a guarantee that the thread that installed the signal handler is the thread that receives the signal. This isn't normally a problem, but the notifier relies on the arrival of an alarm signal to break it out of the select with errno set to EINTR when a user time-out has expired. This will not happen if the signal is deliver to another thread, even though the correct signal handler has been run. In order to have the correct action take place, the application developer must explicitly block receipt of the signals which the notifier is dispatching in all threads but the one running the notifier.

Implications for widget set developers

In theory, widgets sets should require no changes. The widget class functions are hidden from direct invocation through a protected entry point.

In reality, widget sets are not that pure. They add their own data and entry points. For example, the OLIT widget set has a large number of externally accessible data structures and a handful of entry points. Each of the entry points must be protected, and the data structures need to be analyzed for potential access problems.

Many of the assumptions applicable during widget set development are also useful when analyzing mutual exclusion problems. The recommended style of writing widgets, such as using separate include files for public and private declarations, simplifies the analysis. Hiding data structures behind well known entry points or abstract interfaces also makes it easier to identify problem areas.

Unresolved Issues.

At the time of this writing, several problems have not been addressed:

- Vararg functions have not been protected. These functions only require addition of *XtGetToken* and *XtReleaseToken*. The C preprocessor renaming scheme will not work here (at least in a portable fashion) because variable argument lists cannot be passed between functions.

- Only the entry points declared in <X11/Intrinsic.h> have been protected. It is not clear if applications should include private or implementation header files, although some might.

- Currently, there is no safe way to handle signals in the Intrinsics. Threads add a new dimension to this problem because each thread can specify a signal mask. There may be some techniques where this feature is useful. However, more study needs to before the implications are understood.

- Protecting XtAppNextEvent with *XtGetToken* and *XtReleaseToken* may have problems under some circumstances. When the token is dispatched by *_XtTokenDispatch*, XtAppNextEvent essentially becomes unprotected. In the current prototype, other threads may acquire the token and enter this function. Reentering XtAppNextEvent from a I/O notification procedure isn't a wise thing to do even in a single threaded application, so this is not viewed as a problem. To completely protect the toolkit however, this function and others such as XtAppProcessEvent may require an alternate locking scheme.

- Application Contexts have not been used to increase parallelism. The major reason is that the application context is an overloaded abstraction: it is a construct used both for porting to various operating systems, and for providing capabilities for creating "virtual" applications within a single address space. Building multi-threading on top of this construct would only further confuse its definition. The fact that resources, such as the display connection, may be shared by several application contexts increases the difficulty of adding threading based on this construct.

- The pipe created in *XtInitializeToken* is only registered with the default application context. It should be registered with all application contexts when they are initialized.

Conclusions and future directions.

While evaluation is still proceeding, the token-based approach appears to be a simple, effective technique for making the Xt and XView toolkits MT-safe. We have written demo/test programs such as multi-threaded performance meters monitoring hundreds of hosts; it is clear, however, that as with any complex multi-threaded library, one of the most difficult aspects of development will be testing.

After reviewing the internal structures of both Xt and XView, it seems clear that any effort to support significant degrees of concurrency inside either toolkit is a difficult undertaking of uncertain outcome. The design of a new internally multi-threaded toolkit (and the thread-aware Xlib to support it) appears an interesting topic for collaboration.

Author Information

The authors are working on various aspects of windowing technology at SunSoft. They may be reached at *firstname.lastname*@Eng.Sun.Com.

Implementing Resolution Independence on top of the X Window System

Mark A. Linton

Abstract

A resolution-independent user interface system allows applications to support printing and different resolution displays without modifying any code. Because of the lack of direct support in the X Window System, we have implemented resolution independence on top of X in a client library. Our applications specify geometry and drawing requests in a real-world coordinate system, and the library translates the requests to pixel coordinates before passing them to X. We convert *positions* to pixel coordinates rather than *sizes*, avoiding unexpected gaps on the screen but allowing the size of an object in pixels to vary depending on where it is drawn. To support partial update, resolution-dependent information is available to application objects.

Our experience is that resolution-independence does not degrade interactive performance noticeably. Measurements indicate that our implementation of text drawing, which supports character positioning based on printer font metrics, is about 45% slower than drawing text using resolution-dependent calls to the X library.

Mark A. Linton (linton@sgi.com) is a Principal Scientist at Silicon Graphics, Inc.

1 Introduction

Resolution independence in a user interface means that the coordinate system used to specify sizes and positions is not tied to the coordinate system provided by the display. A document editor would ask for the width of a page object to be 6.5 inches, for example, instead of the corresponding number of pixels on a particular display.

The most important use of resolution independence is in WYSIWYG applications, which generate output to a printer that corresponds to the view presented on the display. Resolution independence also allows applications to run identically on screens with different resolutions.

The X Window System protocol, X library functions, and most X toolkits are resolution-dependent, defining graphics and window operations in terms of the pixels on the display. This characteristic of X has made some developers prefer to use other systems that offer resolution-independence, such as NeWS or Display PostScript.

Unlike these other systems, the InterViews toolkit[2] provides resolution independence on top of the X library. Our experience with InterViews is that resolution independence on top of X is convenient, practical, and efficient. In this paper, we describe how to implement resolution independence on top of X and analyze the effect of this approach on performance.

2 Programming model

The basic idea of resolution independence is that all coordinate values are in terms of a physical unit that is unrelated to the display. All graphics requests, window requests, and higher level toolkit operations (such as for geometry management) use coordinates in resolution-independent units. The implementation of these operations must translate the coordinates into pixel positions and sizes for the target device.

InterViews provides a data type called Coord for coordinate values. The unit coordinate is defined to be the size of a typographical point, about 1/72 of an inch. We chose points because they are a common unit in document processing and they are neutral with respect to locale. InterViews also provides scaling and rotation of coordinates, so an object can use other units when desired.

Ideally, Coord would be an abstract data type with the appropriate arithmetic operations. However, our implementation language, C++, does not provide adequate support for small objects. We therefore use a typedef of Coord to the built-in "float" type. We chose to use floating point instead of an integer representing very small units (Microsoft Windows[3] allows an application to use an integer representing a hundredth of a millimeter, for example) because floating point is more convenient for the programmer and the trend in recent CPUs has been to make the cost of a floating-point multiply close to the cost of an integer multiply.

The basic InterViews building block for defining a user interface is called a **glyph**. A **canvas** is a 2-dimensional surface to which a group of glyphs are attached. The glyphs negotiate for space on the canvas, draw on the canvas to refresh their appearance, and damage the canvas to cause an update traversal.

2.1 Canvases and Printers

The canvas class interface is similar to the PostScript drawing model. Operations are provided to specify a path as a list of points and to fill, stroke, or clip the current path. The canvas class also provides operations for drawing text and raster images. Printer is a subclass of Canvas that implements graphics operations by generating the appropriate PostScript text to a file. One can therefore write a single function for drawing to the screen and for generating PostScript suitable for printing. The InterViews document editor, for example, implements the print command by simply creating a printer object and passing it to the draw method for the root object of each page. The objects on the page use the identical code to draw to the printer that they use to draw to the display.

2.2 Fonts

Providing resolution-independent information for fonts introduces two problems. First, the resolution at which a font is designed does not necessarily match the resolution of the display. For example, suppose a user selects the 12-point Times Roman font provided for 75-dpi displays, but the user's display is 90-dpi. The metrics for this font specify a height of 12 points, but the actual height in pixels is only 10 points on the 90-dpi display ($12 * 75/90 = 10$).

Now suppose the user interactively drags a rectangle to be drawn around the 12-point text. If we compute the pixels per coordinate conversion factor assuming 90 dpi when drawing the rectangle, we will determine that the rectangle should be slightly larger than 10 points high. The result will look correct on the display, but on the printer the rectangle will be too small relative to the text.

The two possible solutions to this problem are to ignore the display resolution or to ignore the font metric information. The second solution may require more frequent font scaling, which may reduce the readability of text at small point sizes unless font outlines are available. InterViews implements the first solution, using the font resolution to compute the pixels per coordinate ratio. The conversion ratio also can be specified explicitly through the normal X defaults customization mechanism.

The second problem with fonts is that an application may wish to access resolution-dependent font metrics. For example, a document editor may provide an option to layout characters according to screen metrics, making the text look more regular on the display while sacrificing printed appearance. We solve this problem in InterViews by providing two kinds of font objects, one that returns display metrics and one that returns printer metrics.

2.3 Incremental update

InterViews glyphs may be shared and may overlap transparently (part of an object underneath can show through a transparent part of another object). Glyphs therefore are not allocated X subwindows and must cooperate to update the screen. A canvas manages a "damage" region that represents the update area. Logically, every update requires a full draw traversal over the objects in the window. In practice, some objects will short-circuit the traversal by determining that the damage region does not intersect their bounding boxes.

Unlike other coordinates, a damage region must be resolution-dependent to ensure correct update. For example, suppose object A draws at coordinate 10.5 and a object B draws after A at 10.7. Now suppose that A changes and generates damage for its update. If the destination display maps 10.5 and 10.7 to the same pixel, then the damage region must intersect the bounding box of B or else the overlapping pixel will not be updated correctly.

To support this need, InterViews defines a resolution-dependent region called an Extension. The coordinate units of an extension are points that correspond to pixels on the canvas' device. Using 75-dpi conversion on the example above, 10.5 and 10.7 points are both 11 pixels and would be stored as 10.599 (11 * 72.27 / 75) in an extension.

Ideally, extensions should be computed automatically during drawing. Objects that needed to perform an update could retrieve their extension from the canvas after they were drawn. While this functionality simplifies update management, it complicates drawing and damage area management because glyphs need to be able to incur damage during drawing. Currently, a separate pass is made over the glyphs to compute extensions and incur damage.

3 Converting to pixels

The straightforward way to convert a coordinate to the corresponding number of pixels is to multiply by the pixels per coordinate ratio for the display and then round to the nearest integer. More sophisticated approaches to this problem use techniques such as anti-aliasing to reduce the visual effects of rounding. We have not explored trying such techniques on top of X; we first wanted experience with a simple approach. We therefore round to pixels coordinates and pass the pixel coordinates directly to X. Because the round operation must work for negative values to handle the case of drawing a polygon vertex outside the target window, a test is necessary in addition to an add and truncate. Scaling by the inverse factor is necessary to convert pixels in an X event back to coordinates, but no round operation is necessary.

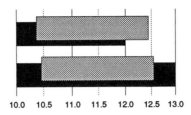

Figure 1: *Rounding positions can yield inconsistent sizes.*

3.1 Placement versus size

Rounding can cause anomalous results on low-resolution devices. Consider drawing a rectangle that is 2 points wide on a 75-dpi display. If the left edge of the rectangle is at 10.4 pixels, then the right edge is at 12.48 and rounding yields a 2-pixel wide rectangle. If instead the left edge were at 10.45 pixels, then the right edge is at 12.53 and rounding yields a 3-pixel wide rectangle. Figure 1 shows this problem visually. The light gray rectangles represent a 2-point wide rectangle and the dark gray rectangles underneath represent the rectangle in pixel coordinates. Rounding on the edges of the upper rectangle yields a 2-pixel wide rectangle; rounding on the lower rectangle yield a 3-pixel wide rectangle.

If we chose to round the size instead of the right edge of the rectangle, then we would always get the same number of pixels. However, we could also get a gap of one pixel between two rectangles that should abut. Figure 2 shows how this gap can occur. The two light gray rectangles at the top are specified in points. In the middle are the two rectangles with sizes rounded to pixel coordinates. At the bottom are the two rectangles with positions rounded.

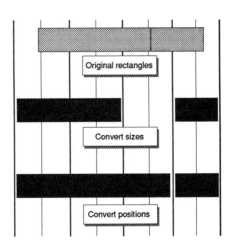

Figure 2: *Converting sizes versus positions.*

The InterViews implementation converts positions rather than sizes. Therefore, objects may not always be the same size depending on their position. Usually, a pixel difference in size is more desirable than a pixel gap between objects that are meant to abut. Some user interface components are not part of a printed representation, such as a text cursor in a document. In this case, it is desirable to specify the object size in pixel units. PostScript provides a "setstrokeadjust" operator to ensure consistent line widths[1]. InterViews simply makes available the display operations that convert between pixels and coordinates. For example, if a border object wishes to be 2 pixels wide on a display, it can ask the display for the size in coordinates of 2 pixels and pass that size to the canvas drawing operations.

3.2 Character positions

Document editors typically place each character at a coordinate position computed by a formatting algorithm. The positions are usually determined from printer font metrics, not display metrics. If the individual character positions are used for drawing, then it is possible that two adjacent characters may overlap on the display.

Our approach is to detect when the coordinate positions of two characters abut in the same line and accumulate the characters into a buffer to send in a single text item to X. When we find a space character, we begin a new text item at the correct position. The effect is that the white space absorbs the differences between display and printer font metrics. We also generate fewer X text items, which improves performance, though we also introduce the extra overhead of comparing coordinate positions for each character request.

Figure 3 shows part of a window dump of the InterViews document editor running on this paper. Figure 4 shows a window dump of a PostScript previewer on the PostScript for the same portion of the paper. The PostScript previewer uses the strategy of positioning each character individually. In the previewer, the word "translates" in the second line has the characters squeezed together. On the other hand, the document editor draws the words "translates the requests" so closely together that one might not realize there were spaces between the words.

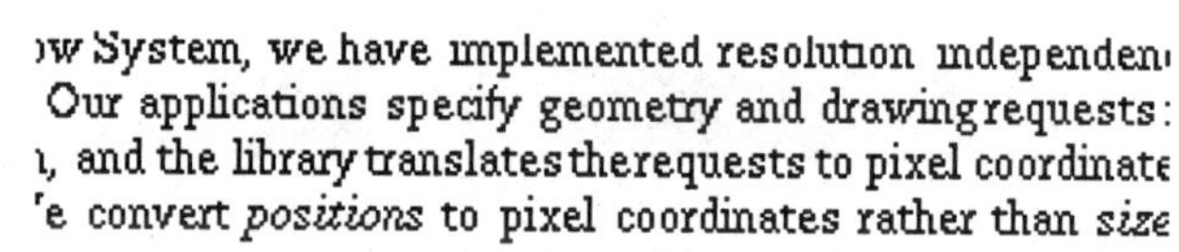

)w System, we have implemented resolution independen
Our applications specify geometry and drawing requests:
ι, and the library translates the requests to pixel coordinate
'e convert *positions* to pixel coordinates rather than *size*

Figure 3: *Words as items.*

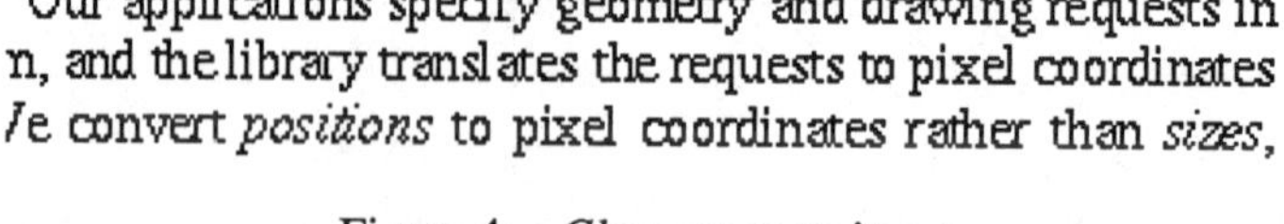

Our applications specify geometry and drawing requests in
n, and the library translates the requests to pixel coordinates
/e convert *positions* to pixel coordinates rather than *sizes,*

Figure 4: *Characters as items*

3.3 Window sizes

InterViews provides a window class for specifying top-level X windows and associated window manager information. The size and placement of a window is in resolution-independent coordinates, which must be converted to pixels before sending a request to X and must be converted back to coordinates in response to an X event such as ConfigureNotify.

Windows have a desired size that most window managers will return in the absence of the user picking a different size. Because the size could have been rounded down in the conversion to coordinates, the objects in the window could get a smaller size than they requested. For example, suppose the natural size for a window is 148.5 points, which corresponds to 154.1 pixels. The window manager will return the requested 154 pixels, which is converted to 148.4 points. As a consequence, some object in the window will need to shrink by a small amount.

Our approach to this problem, though not currently implemented, is to store the round-off error in the window and add it to coordinates that correspond to window edges. This adjustment must be done on Expose events as well as ConfigureNotify events.

4 Performance

To evaluate the run-time cost of resolution-independence, we measured the cost of drawing text through InterViews to drawing text directly with X. Figure 5 shows the measurements of text drawing on an Indigo workstation. The first column is the drawing performance, measured in characters per millisecond. The XDrawText, XDrawString, and XDrawImageString measurements were collected using the x11perf program with the "-polytext", "-ftext", and "-fitext" options, respectively. The XDrawText case draws text from two different fonts, XDrawString draws a single, fixed-width font, and XDrawImageString draws both the text and the background behind the text. The second column contains the relative performance compared to the XDrawText case.

The InterViews benchmark computes the drawing times just like x11perf. The main loop simply calls the character operation on a canvas for each character to be drawn. Because the characters can be any font, this operation is closest in functionality to the XDrawText benchmark.

Benchmark	Characters/msec	Relative to XDrawText
InterViews	45.3	0.55
XDrawText	82.0	1.00
XDrawString	101.0	1.23
XDrawImageString	152.0	1.85

Figure 5: *Text drawing performance.*

Despite the overhead of a virtual function call for each character, copying the characters into a buffer, and testing the current position for each character, the InterViews performance benchmark is only about 45% slower than calling XDrawText directly. This ratio is a reflection of the ratio of CPU speed to rendering speed. If the text rendering were faster or the CPU slower, then the overhead would be higher.

Our experience building applications with InterViews is that the overhead of resolution independence is not noticeable for object such as buttons, menus, and dialog boxes. Objects for which drawing performance is important usually need resolution-independence anyway.

5 Conclusions

Resolution independence is an important capability of a user interface system that is missing from the standard X software. In the past, people have built resolution-independence at a low-level of the system.

Our work shows that it is practical and reasonably efficient to build resolution-independence on top of the existing X protocol. In doing so, we resolved issues involving font metrics, use of resolution-dependent bounding boxes for incremental update, coordinate roundoff for consistent placement, and positioning of characters. The implementation has been available as part of the InterViews distribution since January of 1990. The X-dependent portion of the code is about 6,000 lines of C++, of which about one quarter is in the implementation of the canvas class.

In an environment where the client machine is as fast as the server machine, implementing resolution-independence in the client will perform as well if not better than an implementation in the server. In the case where a server has support for resolution independence, we can simply retarget the InterViews canvas implementation to use the whatever mechanisms are available.

Acknowledgments

Paul Calder designed and implemented the resolution-independent mechanisms of InterViews. Dave Sternlicht wrote the InterViews benchmark program.

References

[1]   Adobe Systems Incorporated. PostScript Language Reference Manual, Second Edition. Addison-Wesley, 1990.

[2]   P. Calder and M. Linton. Glyphs: Flyweight objects for user interfaces. *Proceedings of the ACM SIGGRAPH Symposium on User Interface Software and Technology*, pages 92-101, Snowbird, Utah, October 1990.

[3]   C. Petzold. Programming Windows. Microsoft Press, 1990.

Don't Fidget with Widgets, Draw!

Joel F. Bartlett

Abstract

In their quest to produce tools for the production of uniform graphical user interfaces, almost all designers of toolkits for the X window system have overlooked an important capability. The best way to improve many programs is not to replace text interfaces based on command line flags with graphical buttons, but to provide programs with a simple way to draw pictures. This report describes a graphics server, ezd, that sits between an application program and the X server and allows both existing and new programs easy access to structured graphics. Programs may draw, edit, and sense user events in terms of application-defined graphical objects. When run on workstations with 10 MIPS or faster processors, interactive response is excellent, indicating that ezd's simple structured graphics drawing model can be widely applied. The enthusiastic response of ezd's initial users and the variety of uses to which they have put it to suggest that there is a tremendous pent-up urge to draw with programs and that ezd has lowered the barriers to doing so.

Joel Bartlett is a member of the research staff at Digital Equipment Corporation's Western Research Laboratory.

Introduction

Even though researchers at Digital Equipment Corporation's Western Research Laboratory have been running the X window system [19] for more than five years, most of their programs make no use of graphics. While libraries and interface generators [11] have provided many interactive programs with uniform, configurable, sophisticated graphical interfaces, they have not provided programs with a way to draw.

A typical candidate for easy-to-use 2-D graphics is a printed circuit board router, which takes the physical location of components and a netlist describing their logical connections, and produces a wirelist showing the actual location of wires. The methods used by the grr router [9], are illustrated in the technical report by hand constructed drawings like Figure 1. If similar drawings could have been automatically made during the construction of the router, they would have greatly simplified debugging and improved the designer's understanding of the routing heuristics. However, the designer saw adding graphical output as being too time consuming. Only after the router was completed were graphics added to demonstrate the router's performance.

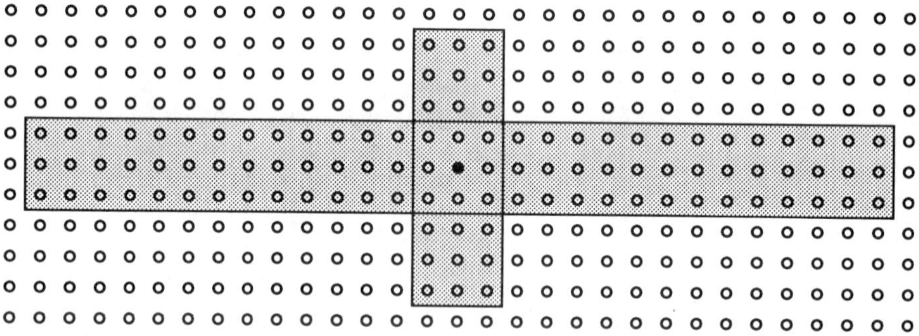

Figure 1: Printed circuit board router

Barriers to using graphics must be lowered to encourage programs to use them. Separating creation of drawings from rendering them on a display is one way to hide complexity from the programmer. Interactive drawing programs like MacDraw[1] and idraw [22] do this by providing users with a high-level, structured drawing model. As users are dealing with graphical objects instead of pixels, objects may be freely overlapped, moved, and edited; the drawing program taking full responsibility for correctly rendering them on the display.

Application programs can be offered these capabilities by providing a graphics server that replaces the drawing program's graphical user interface with a process-to-process protocol. Extensions to this server can allow graphical objects to react to the workstation's mouse and keyboard. For example, a network management system could

---

[1]MacDraw, a trademark of Claris Corporation, is a drawing program for Apple Macintosh computers.

draw a picture showing the host machines and their physical connections. By clicking the mouse on the appropriate graphic, one could get detailed status information about a host system or communication line. One can also use these capabilities to build conventional-looking user interface objects such as push buttons or sliders.

This paper describes such a graphics server, ezd, and reports WRL's experience with it. The challenge in constructing ezd was to make it simple enough to be readily used, yet with enough graphics capabilities and performance to be useful in a variety of applications.

Overview of ezd

Simple graphics should be simple. The same afternoon that one first encounters ezd, one should be able to take an existing program and produce meaningful graphics. Ezd makes this possible by providing a simple, powerful drawing model and application interface, and hiding all details of display management.

High Level Drawing Primitives

Ezd's drawing model is straightforward: graphic objects are ordered into drawings, and drawings are displayed by mapping them onto windows. Graphic objects are created using commands that create lines, rectangles, polygons, arcs, and text in arbitrary colors, stipples, and fonts. The x,y position, size, and line width of each object is specified in a device-independent coordinate system using either integer or floating point numbers. Zero or more of these drawing primitives can be grouped together to form a named object.

The order in which objects are defined is important, as objects are drawn in the order that they were added to the drawing using the *painter's algorithm* [16]: objects are opaque and later-defined objects can obscure earlier-defined objects. When a named object is first defined, its position in the drawing order is established. Drawings may be edited by simply redefining the object. When the object is redefined, its position in the drawing order is retained. Objects can be hidden from view by defining them as a null object with no graphics commands. Finally, an object's position in the drawing order can be changed. Objects may be brought to the top of a drawing, sunk to the bottom, or placed above or below another object in the drawing.

When a drawing is displayed by mapping it onto a window, ezd transforms the application's coordinate system to X's coordinate system. Operations such as panning and zooming are done by changing the mapping of the drawing onto the window. Multiple drawings can be displayed in a window, and multiple windows can display a drawing. A window provides a natural "view finder" for producing a PostScript [2] rendering of the drawings mapped onto it.

Interactive Drawn Objects

Drawn objects are turned into user interface interactors by making them sensitive to mouse and keyboard events. The events reported by ezd are similar to those returned by X, with one key difference: X events are associated with windows, whereas ezd events are associated with application-defined graphical objects.

The application makes objects event sensitive by issuing one or more when commands that designate the object name, the type of event, and the action to be taken when the event occurs. As the mouse is moved across a window, ezd continuously translates the mouse position on the display to a position in an object in a drawing. This translation is done by examining the drawings mapped into the window and finding the topmost object in the topmost drawing that contains the mouse. When the event occurs in an object that has an event handler, the associated *action* is taken. It is either a Scheme [1, 18] expression to be evaluated or a Scheme procedure to be called.

The ezd event model does not support X's notion of a "pointer grab." That is, when a mouse button is pushed, the ezd object containing the mouse does not automatically track the mouse until the button is released. Instead, irrespective of the state of the mouse buttons, all events are always reported to the topmost object that contains the mouse. This mechanism is an adequate replacement for pointer grabs as the mouse position is translated to an object in a drawing using the current definition of the drawing. When an event handler running in the ezd server makes a change to a drawing, the change is immediately reflected in the drawing, before the display is updated. Changes to the area of a drawing under the mouse immediately generate any needed object exit and enter events before ezd processes further X events.

Extension Language

Intertwined with event handling is ezd's extension language, Scheme. When an event is reported to an object, the event handler (a Scheme procedure or expression) is evaluated. The simplest event handler, used in the section *An Interactive Clock Face*, is the expression (log-event). When it is evaluated, it sends a text message containing the event type, window, drawing and object names, and mouse coordinates to the application program via a pipe[2].

More sophisticated extensions can be done by adding new Scheme procedures to ezd. The buttons, slider, and text region used in the section *Weather Forecasts* are drawn with a library of interactors written in Scheme that perform all graphical effects using ezd's basic drawing commands.

---

[2]A pipe is a mechanism for interprocess communication. See [13] for additional information on the UNIX runtime environment.

Loose Coupling to Application Program

A simple drawing model is not enough. The graphics system should neither restrict the application's choice of programming language nor dictate control flow.

Ezd is visible to an application program as a structured graphics server using a simple text-based protocol. Unlike most X-based toolkits, ezd issues no event requests that must be handled by the application program, and thus imposes no requirements on the application's control flow. Ezd only notifies the application program when an event occurs in which the application has explicitly designated interest.

When building an interactive program, this may have little effect on the program's design. For example, the clock face program in the section *An Interactive Clock Face*, requires an event loop. However, the event handling code is simpler than would be required for most other X-based implementations as there are fewer events to handle and the static portions of the drawing never need to be redrawn.

Eliminating mandatory event monitoring allows any program that can print text to produce graphics as well. For example, a video monitor calibration tool was written in the form of a 111-line shell script. It displays a window of instructions and a window containing test patterns. Once the monitor has been adjusted, a mouse click terminates the application.

Automatic Display Management

Once a drawing is mapped onto a window, the application program need not further concern itself with the window as ezd takes full responsibility for maintaining the contents of the window. When a drawing is changed by the application, all views of it are automatically updated. Display updates are deferred until a natural break in the application command stream. The changed portions of each window are then determined, rendered to an off-screen buffer, and copied onto the display. Simple animation is implicit in this display handling method as multiple changes to a drawing are reflected as one smooth, flicker-free change to the window(s) displaying it.

An Interactive Clock Face

The clock face described in this section and shown in Figure 2 demonstrates how ezd's drawing and control ideas combine to produce interactive graphics. Dragging either of the clock's hands using mouse button 1 smoothly changes the time.

The first phase of this 200 line C program (found in [5]) creates a separate ezd process with a pipe named out for requests to ezd, and a pipe named in for event notifications from ezd.

The second phase of the program issues commands to ezd to define the clock face and recognize user mouse actions on it. The first commands issued create a window named clock-window and a drawing named clock, and map the drawing onto the window.

Figure 2: Interactive clock face

```
(window clock-window 200 200 fixed-size)
(set-drawing clock)
(overlay clock-window clock)
(origin clock-window clock 100 100)
(scale clock-window clock 1 -1 1)
```

The origin command sets the origin of the drawing in the center of the window. The scale command changes the default X coordinate system (positive Y goes down) to one in which positive Y goes up and declares that one unit in the drawing is one pixel on the screen.

   The next group of commands define the objects making up the clock face. As later-defined objects can overlap earlier-defined objects, objects are defined from back to front.

```
(object back (fill-arc -100 -100 200 200 0 360 gray95)
             (arc -100 -100 200 200 0 360 gray85))
(object minute)
(text -60 -60 120 120 left up "time" grey60 "times_italic24")
(text -60 -60 120 120 right center "drifts" grey60 "times_italic24")
(text -60 -60 120 120 left down "by" grey60 "times_italic24")
(object hour)
(fill-arc -5 -5 10 10 0 360 black)
(object cover)
```

The first object defined is the background of the clock. It consists of a filled circle edged in a slightly darker gray and is given the name back. Each drawing command specifies the x,y position and size of the object it defines in terms of the application's coordinate system. Next, the minute hand is defined as a null graphical object. Although the command causes nothing to be displayed, it does establish the order of the object named minute in the list of objects in the drawing. Following this come the text commands that display the string "time drifts by". Text is positioned by specifying a position, a rectangle, and two keywords indicating left-right position and up-down position within the rectangle. Finally, the hour hand's order in the drawing is established, the hands' drive shaft is defined, and the null object cover is defined.

The hands are defined by calls to the following procedure. Each time a hand is redefined, ezd automatically updates the display.

```
void  draw_hand( name, length, angle )
      char  *name;
      int   length;
      double  angle;
{
      fprintf( out,
              "(object %s (fill-polygon 0 0 %f %f %f %f %f %f))",
              name,
              25*cos( angle+.25 ), 25*sin(angle+.25 ),
              length*cos( angle ), length*sin( angle ),
              25*cos( angle-.25 ), 25*sin(angle-.25 ) );
}
```

Time is set by dragging either of the hands with the mouse. A drag operation is started by depressing mouse button 1 with the mouse on either of the hands. The hands are made mouse-sensitive by issuing the when commands:

```
(when minute button1down
      (begin (log-event),
             (ezd '(object cover
                     (fill-rectangle -100 -100 200 200 clear)))))
(when hour button1down
      (begin (log-event)
             (ezd '(object cover
                     (fill-rectangle -100 -100 200 200 clear)))))
```

Each command is of the form (when *object event action*). *Object* is the name of an object in the drawing, *event* is the type of event, and *action* is a Scheme expression to evaluate. The event action is a sequence of two procedure calls. The first, (log-event), causes an event record to be written on ezd's default output file that can be read by the application from in. The second issues an ezd command to redefine the object cover as a clear-filled rectangle that covers the entire window.

The drag operation is continued by the user moving the mouse over the window with button 1 held down. Defining cover over all other objects in the drawing and making it sensitive to mouse motion and button 1's release assures that it will track all mouse motion in the window until the button is released.

```
(when cover motion (log-event))
(when cover button1up (ezd '(object cover)))
```

Once these commands have been sent to the ezd server, the program enters its third phase, monitoring events by reading text messages from in. Note that the only events reported by ezd are those that the application has explicitly asked for.

To illustrate the interaction between the application and ezd, the actions taken when a user sets the time are explained. When the user presses mouse button 1 down on one of the hands, ezd logs the event to the application and redefines the object cover. The application detects this event by reading the text:

```
(BUTTON1DOWN CLOCK-WINDOW CLOCK HOUR 2 34 102 66)
```

As cover is now the top object on the drawing, mouse motion events are reported to it and relayed to the application as strings of the form:

```
(MOTION CLOCK-WINDOW CLOCK COVER 4 34 104 66)
```

Using the hand from the button-1-down event, and the mouse position from subsequent motion events, the application redefines both hands to reflect the new time. This process continues as the user drags the mouse until button 1 comes up. When button 1 comes up, the drag is complete and `cover` is redefined as a null object.

Applications of ezd

The true test of any graphics system is not the elegance (or lack thereof) of its drawing model or implementation, but the applications that users are able to construct with it and their ease of construction. This section describes four applications representative of work done at WRL. They demonstrate that ezd has been easy to use and can be used for real problems.

Heap Memory Map for Garbage-Collected C++

A generational garbage collector for C++ [4] is able to do significant heap compaction in spite of the fact that the roots are ambiguous. An excellent way to demonstrate the collector's performance is to display a map of the heap as the program runs. Each 512-byte page of the garbage-collected heap is represented in Figure 3 by a small rectangle whose color denotes the state of the page: free, a member of the stable set, or recently allocated to the current generation. As each page is allocated, the associated rectangle is defined. During garbage collection, retained data is compacted by copying it from recently allocated pages to newly allocated pages in the stable set. At the end of garbage collection all pages not in the stable set are marked free.

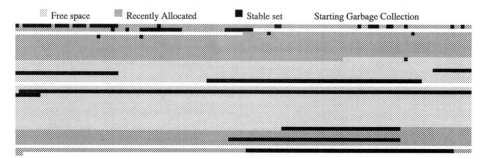

Figure 3: Heap memory map

In order to provide a heap map for arbitrary C++ programs, it is important that the map's presence not affect the control flow of the program. The C++ program never receives a request from ezd as ezd handles all X events and user interaction. Even though the user may stop the display and step it through a garbage collection via a pop-up menu, the only effect on the C++ program is that it may block if it fills the pipe to ezd.

This application is typical of the type of "quick and dirty" drawing that one can produce with ezd: take an existing program and quickly modify it to draw a picture about some aspect of its computation. In this case, the heap map was implemented in part of an afternoon using less than 100 lines of C++.

High Density Data Representation

While ezd was designed to be a program-driven drawing system for displays, its ability to generate PostScript images makes it valuable for document graphics as well. David Wall examined how well estimated and real program execution profiles predict program behavior [23]. He compared five types of profiles produced by eleven different methods against the actual profiles for multiple runs of eleven programs. In order to reduce this volume of information to something from which he and his readers could draw conclusions, he devised a graphical notation (shown in Figure 4) consisting of arrays of pie charts[3]. In order to easily produce the 2,508 pie-charts found in his paper, Wall created a little language to specify them[4] and a compiler to convert it to ezd commands.

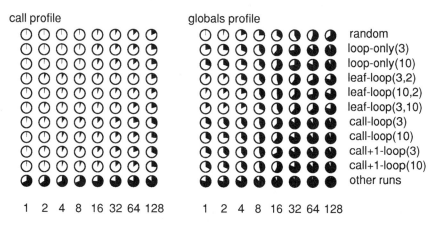

Figure 4: Program execution profile estimates

Weather Forecasts

National Weather Service forecasts for the United States are sometimes available for network access. The ezd application shown in Figure 5 was constructed to fetch such forecasts for the contiguous 48 states. The mouse-sensitive diamonds on the map identify cities that issue forecasts. When the mouse is positioned over a diamond, text describing the region covered by the forecast is displayed. When the mouse is clicked on a diamond, the forecast is obtained via the network and displayed in the text area at the bottom of the

---

[3]For other elegant examples of this technique of using "small multiples," the reader should consult [20] and [21].

[4]More examples and a discussion of the virtues of little languages for specifying documentation graphics are found in [7].

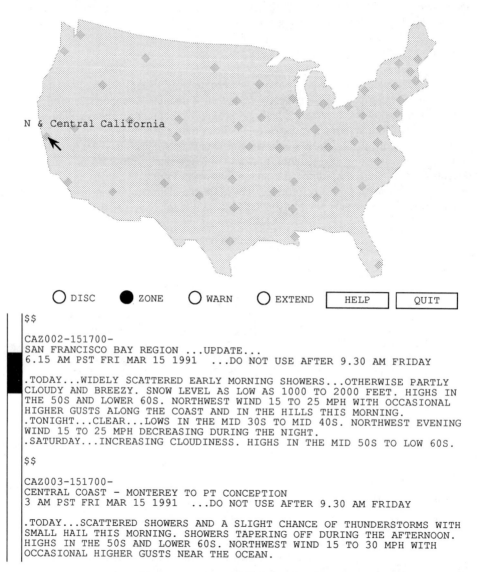

Figure 5: 48 states' weather forecasts

window. The text is scrolled using the scroll bar on the left of the text and can be copied into other X applications with the mouse.

BIPS Router

For the last two years, the majority of researchers at WRL having been working on BIPS, a custom bipolar processor with arithmetic unit, floating point unit, address translation buffers, memory management unit, and first level cache all on one die. The CAD tools being constructed for this project allow schematics and hints about layout to be automatically converted to a chip. As can be expected, automatically routing the chip is a difficult problem. Early on in the project, Jeremy Dion and Louis Monier reached the limits of their patience with debugging using conventional tools and chose to try graphics to observe the router in action. Their initial efforts took less than a day to implement and produced pictures similar to that show in Figure 6, which contains over 2000 graphical objects.

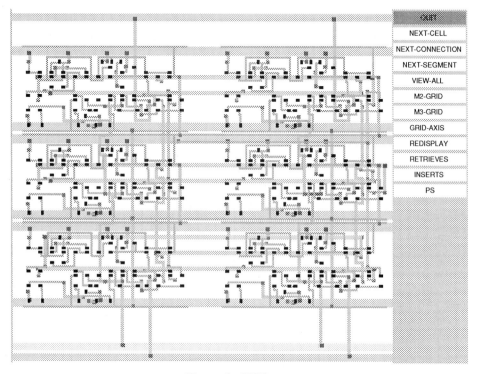

Figure 6: BIPS router

The chip is represented in ezd in a natural way: each layer of the chip is a drawing. The drawings are then overlaid into the window in the same order they appear in the chip. As wires are allocated, the area is defined in the appropriate drawing. When wires are ripped up, the objects representing them are redefined as null objects and ezd takes care of correcting the display. The control panel on the right of the drawing allows debugging options to be selected and the router to be stepped. Since ezd runs as a separate process, the graphics window remains intact even when the router is stopped at a breakpoint.

Comparison With Other X-based Tools

Ezd's power and ease-of-use come from a combination of a high-level drawing model with a server that takes full responsibility for display management. Neither the most prevalent X toolkit, Xt [3][5], nor PostScript-based systems such as NeWS [10] provide structured graphics. One toolkit, InterViews [14], provides a class of structured graphics objects for use by applications, but it does not use structured graphics for drawing user interface interactors.

None of these other tools offer ezd's "event-free" graphics. All their clients must handle events generated by the X server and take responsibility for redrawing damaged portions of the application's windows.

Ezd's embedded language allows good interactive performance by handling events in the server and provides a mechanism for user extensions to ezd. Other graphics systems such as SCIX [12], a shell for GL [6], and WINTERP [15] have also used Lisp dialects as extension languages. Another system that has made extensive use of a server embedded language is NeWS. Two advantages that ezd has over NeWS and other PostScript-based systems are that large extensions to ezd written in Scheme may be compiled and linked into ezd, and that Scheme was intended for human consumption.

While ezd is strong in the previously mentioned areas, it is weak in others. Its graphics primitives are not as powerful as those found in PostScript based systems that allow arbitrary scaling and rotation of all graphics, including text. It is not oriented towards building predefined, uniform user interaces. Unlike most X toolkits, it provides no mechanisms for event translation, automatic window layout, or application customization. Finally, even on the fastest machines, structured graphics may not have the desired performance. An early ezd user wanted to draw tens of thousands of points and line segments on a persistent display. The application never needed to erase or interact with any object. Ezd was too slow and required too much memory to represent the drawing; the user ended up with a solution based on Xlib.

The Return of Interactive Structured Graphics

Given WRL's positive experience with ezd, it is natural to ask: why haven't others provided simple access to structured graphics? The record suggests that they have, but there were problems. In the early 80's, there were attempts to build graphical user interface systems using GKS [11]. Two things probably contributed to their demise. First, there were both functional and performance limitations to making systems using structured graphics interactive. The graphics systems were focused towards high-quality output, rather than toward rapid display and handling user interaction. Second, while these systems thought in terms of a single application window, systems done at Xerox PARC encouraged people to think in terms of multiple interactive windows sharing the screen. The performance demands of this type of environment seemed to preclude the use of structured graphics.

---

[5]Xt is a a toolkit built on top of Xlib, X's low-level C library. In conjunction with the toolkit, one uses a library of *widgets* such as Motif [17]. A widget is a predefined component of a user interface that typically consists of both a graphical "look" and an interactive "feel", e.g. a push button or pop-up menu.

For low-performance machines and simple interactive objects like buttons, a policy of differentiating between structured graphics and interactive interface objects makes sense. As computers get faster and interactive objects more ornate, there is less reason to separate interactive interface objects from other structured graphics. Instead, one wants "interactive drawings" that are representative of the application problem domain with user interface controls forming a natural part of the drawing. The only graphics changes required to turn the BIPS router display into a browser is the addition of a few ezd commands to make the wires sensitive to mouse clicks. Other efforts in this area include Unidraw [22], a set of tools for constructing application specific graphical editors, and Xerox PARC's "Embedded Buttons" architecture that is exploring the use of text and graphics editors to construct user interfaces [8].

Conclusion

Ezd applications offer evidence that the ezd's approach to program graphics can be scaled beyond toy problems. The weather program contains an interactive map and some very conventional user interface interactors constructed with ezd. The push buttons and radio buttons provide immediate response and appear similar to those provided by the other X toolkits. Even though they're constructed using structured graphics, the slider moves smoothly and the text smoothly scrolls at an acceptable speed. The BIPS router is able to display portions of a chip being routed using drawings consisting of thousands of graphical elements. While one would not confuse the speed and detail of the circuit drawing with one produced by a "real" VLSI CAD tool, its speed is adequate and the information presented by it has proven to be invaluable to the construction of the router.

The individual graphics ideas embodied in ezd are not novel. What is novel is making them available to any program via a server interpreting a simple, text-based protocol. The enthusiastic response of ezd's initial users shows the demand for simple-to-use 2-D structured graphics, and today's 10 MIPS or faster workstations allow it to be provided with good interactive performance.

Software Information

The ezd server is available for use outside Digital Equipment Corporation. It may be copied via ftp from the directory /pub/DEC/ezd on the system gatekeeper.dec.com. See the copyright statement included in the source for the conditions governing its use.

Author Information

Joel Bartlett is a member of the research staff at Digital Equipment Corporation's Western Research Laboratory. Besides easy-to-use graphics, his research interests include garbage collection and portable Scheme implementations. His Internet address is bartlett@decwrl.dec.com.

References

[1] Harold Abelson and Gerald Jay Sussman with Julie Sussman.
Structure and Interpretation of Computer Programs.
The MIT Press, 1985.

[2] Adobe Systems Incorporated.
PostScript Language Reference Manual - 2nd edition.
Addison-Wesley Publishing Company, Inc., 1990.

[3] Paul J. Asente and Ralph R. Swick.
X Window System Toolkit.
Digital Press, 1990.

[4] Joel F. Bartlett.
Mostly-Copying Garbage Collection Picks Up Generations and C++.
Technical Note TN-12, Digital Equipment Corporation Western Research
Laboratory, October, 1989.

[5] Joel F. Bartlett.
Don't Fidget with Widgets, Draw!.
Research Report 91/6, Digital Equipment Corporation Western Research
Laboratory, May, 1991.

[6] Brian Beckman.
A Scheme for Little Languages in Interactive Graphics.
Software-Practice and Experience 21(2):187-207, February, 1990.

[7] Jon Bentley.
More Programming Pearls.
Addison-Wesley Publishing Company, Inc., 1988.

[8] Eric A. Bier and Aaron Goodisman.
Documents as User Interfaces.
In *EP90, Proceedings of the International Conference on Electronic Publishing,
Document Manipulation, and Typography*, pages 249-262. Cambridge
University Press, 1990.

[9] Jeremy Dion.
Fast Printed Circuit Board Routing.
Research Report 88/1, Digital Equipment Corporation Western Research
Laboratory, March, 1988.

[10] James Gosling, David S. H. Rosenthal, Michelle J. Arden.
The NeWS book: an introduction to the Networked Extensible Window System.
Springer-Verlag, 1989.

[11] H. Rex Hartson and Deborah Hix.
Human-Computer Interface Development: Concepts and Systems for Its
Management.
ACM Computing Surveys 21(1):5-92, March, 1989.

[12]   Hakan Huss and Johan Ihren.
       SCIX A Scheme Interface to the X Window System.
       Royal Institute of Technology, Stockholm, March 1990, available from
            huss@nada.kth.se or johani@nada.kth.se.

[13]   Brian W. Kernighan, Rob Pike.
       The UNIX Programming Environment.
       Prentice-Hall, Inc., 1984.

[14]   Mark A. Linton, John M. Vlissides, and Paul R. Calder.
       Composing User Interfaces with Interviews.
       IEEE Computer 22(2):8-22, February, 1989.

[15]   Niels P. Mayer.
       The WINTERP Widget INTERpreter - A Lisp Prototyping and Extension
            Environment for OSF/Motif-based Applications and User-Interfaces.
       LISP Pointers 4(1):45-60, July-March, 1990.

[16]   William M. Newman, Robert F. Sproull.
       Principles of Interactive Computer Graphics, Second Edition.
       McGraw-Hill Book Company, 1979.

[17]   Open Systems Foundation.
       *OSF/Motif Series (5 Volumes): Motif Style Guide; Programmer's Guide;
            Programmer's Reference; User's Guide; Application Environment
            Specification; User Environment Volume.*
       Prentice-Hall, 1990.

[18]   Jonathan Rees, William Clinger (Editors).
       Revised[3] Report on the Algorithmic Language Scheme.
       SIGPLAN Notices 21(12):37-79, December, 1986.

[19]   Robert W. Scheifler and James Gettys with Jim Flowers, Ron Newman, and
       David Rosenthal.
       X Window System.
       Digital Press, 1990.

[20]   Edward R. Tufte.
       The Visual Display of Quantitative Information.
       Graphics Press, 1983.

[21]   Edward R. Tufte.
       Envisioning Information.
       Graphics Press, 1990.

[22]   John M. Vlissides and Mark A. Linton.
       Unidraw: A Framework for Building Domain-Specific Graphical Editors.
       Technical Report CSL-TR-89-380, Stanford University, July, 1989.

[23]   David W. Wall.
       Predicting Program Behavior Using Real or Estimated Profiles.
       In *ACM SIGPLAN '91 Conference on Programming Language Design and
            Implementation*, pages 59-70. June, 1991.

A Macro Facility for X

Object Specific Event Simulation

Kuntal Rawal

Abstract

This paper describes a Mouse and Keyboard event capture and playback mechanism used to implement a macro facility under X Window System[1]. The mechanism allows an arbitrary event sequence to be bound to a key press event. Pressing the key activates the macro much like a normal accelerator. The mechanism also has the ability to register and replay nested macros to arbitrary depth; macros bound to different keys can be combined and bound to a single key. The mechanism is provided as part of the toolkit; any program bound to the toolkit gets the macro mechanism for free, allowing the end user to create, save, and delete macros. Macros are preserved across multiple invocations of a program. The file format used is that of the X resource manager.

Whereas most simulation techniques break down when window positions are moved or resized, this implementation can play back events even after the windows/objects have had their origins shifted, have been resized, or some other attributes have changed.

Kuntal Rawal is a Software Engineer at Solbourne Computer, Inc., 1900 Pike Rd., Longmont, CO 80501

Introduction

Event simulation has gathered importance with the advent of user interfaces where user interaction is not limited to keyboard commands, but includes mouse usage. Event simulation finds application in everyday usage where the user needs a short-cut to actions performed repeatedly, in automated demos, and in automated testing. The problem can be divided into two parts:

1. Capturing keyboard and mouse events.
2. Playing back previously captured events.

Keyboard events can be captured relatively easily by recording which keys are pressed. To sufficiently capture the state of the mouse, one needs the (x, y) position <u>and</u> the condition of the buttons of the mouse. One of the most difficult aspect is that we would like to capture the position so that even if user customizable attributes are changed (font, borderwidth, object location, or object size) the captured event should still play back reasonably well. Recording the mouse position as x and y coordinates is not sufficient to achieve this goal.

This paper describes a scheme to record each position in an *object specific* manner to achieve the independence from user customizable attributes. Each recorded event has an event specific part and optional object specific information.

Currently this scheme is implemented as part of the OI^2 Toolkit [Aitk90], but the same techniques can be used under any other toolkit to provide similar functionality.

The scheme presented is useful in automating frequently employed actions by an everyday user, in automated demos and in a limited way in automated testing.

The first section describes the general technique used to create, register, execute, save and read the macro. The second section discusses the event specific aspects. The third section describes the object specific information needed for an event with examples of a text and a menu object.

1.0 General Technique

Each application gets a *macro object*. The macro object consists of scrolling menu containing existing macros; and a menu with options to create, save, delete, read or execute a macro. A macro object contains a list of *macros* that are currently defined. Each macro consists of a number of *action objects*. An action (object) can be a KEY_PESS action or a BUTTON_MOTION action. Each action consists of a series of *events*.

1.1 Creating a Macro

When the user begins building a macro, the macro object sets a flag indicating that events are to be recorded. In the main event dispatch loop for the toolkit, if the macro object's capture flag is on, the event is sent to the macro object's capture routine. In the capture() function, the event is passed on to the respective action object to record the event. The action object records the 'event generic' part. In order to capture the object specific part the action object's capture function calls the user interface object's (the object where the event occurred) capture function. This function returns the object specific part to save. Depending on the object, it might use a default capture function or a specific one. Object specific data is further explained in section 3.

When the user is finished recording the events, he/she registers the macro.

1.2 Registering a Macro

Each macro is registered as an accelerator on the top level object. All macros cause the same function to fire. The macro keys are converted into a quark and passed to the called function, which uses it to find the appropriate macro. The new macro accelerator is merged with all the existing accelerators on the top level object. The following lines illustrate this point:

```
static char *trans = "#override \n
           %s";
...
sprintf(accstr, trans, macro->key()) /* key()=> 'Ctrl F12'*/
sprintf(tmp_string, "%d", XrmStringToQuark(macro->key()));
sprintf(accel_str, "%s: OI_exec_macro(%s)", accstr, tmp_string);
top_object->merge_accelerator(accel_str);
...
```

1.3 Executing a Macro

The toolkit maintains a macro stack. This is a stack of macros which are currently executing. This allows us to nest the macros so that a macro can call a series of other macros.

Depending on object specific data, XWarpPointer is used to set the location of the mouse pointer. An event is sent to the window using the XSendEvent call. After each event is sent, it is necessary for the macro to return to the main processing loop of the Toolkit in order to process the event generated by the macro. This means that when a macro is playing back the events, it should be able to maintain its state between invocations. Each macro maintains the current action and each action maintains the next event to dispatch.

1.3.1 Timing Each Event

A select() call is used to wait for the time delay associated with each event. This ensures that other events are not blocked while playing back the macro. The event dispatch uses the previous event's time of execution, current event's time delay, and the current time for computing the final time delay.

1.3.2 Object Map State

Consider an example of a sequence of events which consists of a button press on a cell which activates a dialog box and the user starts typing into the dialog box. When playing back this sequence the dialog box should be mapped before the key press events are sent. This is ensured by a call to XGetWindowAttributes to make sure that the map state is IsViewable. A resource controlled time-out value is provided for the maximum amount of time to wait for an object be viewable before terminating the macro.

1.4 Saving and Reading a Macro

Macros are saved in a file in a format resembling X Resources. This makes it easier to read the file using the existing resource manager reading, writing, and parsing functions. The following is an example of a macro saved in a file:

```
!
! Macro File for smac. Created on Fri Nov 22 19:25:58 1991
!
*smac*Macro: F12
!
! <Key> F12
!
*smac*macro.F12.items: item1
*smac*macro.F12.topObject: TestWindow

*smac*macro.F12.item1.type: KeyPress
*smac*macro.F12.item1.number: 2
*smac*macro.F12.item1.KeyPress_0.name: TestWindow/mytxt
*smac*macro.F12.item1.KeyPress_0.keySymbol: 111
*smac*macro.F12.item1.KeyPress_0.modifiers: None
*smac*macro.F12.item1.KeyPress_0.time: 0
*smac*macro.F12.item1.KeyPress_1.keySymbol: 107
*smac*macro.F12.item1.KeyPress_1.modifiers: None
*smac*macro.F12.item1.KeyPress_1.time: 420
```

This tells us that there were two keys associated with the macro attached to F12 key. The key presses were in the object named 'mytxt' which is a child of 'TestWindow' and both the key presses were in the same object since 'KeyPress_1' does not have a name specified. Time delays are stored in milliseconds. Accelerator for the macro is installed on 'TestWindow' (topObject).

Macros are read from the file using the standard toolkit calls to get resources.

1.5 Event Translation

Not all the event objects have their own window. For example, menu cells do not have a window. Thus the event received would be with the window id of the menu. Therefore before the event information is saved, the event location needs to be translated with respect to the actual child object.

Similarly, before simulating the event, the nearest parent object with its own window is looked up and the event location is translated with respect to this parent object.

2.0 Events and Actions

A Macro can contain two types of actions:
1.   KEY_PRESS: This is a sequence of key presses.
2.   BUTTON_MOTION: This is a ButtonPress followed by ButtonMotion (optional) followed by a ButtonRelease.

2.1 KEY_PRESS Action

Each KEY_PRESS action contains the following items:

```
  ..
  Keysym key_sym;          /* Key symbol of the key pressed. */
  int    modifier_status;  /* Modifier status: Ctrl, Shift etc. */
  Time   time;             /* Time delay from the previous event */
  char   *object_name;     /* Object to send the event to. */
  char   *object_specific; /* Object specific event info. */
  ..
```

The example in section 1.4 shows how it is stored in the file. String 'object_specific' is explained in section 3.0.

2.2 BUTTON_MOTION Action

Each BUTTON_MOTION is stored as a button-press, optional button-motion, and a button-release. The button press and button release each have following data:

```
int      button_num;      /* Button which was pressed or released */
int      modifier_status; /* Modifier status: Ctrl, Shift etc. */
char     *object_name;    /* Object to send the event to. */
char     *object_specific; /* Object specific event info. */
```

Each button release contains additional time stamp information to indicate the time delay between the button release and the previous event.

```
Time     time;            /* Time delay from the previous event */
```

Besides containing the details for button press and button release, a BUTTON_MOTION action contains ButtonMotion event related data. Each ButtonMotion event contains:

```
int      modifier_status; /* Modifier status: Button1 etc. */
Time     time;            /* Time delay from the previous event */
char     *object_name;    /* Object to send the event to. */
char     *object_specific; /* Object specific event info. */
```

An example of the action saved in a macro file is:

```
..
*smac*macro.R15.item0.type: ButtonMotion
*smac*macro.R15.item0.ButtonPress.name: TestWindow/optionMenu/cell1
*smac*macro.R15.item0.ButtonPress.objectSpecific: (0.440000, 0.545455)
*smac*macro.R15.item0.ButtonPress.buttonNumber: 1
*smac*macro.R15.item0.ButtonPress.modifiers: None

*smac*macro.R15.item0.ButtonMotion.number: 2
*smac*macro.R15.item0.ButtonMotion_0.name: TestWindow/optionMenu/cell1
*smac*macro.R15.item0.ButtonMotion_0.objectSpecific:(0.52000,0.545455)
*smac*macro.R15.item0.ButtonMotion_0.modifiers: Button1
*smac*macro.R15.item0.ButtonMotion_0.time: 40
*smac*macro.R15.item0.ButtonMotion_1.name: TestWindow/optionMenu/cell1
*smac*macro.R15.item0.ButtonMotion_1.objectSpecific:(0.64000,0.545455)
*smac*macro.R15.item0.ButtonMotion_1.modifiers: Button1
*smac*macro.R15.item0.ButtonMotion_1.time: 40

*smac*macro.R15.item0.ButtonRelease.name: TestWindow/optionMenu/cell1
*smac*macro.R15.item0.ButtonRelease.objectSpecific:(0.640000,0.545455)
*smac*macro.R15.item0.ButtonRelease.buttonNumber: 1
*smac*macro.R15.item0.ButtonRelease.modifiers: Button1
*smac*macro.R15.item0.ButtonRelease.time: 80
..
```

3.0 Object Specific Data

The data contained in this part of the captured event is specific to the object to which the event is sent. Its purpose is to convert and store the mouse pointer position in a manner which is independent of the relative positions of parts of the object, changes in the size of the object due to a change in any of its attributes, etc.

For an object like a box, the object specific data is a ratio of (x, y) mouse pointer location with respect to the size of the object. For example, if the box has the size of 200x200 and the mouse pointer location is at 80, 100 then for a box with this event, the object_specific string takes the form: '(0.4, 0.5)'. An entry in the macro file would look like:

```
...
smac*macro.F12.item0.ButtonPress.objectSpecific:  (0.4, 0.5)
...
```

This ensures that the 'relative position' of the event remains the same for an object irrespective of the size of the object. This is the minimum level of object specific information that is stored in an object.

However some objects need more or different information than this. An example of an object needing different information is a text object. Instead of storing the ratio of the relative position for where the button press occurred, it stores the column and row position. This ensures that any change in the font, for example, will not affect the event simulation.

In a more complex case of a menu, it stores the information relative to the cell the pointer is closest to, whether the pointer is inside or outside the menu, etc.

Following sections describe object specific data stored by the text and menu objects.

3.1 Text

Text objects save the position either as a (column, row) or as a relative position depending on where the event occurred. *Figure 1* describes three cases which determine how the object specific data is stored.

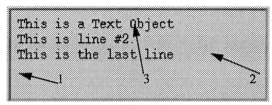

Figure 1

1.   When the event is not on any line, the relative position in the form '(0.468, 0.984)' is used. The decimal point indicates that the position stored is relative.

2.   When the event is on a valid line but not on any character then the data is stored in the form (relative-position, line-number), e.g. (0.468, 10).

3.   When event location is on a valid character, the data is stored in the form (character-position, line-number), e.g. (10, 20).

3.1.1 Example

Figure 2 shows how the same macro to select a text from the same text object, but running with different attributes in two different instances, selects the same characters. Text in *Figure 2-A* has the font 12x24 and Motif[3] focus cursor width of 2 pixels. Text below it (*Figure 2-B*) is running with a 12pt courier font and the Motif focus cursor width of 5 pixels. However the macro to select the text worked exactly the same in both the cases.

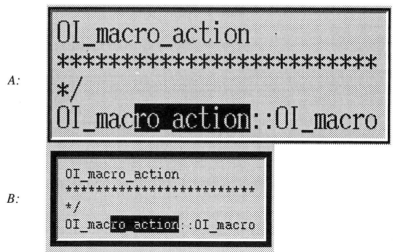

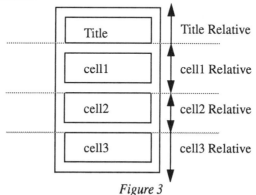

Figure 2

3.2 Menu

The discussion of object specific information for menus is restricted to the Motif model. Under OPEN LOOK[4] additional information is needed to cover the case when the event location is inside the pushpin.

The menu may need to know the object specific information with respect to the menu cell and the title of the menu. Also a menu may have a vertical or a horizontal orientation. Relative positions with respect to cells and the title are used to save the menu's object specific information. In most of the cases, the title is not an active part of the menu. A resource is provided to control if the title relative positions are desired or only cell relative positions are to be recorded. *Figure 3,* below, describes the relative positions used to save the information.

Figure 3

Each of the object specific strings are also preceded by 'In' or 'Out' strings to indicate if the event occurred inside or outside the menu. The first relative position is the distance along the major axis of the menu. This allows for correct simulation even if the menu orientation changes between record and playback. Following is an example of an object specific data stored for a menu object:

```
...
*smac*macro.R15.item0.ButtonMotion_1.objectSpecific:In(cell1,1.04,.12)
...
```

If this was recorded for a vertical menu, then 1.04 is the relative y-position (major axis) and 0.12 is the relative x-position. The positions are relative to cell1. This indicates that the ButtonMotion event was below cell1 but not inside cell2. If the menu orientation changes to be horizontal during simulation, 1.04 would become relative x-position and 0.12 would be relative y-position. This would still place it between cell1 and cell2 for a horizontal menu.

If the event was inside the title it might look like:

```
...
*smac*macro.R15.item0.ButtonMotion_1.objectSpecific:InTitle(,.44,.12)
...
```

Or if it was inside the menu but to the left of the title (for a vertical menu) then it might look like:

```
...
*smac*macro.R15.item0.ButtonMotion_1.objectSpecific:InTitle(,.12,-0.04)
...
```

3.2.1 Example

Following example shows a macro which fires a cell in a pulldown menu. The same macro is used to fire the cell in two different instances which appear quite different as *Figure 4*, below, shows.

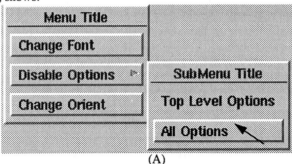

(A)

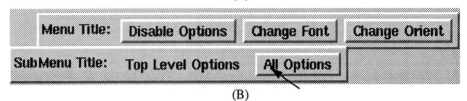

(B)

Figure 4

In this example not only the orientation of the menu has changed but also the ordering of the first two cells is reversed. The macro still simulates correct behavior.

3.3 Handling Object Specific Data

The object specific part is saved by passing the event to the object where the event occurred. The object's capture function returns a string of the form 'In(cell1,1.04,.12)'. This is saved as the object specific part of the event. When simulating the event, the object's decode function is called with the object specific string; it returns the corresponding (x, y) co-ordinates which are used in the XSendEvent() call.

3.4 Invalid Events

Consider a menu event:

```
...
*smac*macro.R15.item0.ButtonMotion_1.objectSpecific:In(cell1,1,.02,.12)
...
```

If somehow the space between the menu and the cell has become zero at the time of simulating the event, then there aren't any valid (x, y) locations that can satisfy this event. It becomes an invalid event. Each object can determine what to do with any invalid events. Currently menu ignores such an event.

This area needs further work to determine if it is possible to provide a user defined option to determine the course of action under these conditions.

4.0 Summary

The proposed scheme consists of:
1. Add necessary hooks to the toolkit in the main event dispatch loop to save and simulate the event.
2. Provide functions to capture, save, read, and execute the events.
3. Provide functions to translate the event from a non-window object to the nearest parent windowed object and vice versa.
4. Provide generic (default) object specific capture and decode functions.
5. Provide particular capture and decode functions to objects that need different object specific information.

The proposed scheme is still under development. Some of the areas which need further work are:
1. Reducing the size of the macro file and reducing the load on the resource manager.
2. Exploring various options for invalid event handing.
3. Fine tuning object specific event data.
4. Explore the extensions to include PointerMotion etc. for use in automated testing.

5.0 Acknowledgments

I would like to thank Gary Aitken for his valuable input and suggestions on this project. I would also like to thank all other members of the User Interface group, especially Tom LaStrange, who with their 'can you do this?' questions have helped make this a useful and a workable scheme.

6.0 Author Information

Kuntal Rawal is a software engineer at Solbourne Computer, Inc. and currently works on the OI Library. Prior to working at Solbourne, Kuntal was a consultant to Tektronix, doing X Server testing. He graduated with a degree in Electrical Engineering from Indian Institute of Technology, Bombay, India. He can be reached at (303) 678-4352 or kuntal@Solbourne.COM.

7.0 References

[Aitk90]

Aitken, Gary, *OI: A Model Extensible C++ Toolkit for the X Window System*, 4th Annual Technical Conference on the X Window System, 1990.

---

[1] **X Window System** is a registered trademark of Massachusetts Institute of Technology.

[2] **Object Interface Library (OI)** is a registered trademark of Solbourne Computer, Inc.

[3] **Motif** is a registered trademark of the Open Software Foundation.

[4] **OPEN LOOK** is a registered trademark of AT&T.

Testing Widget Geometry Management

Daniel Dardailler

Abstract

The complexity of the Xt geometry management and the variety of OSF/Motif layout policies combine to make the understanding of the layout activities in any Xt/Motif based application a very difficult task. This paper presents a set of tools intended to help programmers follow the complex flow of geometry requests and check the compliance to the Xt specifications of a program or a widget set library. A first technique using a specialized widget is described, and then a library-based system is presented. The advantages and drawbacks of both approaches are then discussed in a separate section.

Introduction

Debugging large Motif applications is not a simple task and the first thing OSF usually asks from the programmers reporting bugs is to extract from their large application a minimal program that shows the same anomaly. While this technique usually works fine for most defect issues, layout problems still remain very complex to track down, the problem residing most of the time in the toolkit itself, in the form of untested combinations of nested Composite and Primitive widgets.

Even the simpler of those geometry-related problems almost always involve stepping through the widget code, and if a C interpreter (like Saber) is not available, the developer usually needs to re-build the library -g before actually starting to debug. In addition, with or without re-compilation needed, once the test is ready to run in the symbolic environment, the engineer may have forgotten the "magic" of the Xt

Daniel Dardailler (daniel@osf.org) joined the Open Software Foundation in 1990 as a Senior Software Engineer in the User Environment Components group. His responsibility in the OSF/Motif project includes the geometry management of most widgets. He holds a Ph.D. in Computer Science from the University of Nice/Sophia Antipolis.

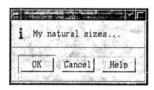

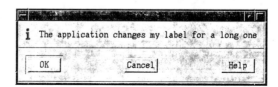

Figure 1: Dynamic re-layout in Motif with Xt.

geometry management, and he may spend valuable time deciding where to put his break-points. As the resources in disk space (for the debug libraries) and engineering become scarce, this type of overhead becomes unacceptable.

The idea of this work is to provide a very flexible framework that allows the application's developer and/or the toolkit's developer to track most geometry management problems without even having to recompile the original code.

By just relinking with a special library, the developer is now able to point to a particular area in a widget tree instance (using pseudo-resource descriptions in a file or an interactive tool like **editres**, the X resource editor), and he will get a report of the geometry flow for this specific zone of the application.

The next chapter briefly presents some aspects of the Xt geometry management. The knowledge of the layered X architecture with the Intrinsics providing the widget abstraction is required.

Xt geometry management

Why is the Xt geometry management so difficult to understand?
Mainly because it is powerful.

If you look at a MacIntosh or a Windows 3.0 screen, you'll see that there is almost no dynamic layout. Either the applications include a scrollable viewport, and everything is clipped when the top level window gets smaller, or there is no scrolled window and user's resize handles aren't present. There is in both toolkits a way for the application to be called back when the top level window is resized, but since no generic mechanism is provided to handle the re-layout, few applications take advantage of these resize notifications.

In Xt, on the other hand, the toolkit provides all the mechanisms for doing dynamic re-layout. The key point is that the preferred geometry of a composite is computed from its children's preferred geometry (which themselves may be composites).

Figure 1 illustrates the different kind of "traversal" that Xt geometry management can perform on a given application widget instance tree.

The first message box layout (top-left, "natural sizes") results from a initial bottom-to-top flow that is implemented as a postorder top-down traversal. The push buttons and the message label are first asked their preferred sizes, the message box then arranges all its children and computes its own geometry, which is eventually used to size the top level shell window.

In the second layout (top-right, "resized by the user"), a top-to-bottom chain of reconfiguration orders is shown. When the top-level shell window is resized, it resizes its unique message box child. In turn, the message box accommodates its own layout to its new boundaries: the preferred geometry of the label is asked and given the room left in the manager, an alternate button-placement algorithm is used.

The last window is an example of bottom-to-top request-flow. When the application changes the message label, Xt manages to have the parent (the message box itself) informed. As a result of the grow request made by the label, the message box computes a new push buttons layout and asks the top level shell window to become larger. The shell widget itself needs to communicate with the window manager (as it is a different process in the X architecture) and if the size changes are accepted as is, the re-configuration eventually occurs.

Xt, like the X protocol, provides generic mechanisms, not policies. The widgets have to implement their own layout algorithms within the Xt framework. The generic way for a widget to resize another widget (usually a child) is thru a call to XtResizeWidget, but most widgets have private layout policy resources (orientation, packing, visibility, etc) that control *their own geometry* inside the new boundaries. The level of complexity and the bugs found in the manipulation of these resources are orthogonal to the Xt geometry management mechanisms, but one should understand both dimensions in order to maintain the widget set code.

The Application Programmer Interface provides three basic mechanisms:

- a way for a parent widget to reconfigure the size and position of a child widget: XtConfigureWidget (with its variants XtResizeWidget and XtMoveWidget). It's a top-to-bottom order.

- a way for a child widget to request a change in geometry: XtMakeGeometryRequest (and its variant XtMakeResizeRequest). It's a bottom-to-top flow.

- a way for a parent widget to ask its preferred geometry to a child: XtQueryGeometry.

Composite widgets need in turn to implement a GeometryManager method that receives and possibly makes calls to XtMakeGeometryRequest, and a ChangeManaged method that handles the changes in the list of children. The actual space allocation is implemented in the Resize method.

Not to help the overall understanding, the structures used in the API (XtWidget-Geometry, XtGeometryResult) are shared by the request and the query geometry functions but with different semantics...

If I add that all this stuff happens simultaneously and often requires inter-process communications (client/X server/window manager), you'd be convinced that a new tool was needed!

The GeoTattler widget

This chapter describes a new widget, the GeoTattler, whose purpose, once inserted in a widget hierarchy, is to check the compliance to the Xt geometry management specifications of its child and its parent. It does that by reporting in a human-readable form the flow of requests and the inconsistencies occurring during the up and down process of the Xt layout mechanism.

A special section is dedicated to a complementary library, libGeo, which includes the GeoTattler code and an XtCreateWidget wrapper that uses Xt subresources to determine where to insert a GeoTattler widget in the application widget hierarchy at startup time.

Description

The basic idea is to create a new composite widget, the GeoTattler, an instance of which is inserted between a parent and a child widget, for the purpose of tracing and reporting their geometry management negotiations, now routed through the GeoTattler class methods.

This idea of inserting an active component into the flow of a given process for debugging purpose has already been proven useful, at the X protocol level, by the success of the **xscope** or the **xmon** program.

GeoTattler is going to "fake" the child from the parent's point of view, and fake the parent from the child's point of view. It can easily detect, for instance, actions such as the parent resizing the child, since GeoTattler will be resized first and will have to resize the child itself; at this time, it can report the geometry request coming from the parent before passing it to the child.

The GeoTattler has of course all the methods needed to handle geometry management properly: Initialize, Resize, GeometryManager, ChangeManaged, and Query-Geometry.

In addition, since the current design forces the GeoTattler to have only one child, it has an InsertChild method which controls that number. We believe it's better to use a higher level set of facilities to test the behavior of several children in a same parent (like the use of subresources described in the next section).

Look at the Xt specification (R4/R5), chapter 6: *Geometry Management*, and you'll see that it is full of *shoulds* and *musts*, and that there is in fact a very formal protocol hidden behind these 12 pages of esoteric English text :-) Given this complexity, it would also be interesting, to not only trace, but also to test whether the parent and the child react properly to geometry management actions.

The technique of testing used in the GeoTattler is very simple: it has a certain number of flags stored in the instance widget, and the geometry related class methods set and check them at the right time.

Let's start by the current list of predicates the GeoTattler is able to verify and then we will describe the implementation of the first one in detail.

- The parent has a compliant XtGeometryDone or XtGeometryYes policy (it calls the resize proc of the child on acceptance of a geometry request or not).

- The child is not requesting its parent from its resize proc (might result in infinite loop).

- The parent is not considering an unmanaged child.

- The child deals properly with the XtGeometryAlmost proposal.

- The parent always accepts its own last XtGeometryAlmost proposal .

- An XtGeometryNo or an XtGeometryAlmost reply from the parent didn't change the current geometry.

- The XtCWQueryOnly bit set doesn't change the current geometry either.

- A widget is not making a geometry request from its SetValues method (thus allowing a subclass to change the behavior).

- A child QueryGeometry is conformant to the specification for XtGeometryNo, XtGeometryYes and XtGeometryAlmost.

Because of the Xt specifications being frozen too early in the life time of the Intrinsics, the XtMakeGeometryRequest function is not able to report if the parent has effectively resized the requestor child. The managers' GeometryManager method can return either XtGeometryDone or XtGeometryYes, but the Intrinsics will change any Done to Yes before returning from XtMakeGeometryRequest.

From the child's point of view, after a request has been accepted, this means that either it trusts its widget set policy (if there is one) and always, or never, call its resize proc itself, or it has to track the calls to its own resize method to see if it needs to re-layout (because its parent didn't do it yet).

That's exactly what the GeoTattler simulates. In its resize method, it sets an instance boolean True and its Geometry Manager sets it False before making (passing really) a request to its parent. If the boolean value is True after the return of XtMakeGeometryRequest, the parent is a XtGeometryDone, otherwise, its a XtGeometryYes. Note that this doesn't mean that the parent returned XtGeometryDone or XtGeometryYes to Xt; it can be wrong in its interpretation of its own reply.

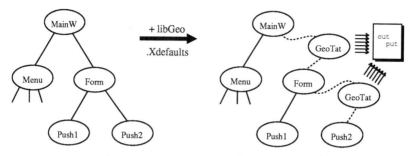

Figure 2: Widget tree modification.

The Motif widget set has moved to a coherent XtGeometryYes policy for all its manager in the 1.2 release, so this is particularly important to check before incorporating any new manager in the toolkit.

The GeoTattler is a subclass of the Motif XmManager, and it is really specific to the Motif toolkit due to its constraint resources set (see the Discussions chapter for details). As a Motif manager subclass, it also inherits other features of XmManager including Gadgets handling and Motif keyboard traversal management. Adapting the GeoTattler for a different Toolkit, though, would not be difficult.

How to use the GeoTattler: libGeo

The GeoTattler widget is fairly transparent in the sense that it never mentions its own name in the output trace. It's always in the form: "`parent` is doing something to `child`", even if the truth is that `parent` is doing something to the GeoTattler, which in turn is doing something to `child`.

The goal of the libGeo library is to extent this transparency to the application itself, so that the GeoTattler be usable without recompiling any program.

Let's describe how it works from the user point of view (the user being a developer who wants to check the geometry behavior of an application) and then we'll describe the implementation.

Let's consider a very simple hierarchy of widgets: a main window containing a menubar and a form with 2 buttons in it (as illustrate in the left part of figure 2).

The initial production line for this test is:

```
cc -o sample sample.o -lXm -lXt -lX11
```

where sample.c is the application creating the widgets, Xm is the motif library, Xt the X toolkit Intrinsics and X11 the X library.

The first thing to do is to re-link the program with the Geometry tester library inserted before Xt:

```
cc -o sample sample.o -lXm -lGeo -lXt -lX11
```

By doing just that, the behavior shouldn't have changed.

Then, if these lines are added to the resource environment (i.e the .Xdefaults file):

```
*XmForm*geoTattler: ON
sample*Push1.geoTattler: OFF
```

the widget tree becomes as illustrated in the right part of figure 2 and the program produces this specific output:

(after an XtSetValues (..XtNwidth..) on Push2 by the application)

```
"Push2" is doing a geometry request:
      - width wants to move from 226 to 284
   to its parent "Form".
"Form" is resizing its child "Push1" to (200,32)
"Form" replies Yes to the request.
```

(after a resize of the toplevel shell by the user)

```
"sample" is resizing its child "Form" to (300,200)
"Form" is asking "Push1" for its preferred geometry
"Form" is asking "Push2" for its preferred geometry
"Form" is resizing its child "Push1" to ..
      etc, etc...
```

The XtNgeoTattler resource (really a pseudo-resource), with the Boolean values ON and OFF (default) is the only new external interface the user needs to learn. Since the implementation uses a standard function to retrieve the value, the matching rules (bindings, class or instance name, conversion) and the specification niceties of the X resource manager apply.

The semantic of this resource is that if a widget has the attribute XtNgeoTattler set, it is reparented to a GeoTattler widget.

The libGeo.a archive is made of only two modules: the GeoTattler widget itself, GeoTattler.o, and a module GeoCreate.o that simply replaces the XtCreateWidget function. Instead of just calling the internal _XtCreateWidget routine, it now calls XtGetSubResources with the class, name and parent of the widget being created and if a geoTattler resource has been set, a GeoTattler is created as a child of the given parent and the widget itself is created as the child of the GeoTattler.

Two additional hooks are provided for the realization and the destruction of the tree at creation time. If the parent is already realized, the GeoTattler needs also to be realized, since its child can be realized at any moment in the future and an X protocol error would be generated if the GeoTattler was not realized. A destroyCallback is also added to the child, so that it will destroy the GeoTattler if it is being killed before its original parent.

```
#define XtNgeoTattler "geoTattler"
#define XtCGeoTattler "GeoTattler"

typedef struct { Boolean geo_tattler ;} GeoDataRec ;
static XtResource geo_resources[] = {
    { XtNgeoTattler, XtCGeoTattler, XtRBoolean, sizeof(Boolean),
      XtOffsetOf(GeoDataRec, geo_tattler),
      XtRImmediate, (caddr_t) False }
} ;

Boolean _GeoIsTattled (Widget widget)
{
    GeoDataRec geo_data ;
    Boolean is_geotattled ;

        /* First check for a matching widget in the cache */
    if (_is_geo_cached (widget, &is_geotattled)) return is_geotattled ;

        /* no widget found in the cache, look in the database */
    XtGetSubresources(widget, (XtPointer)&geo_data,
                    XtName(widget), XtClassName(widget),
                    geo_resources, XtNumber(geo_resources), NULL, 0);

        /* now add this guy in the cache */
    _geo_cache(widget, geo_data.geo_tattler) ;

    return geo_data.geo_tattler;
}
```

Figure 3: _GeoIsTattled implementation.

The libXtGeo library

While developing the XtCreateWidget wrapper for the GeoTattler, it appeared that modifying the Xt library was an easy and very powerful way to see what really happens at the Intrinsics level (obvious, isn't it?).

Description

Following this idea, the Xt modules (R5 MIT implementation) dealing with geometry management were isolated:

- Geometry.c, of course, for the basic mechanisms.

- Manage.c, for the ChangeManaged calls.

- Intrinsic.c, for XtRealizedWidget which calls ChangeManaged.

```
void XtConfigureWidget(w, x, y, width, height, borderWidth)
    Widget w;
    Position x, y;
    Dimension width, height, borderWidth;
{
    XWindowChanges changes, old;
    Cardinal mask = 0;

    _GeoPrintTrace(w,"%s is being configured by its parent %s\n",
                   XtName(w), XtName(XtParent(w)));
    _GeoTabTrace();

    if ((old.x = w->core.x) != x) {
        _GeoPrintTrace(w,"x moves from %d to %d\n",w->core.x, x);
        changes.x = w->core.x = x;
        mask |= CWX;
    }

    ..... same tests for w->core.y, width, height and border_width ...

    if (mask != 0) {
        if (XtIsRealized(w)) {
            if (XtIsWidget(w)) {
                _GeoPrintTrace(w,"XConfigure %s's window.\n", XtName(w));
                XConfigureWindow(XtDisplay(w),XtWindow(w),mask,&changes);
            }
            else {
                _GeoPrintTrace(w,"ClearRectObj called on %s.\n", XtName(w));
                ClearRectObjAreas((RectObj)w, &old);
            }
        } else {
                _GeoPrintTrace(w,"%s not Realized.\n",XtName(w));
        }

        _GeoUnTabTrace();

        if ((mask & (CWWidth | CWHeight)) &&
            XtClass(w)->core_class.resize != (XtWidgetProc) NULL) {

            _GeoPrintTrace(w,"Resize proc is called.\n");

            (*(w->core.widget_class->core_class.resize),w);
        } else {
            _GeoPrintTrace(w,"Resize proc is not called.\n");
        }

    } else {
            _GeoPrintTrace(w,"No change in configuration.\n");
            _GeoUnTabTrace();
    }
} /* XtConfigureWidget */
```

Figure 4: Modified version of XtConfigure Widget.

- SetValues.c, which makes geometry requests at the end of the chain.

- Shell.c, for the Shell RootGeometryManager.

The new library, libXtGeo.a is made of a modified version of these five modules.

Note that the Create and VarCreate modules are not needed anymore, since the XtGetSubResources work is now done dynamically. A function _GeoIsTattled that takes a widget is provided for this purpose. It first looks in a cache to see if the triple [widget, widget_name, class_name] matches something, and if not, it calls XtGetSubResources and caches the result (implementation shown in figure 3) .

In addition, the libXtGeo library includes a module which provides 3 public functions:

- _GeoPrintTrace, which takes a widget and a printf specification. This function uses _GeoIsTattled(widget) to determine if the trace is wanted.

- _GeoTabTrace, which adds a tabbing to the indented output.

- _GeoUnTabTrace, which pops a tabbing.

The modifications made to the Xt modules themselves are fairly straightforward: before any interesting action, the libXtGeo functions are called (figure 4 shows the new XtConfigureWidget routine, from Geometry.c).

The output trace given by libXtGeo is much more complete than with the GeoTattler. Tracking the calls to the shell root geometry manager and made by the shell root geometry manager, for instance, is only feasible at this level.

In addition, and since the "black box" was opened, the Editres event_handler was added to Shell.c (so that the widget hierarchy be easily viewable) and a hack was added to XtSetValues in order to perform dynamic setting of the geoTattler subresource. The result is the following: providing that your application has been linked with libXtGeo, you can **interactively** turn ON and OFF geometry management report using the `editres` resource editor.

How to use libXtGeo

The libXtGeo library provides the programmer with the same interface (XtNgeoTattler:ON/OFF) than the GeoTattler package. Programs only need to be re-linked with -lXtGeo before -lXt and the resource environment to be modified as well.

Let's consider the report generated by a single push button inside a shell, when the activate callback of the button calls XtSetValues to change the label string to `GoodBye world` (as shown in figure 5).

With the following .Xdefaults file:

Figure 5: Bottom-to-top resize request.

```
# original label string
geo_push*push.labelString:Hello World.\n\
                          Click to see some changes\n\
                          in geometry.
# needed to allow bottom-top requests to succeed
geo_push*allowShellResize:True
# we want exhaustive report for this demo
geo_push*geoTattler: ON
```

the output is (when the user clicks on the button and the setvalues on the label is performed):

```
XtSetValues on "push" sees some geometry changes.
    "push" is making a geometry request to its parent "geo_push".
        Asking for a change in width: from 235 to 127.
        Asking for a change in height: from 58 to 26.
        Go ask the geometry manager.
            "geo_push" is making a geometry request to its parent Root.
                Asking for a change in width: from 235 to 127.
                Asking for a change in height: from 58 to 26.
                Go ask the RootGeometryManager.
                    Configuring the Shell X window :
                            width = 127
                            height = 26
                    ConfigureNotify succeed, return XtGeometryYes.
            Root returns XtGeometryYes.
            Reconfigure "push"'s window.
    "geo_push" returns XtGeometryYes.
    XtSetValues calls "push"'s resize proc.
XtSetValues calls XClearArea on "push".
```

For regular applications (hundreds of widgets), this kind of report becomes very dense and the geoTattler:OFF value is used to **focus** on very specific area of the widget tree.

Discussions

GeoTattler issues

Since the design principle of the GeoTattler widget is to insert additional widgets in a widget's tree, it also modifies the underlying hierarchy. A side effect is that it breaks the behavior of applications and toolkits that were relying on specific properties of this hierarchy.

Inter-dependence between widget classes is the first point we have to look at. In Motif especially, there are a lot of places where the XmIs *Class* macros are used, and introducing a GeoTattler somewhere in the instance tree is often an issue.

The RowColumn widget, for instance, has an XmNentryCallback resource which is used to revector the activateCallback of all its Buttons children. It does that by checking the class of the children before systematically adding its own callback. If one of the button is reparented to a GeoTattler, which is not a button and has no activateCallback anyway, the entryCallback won't work anymore for the button child of the GeoTattler. Another example is the BulletinBoard widget which checks if its parent is a DialogShell before reporting its dialogTitle attribute up one level.

Note that these widget class inter-dependencies wouldn't be present if we had a general *widget property mechanism* in the Intrinsics (eg. Traits).

Another problem is found in the resource file themselves, when they become very specific about the hierarchy. Things like:

```
myapp*XmFrame.XmPushButton.shadowThickness: 0
```

won't work anymore if a widget is systematically inserted in the hierarchy:

```
myapp*XmPushButton.geoTattler: ON
```

The new description is breaking the initial parent-child relationship between the frame and the push buttons (since all PushButtons are now reparented to GeoTattlers). But since the resource file can easily be updated when the geoTattler resource itself is added, this problem can be considered as minor.

A much more nasty issue appears with constraint resources.

Constraint resources are maintained by the parent for the child, and if the parent class changes, they are not maintained anymore.

Consider a PanedWindow for instance, it has a XmNpaneMax constraint resource which controls the maximum size the user can resize a particular pane (the pane child the resource is set for). If this pane child is reparented to a GeoTattler, the GeoTattler then becomes the child of the PanedWindow and the paneMax constraint originally set on the child is lost. For constraint resources that are related to geometry management (like Form attachments), it is a very serious problem, even in a test environment.

The only solution to this problem we have found so far is to make the GeoTattler itself a constraint widget (which it was already, as a subclass of the Motif XmManager) with a set of constraint resources equal to the union of all the constraint resources present in the widget set tested.

At creation time, when the GeoTattler ConstraintInitialize method is called, we check the current constraint resource values against their default; if they have changed, we report the change to the parent of the GeoTattler (using XtSetValues on the GeoTattler itself). The same code is used at ConstraintSetValues time to track the change between the current and the new constraint attributes.

This is not a generic solution but it works well for a given toolkit at a given time. It is also very localized code, easy to adapt for new Constraint widgets.

Toolkit approach issues

The main concern with the modified toolkit approach is the maintenance of the code, since the original Xt continues to evolve and we are not planning on having MIT adopt our code. But since the libXtGeo is only a subset of the entire Xt and we (the OSF/Motif team) are working in close relationship with the X consortium for Xt specifications, this is not a big problem as long as we maintain libXtGeo ourselves.

A clear advantage of libXtGeo over the GeoTattler is its independence of the widget set tested. libXtGeo is more than a simple DEBUG version of Xt (outline output, geoTattler sub-resource specification, specialization in Geometry Management) but it is still to be used as a replacement of a part of Xt, on top of which the widget sets are built.

Conclusion

I have used only libXtGeo in my tests for Motif and it has already proven to be **very** helpful. Anyone developing a new widget or debugging an application that has layout problems might be interested by this tool (freely available on the server `export.lcs.mit.edu` in the archive `contrib/libXtGeo.tar.Z`).

The GeoTattler work wasn't done in vain though. It gave us a better understanding of the consequences of modifying a genuine widget instance tree (and there are other examples of such a technique, like the self-moving widget).

Both the GeoTattler widget and the libXtGeo package give information about the current flow of requests in the widget set, but using these tools, you'd never really perform an *exhaustive* checking of the geometry managers. If the XtCWQueryOnly flag is never used by any child widget, for instance, there is no way to find out that composite parents in a widget set are not properly dealing with query only requests.

Another test bed needs to be built, with an enhanced version of the GeoTattler as the central component. The final program would resemble a small interface builder, allowing the user to create various hierarchies of widget classes, embedded with GeoTattlers. It would let the operator activate very specific geometry actions, thus really **validating** the geometry management of any component.

Bibliography

Robert W. Scheifler, James Gettys. *The X Window System. C library and Protocol Reference*. Second edition. Digital Press. ISBN 1-55558-050-5.

Paul Asente, Ralph Swick. *The X Window System Toolkit.* Digital Press. ISBN 1-55558-051-3.

Open Software Foundation. *OSF/Motif 1.1 Programmer's Reference.* Prentice Hall. ISBN 0-13-640681-5.

Dan Heller. *Motif Programming Manual.* Volume Six - O'Reilly & Associates, Inc. ISBN 0-937175-70-6

Kee Hinckley and Andrew Schulert *Geometry Management with Xt: Advice for Widget Authors.* Xhibition 91 Conference Proceedings, June 1991.

Hubert Rechsteiner. *The Self Moving Widget.* Xhibition 91 Conference Proceedings, June 1991.

Migrating Widgets

Christian P. Jacobi

Introduction

As a building block for ubiquitous computing [8] we need windows moving from display surface to display surface. We have modified the Cedar XTk [2, 3, 7] toolkit to support migrating widgets. (The Cedar XTk toolkit is similar in spirit to Xt [1], however, it is much simpler).

Previous attempts to implement migration of X windows have either too completely hidden migration from clients who might need to know about it, or required extensive application support. We have chosen a different, novel approach by letting the toolkit handle the migration. It exposes the knowledge but not the work of dealing with X windows [5] to clients; it allows them to take full advantage of the complete X protocol if they wish while at the same time not imposing costs when only simple features are required.

The obvious solution, to migrate X windows directly, does not work well because information about X windows is cached in many different places. Our solution to this problem is to migrate X "widgets" instead. What makes our solution work for migrating applications is that there is typically a container (shell) widget behind an X window application and it suffices to migrate that widget.

Widgets adhere to a protocol by which a request to migrate to a different X server can be received. This architecture has been chosen with the desire to enable migration while at the same time maintain a simple standard architecture for the toolkit without the cost of migration when not used.

Christian Jacobi is a member of research staff, Xerox Palo Alto Research Center.

We do not claim that the approach to use the toolkit shall be used exclusively. In fact, most important ubiquitous computing applications might have an application-specific method of migrating. However, this toolkit approach is a welcome simplification for the applications which won't need to worry about migration.

The work might be divided into 3 parts.

1) An infrastructure by which migration requests are issued.

2) A protocol by which a shell (or an application) is told that migration is requested.

3) The actual implementation of migrating widgets.

1) Infrastructure

The simplest implementation is a push tool. This tool runs (displays) on a particular X server and allows the user to push applications to other servers. By using the same server as the application, many problems are avoided. We don't have to find the current X server. Security is dealt with very simply.

Another implementation we tried is to make the application follow the location of an active badge. This opens a big can of worms. Security has to be mentioned but, there is much more. Which applications should follow a badge?

There are some window manager issues. Much more research in this area is required. Migrating widgets proves to be only a building block in a bigger picture.

2) Protocol

We have defined a very simple external protocol, somewhat inspired by ICCCM [6] protocols. Using this protocol migration of shell widgets can be requested externally.

Another, internal protocol allows the application to register who implements migration. While we have some applications which do this on the application level, we will concentrate mainly on the implementation by the toolkit. An application might even specify that it won't allow migration of its widgets at all.

Another external protocol might be desired which is invoked by other means then using the X server. Remembering on which X server an application is displayed at a particular time has turned out to be a difficult problem.

3) The actual implementation

XTk presents migration to the application in a manner similar to how conventional toolkits present window resize.

XTk uses phases similar to Xt's [1] phases for creating widgets, geometry negotiation and realize. However, it needs some new phases for binding to a particular screen, for forgetting a particular screen, and, for shutting down asynchronous access.

One implementation challenge is to gracefully shut down the connection to an X server in such a manner that no errors occur and the widget can be reused on a different connection. This implies some careful synchronization as the applications normally access XTk widgets asynchronously [3].

Certain features have to be specified indirectly and generated at the bind-screen phase only. This is extremely valuable in our environment which uses X servers with very different characteristics. (Resolution, size of screen, fonts, keyboard mapping, color, server version, used window manager, etc.)

Alternatives and related work

Applications can create new connections themselves when they want to migrate the display. This is frequently the most powerful mechanism. Many good applications know how to run on quite different platforms. This might allow us to use similar schemes for migration and for simultaneous display on multiple screens. In general the application level is the easiest place to implement migration. The drawback is that it has to be done in multiple applications. However, the large majority of applications may not want to care about these problems. Should migration of widgets get more popular this might be a more frequently chosen method of implementing migration.

Some simple applications which do not carry state with their windows can accomplish such migration very easily by shutting down and restarting, migrating the process instead of the window. For example a clock application could implement migration by stopping and restarting on the new server. This can be extended to applications which can store their state on files. The ongoing display manager efforts might be helpful in this respect.

A pseudo server could be used which actually displays the window on some real server without telling its clients about it. This is a very powerful technique as it would allow handling nearly every application, at least in parts. However, it is not the best solution to the problem. It can require higher communication bandwidth and it does require large similarities between servers. We do not envision how ICCCM selection transfers could be implemented with this method.

Migration can be built into Xlib. Xlib could keep track of a mapping of resource ids between what the client uses and what the currently used server requires. On migration Xlib would have to create the window forest with exactly the same topology on the new server. We expect problems on implementing ICCCM selection transfers. We believe that this scheme requires large similarities between servers. We wouldn't believe this method to be feasible unless it weren't already implemented.

This approach of course limits its usefulness to applications which use that particular Xlib interface to access X windows. A similar limitation is found on the next few solutions. There this limitation is obvious; we mention it at this place because here it is not really expected.

Migration could be built and hidden in the toolkit. E.g. Trexel [4] allows to migrate its shell windows from one server to an other. However, the Trexel protocol is a complete window system protocol in itself and does not depend necessarily on X windows. It does not expose X-ishness to its clients; this can be viewed both as an advantage or a disadvantage.

Our XTk toolkit handles migration without hiding the X protocol to applications.

One limitation of the usefulness of this approach is that the XTk toolkit is not very popular. However, the idea's used in XTk could apply as well to some more popular toolkit.

Our XTk toolkit, (or more accurately: its infrastructure) allows us to choose between different methods of doing migration. In spite of a small number of applications, we do actually take advantage of using multiple methods for migration.

Defining a new window system architecture which would make migration simpler is certainly a possibility. However, we do not believe migration alone justifies such drastic measures.

Some little problems to solve

Resource identifiers are defined in a server dependent way. X Windows uses identifiers for fonts, graphic contexts, windows, atoms, visuals, colormaps, cursors, and, pixels. When using an identifier for an analogue feature in a different connection, the numerical id value will be different.

The actual data behind a resource identifier is different on another server. Cursors, tiles, off screen bitmaps must have initialized contents. An atom might be internized on one server, and might not be on the other.

Graphics contexts might allow bit-blit on one server, but after migration a stipple sits in an off screen bitmap of the wrong server.

Timestamp's have a server relative base. Many protocols depend on timestamp comparisons.

Keyboard mappings are server dependent. Our experimenting showed that most standard applications do not act on key map changes.

Different servers are not identical. Colormaps, screen resolution, number of extension devices might differ. Does the new server have the same font names? Do the corresponding fonts have the same metrics? While most sites may have resolution differences of a few tens of percents, our environment presents resolution and screen size differences of factors ten and larger.

Disrupting ongoing transactions.

What happens when migration is initiated while a (ICCCM) selection transfer is in progress?
Grabs, Selections, InputFocus have to be released on migrations.

External dependencies.

Some applications depend on particular window managers; does the destination of a migration run the expected one?

Resource database may be different. We do not imagine that all resource databases on a site are maintained equally for the benefit of migration.

Most applications read the resource database only at widget creation time.

Just for the fun of it: The bell might use a different pitch on a different server.

Most of these troubles do not cause problems which can't be solved. However finding solutions which allow current application to work unchanged are much harder then finding conventions by which new applications could handle these problems.

Infrastructure and user interface

We believe that the infrastructure is an area of much required research. At this date we provided interfaces at varying levels and didn't really care how the operations had been invoked. We will introduce a small list of infrastructure problems.

In a general framework we should not really focus on moving windows but on moving information to be presented. Nevertheless, the ability to migrate a window is a useful step.

Which windows should follow you around? All windows? Your calendar? The broken world you are debugging right now? How can we specify those windows which should follow? Where do we have to be to specify which windows should follow? How can we get a window back which was migrated some place?

Should the window appear at a particular place on the screen? A billboard-like display should find the right place without window manager involvement. Better: Will we have to write our own window managers? Should screens have an area where window managers place intruding windows? Think about social context. In a meeting with a large shared screen participants might move their windows right into the center; reminders for certain people, or windows of non participants should get tiny spaces in a predefined area.

Should we use gestures to migrate a window? Should the gesture imply what destination should be used?

Should we push a window to go to some other server. Should we call the windows we want from the new server?. Should a window follow a badge automatically?. Do we want a global database knowing which window is displayed on which server?

We need more communication means then just a window. We could want to build up a phone connection with the person to share a window. Video is getting popular and could be required in addition. Should an arriving window announce itself with a beep?

We will need an authorization scheme which allows more tuning then just enabling and disabling a particular host.

Moving windows is a nice step; but we need more. The infrastructure as well should be prepared for shared windows.

Protocol for migration requests

Shell widgets provide a simple external interface to the migration capability. Some of the reasons this protocol is simple, are that it doesn't have to worry much about race conditions or property ownership. Migration will cause destruction of the old windows. This will free all properties automatically and prevent further events from being received.

If migration was treated carelessly, horrible infrastructures might show up. One design flaw to be avoided is the enumeration all the X servers of a location. It might not be avoidable to enumerate all top level application windows on a particular server just to find the window id of the widget to migrate.

Using X Windows for transmitting requests for migration has the problem that it requires an existing X Windows connection, and, knowledge to which server this connection leads. In addition, if a connection breaks down the communication means to build a new connection are lost.

It would be better to define a network protocol for migration requests. The name or identity of the window would not change when migrating to a new X server. If X Windows features are used, a window would automatically address exactly one instance of an application. It trivially would specify the window to be used. A network protocol would need a means to identify the instance of the application and, which window of it is to be addressed. A simple tool on the window manager level which pushes windows around could avoid these problems. Unfortunately, real usage in X Windows level protocols involves problems like enumerating top level windows of applications, and, checking the identity of windows by looking at properties.

Neither choice of X Windows, or a network protocol makes a difference as to authorization of migration requests. The X servers authorization scheme is no real help. Using the X Windows mechanism is easier for the first implementation, however.

Protocol for migration implementation

It is actually useful to have different implementation choices for migration. The choice of how to migrate best is not obviated by the possibility of automating migration by the toolkit. Actually the choice is quite hard and can involve features like bandwidth requirements, ease of restart, dependency of specific hardware, etc. Sometimes it will be advantageous to migrate computation instead of simply migrating the display.

The actual implementation

In XTk any widget can migrate, not only shell widgets. Migration of shell widgets is powerful enough for many applications. However, we decided to use the same mechanisms to implement reparenting sub-widgets.

Toolkits typically involve phases. Xt uses a phase to create and link the widget data structures. Another phase is realization. Realization can be viewed as a first step doing geometry negotiation and a second step creating the actual windows. Such phases typically walk both the topological window tree, and, the inheritance list (or tree).

We introduce some new phases. A bind screen phase binds a widget to a particular screen without any geometrical layout done. The lose screen phase undoes the binding. We further need an unrealize phase and some shut down phases.

Binding a screen must establish the locking (See separate section). It might serve as the place to check for resolution, fonts, colormaps cursors pixels etc. Note, that in a geometry negotiation phase knowledge of font sizes can be crucial.

The shut down phases are considerably more complex. The basic reason is simple: On shut down we have to leave the data structures intact because there is the possibility of accessing a new screen. Also, we have to wait for all processes involved in the shut down, as we don't want them to interfere with a future screen. We actually introduce at least two phases for the shut down of asynchronous graphic operations.

The increasing number of phases does not bother application programmers; many applications do not need to see all phases explicitly. Operations to include or remove widgets to a parent widget will automatically invoke the bind screen or loose screen phases if the parent is bound. Most of the destructive phases like the termination phases, unrealize, loose screen, destroy phase are necessary only to widget writers. All phases have call back procedures to make them accessible to clients which care.

Locking, robustness

Our actual implementation of XTk supports multi-threaded applications [3]. It has different locking requirements then Xt in principle. We will limit this paragraph on locking requirements to topics influenced by the migration possibilities.

Furthermore, in Cedar we are running different "applications" in the same address space [2]. Maybe "application" should be called an area of trust: how much code is allowed to wedge because of a programming error in some place. Such environment properties force us to have stronger mechanisms to ensure robustness. The way this interacts with migration is that we do not really know whether migration (reparenting) of a widget is within the same "application" or whether we change the "application".

We use a certain monitor lock to protect changes to the structure of widgets. There are different locks to protect non structural data of widgets. In particular graphics operations do not need to acquire the structure lock. We are severely serializing structure changes to allow for very unstructured asynchronous graphics operations. In particular, we do not need synchronization of resize and graphics; the X server is doing that for us.

The structural monitor lock is logically defined by the shell widget. As a consequence, migrating a widget could involve changing the lock responsible for protection of the widget tree. We admit, this looks complicated; however we failed to find a simpler solution which strictly limits damage on deadlock to the application involved. One obvious problem with this locking scheme is that in the phases where no screen is bound to a widget no structural lock is defined. In these phases we leave the locking to the application composing the widget tree. This has never been a problem; in fact the opposite would have. Many applications try to compose a widget tree from a place where they can not acquire the right lock (without risking deadlock). With the current scheme such applications simply construct the widget tree sequentially without locking. They then fork a process to bind the screen and realize the widgets.

We will describe the two shut down phases to stop asynchronous graphic operations.

The first shut down phase basically sets some flags that no more asynchronous graphics operations must be started.

The second phase will make sure that no asynchronous paint operation is under way. For some complex widget classes or applications this is either difficult, inefficient, or risking a wedge. For these cases the second phase will collect the monitor locks which are used by the different asynchronous paint operations.

If there are such collected monitor locks, a third step causes a wait until each of the collected monitor locks was free once. If applications have programming errors causing wedges, it will likely cause the "third step" to fail. We do set a (quite large) timeout on this step.

To make this work it is essential that there are two distinct steps. Providing three steps to implement this basically two step procedure might be redundant, but we have never been sorry about providing the choice. For most widget classes it is very obvious which two steps to use. Different widget classes differ in their choice.

Other costs of the migration features.

As many X resources are server specific, migration requires the need to recompute such resources. There are not many problems which can not be solved using one more level of indirection. Instead of simply setting a resource field of a widget we have to choose one of the following options.

Use closures to describe the feature. The closure is invoked at bind-screen time.

Register a call back for bind-screen to set the feature. This is not such a new requirement. In conventional toolkits the widgets could also be composed before the connection is set up. (At least pre-migration XTk was arranged this way).

Use a name; at bind-screen time the actual resource is looked up with the name.

Default the field. The widget class will do the right thing.

Screen dependent widget fields are cleared out at loose-screen time. We made this choice instead re-initializing fields at bind-screen time to simplify applications which explicitly disable migration. This is a step to hide the cost of migration when it is not used.

Conclusions.

We have implemented this migration scheme. We are still working on the infrastructure. So far we have not learned the lessons of migration for the actual purposes it was envisioned. The missing infrastructure makes statements about migration for ubiquitous computing premature. However, migration has been widely used for many different purposes. The two most frequent uses so far are debugging and demos (of other things then migration).

Migration was used for debugging by migrating the debugger window to the machine we are debugging, or, the other way around. It has also been frequently used to migrate a debugger window to a person giving advice.

Demos are a good client of migration because people set up their own machine for the demo and simply migrate the windows to the demo machine.

Some people use this migration scheme to migrate their windows to their home machine (over 56kbit phone line) when they are leaving the office.

Migration is seen as a small step towards our goal of ubiquitous computing.

Migration was of little cost to either intrinsics, widget sets or applications. When migration was introduced for XTk, it caused large parts of it to be redesigned or rewritten; however it didn't make XTk actually more complex. Most widget classes did have to be updated; some of this was error prone. Most applications only needed trivial edits, at least when they did not use the migration.

References.

1. Asente, P. J., Swick R. R., X Window System Toolkit, Digital Press.

2. Jacobi, C., An Xlib for Cedar, 3th Annual Technical X Windows Conference, 1989.

3. Jacobi, C., Opportunities with Lightweight Processes for X Window Clients, 4th Annual Technical X Windows Conference, 1990.

4. Nelson G., Systems Programming with Modula-3, Prentice Hall

5. Scheifler, R. W., Gettys, J., The X Window System. ACM Transactions on Graphics, (5)2, April 1986.

6. Rosenthal D., Inter-Client Communication Conventions Manual, MIT X Consortium Standard.

7. Swinehart D., Zellweger P., Beach R., Hagmann R., A Structural View of the Cedar Programming Environment, ACM Transactions on Programming Languages and Systems, (8)4, Oct 1986.

8. Weiser M., The Computer for the 21st Century, Scientific American, (256)3 Sept 1991.

Implementing Drag & Drop
for X11

Gabe Beged-Dov, Ellis S. Cohen

Abstract

This paper describes issues in the design and implementation of a protocol to support drag and drop between $X11^{TM}$ clients. We use standard X11 mechanisms for communication, while achieving good performance across a wide range of hardware configurations.

A dynamic protocol requires messaging between clients during dragging. It allows a potential destination client to dynamically determine whether the pointer is over a drop site that is valid for the object being dragged, and permits the destination client to provide sophisticated drag-under effects when it is.

A preregister protocol requires destination clients to store information about drop sites in a database which is read by the dragging agent, avoiding messaging overhead. The preregister protocol permits a wider range of drag-over effects, and gives good performance on low-end machines and over high-latency connections at the cost of limiting the kinds of drag-under effects available.

Our design supports both dynamic and preregister protocols, and allows the choice to be made based on the wishes of the user and of both clients involved. It is currently implemented as a prototype integrated with the $OSF/Motif^{TM}$ toolkit. The toolkit implementation is designed so that, except for code to implement additional drag-under effects when the dynamic protocol is used, identical client code can be used with either protocol.

Gabe Beged-Dov is the lead architect for the Drag & Drop project at Hewlett-Packard.
Ellis S. Cohen is the principal architect for OSF/Motif at the Open Software Foundation.

Introduction

Drag & Drop allows a user to use the mouse to "pick up" a source selection or "object", "drag" it elsewhere on the screen, and "drop" it on some destination, typically to transfer the source data to the destination or to apply some operation (represented by the destination) to the source object.

Drag & Drop implementations have been available for some time. The Macintosh Finder^{TM} [1] is probably the best know example; Unix file managers for X11, such as HP VUE^{TM}, IXI's X.desktop^{TM}, and Visix's Looking Glass^{TM} [2] provide similar functionality.

Drag & Drop is simplest to implement when both the source and the destination are part of the same application. When they are in different applications, messaging is required, at the very least, to provide information about the drop and arrange for the transfer. HP VUE, IXI's X.desktop, and OPEN LOOK^{TM} [3], all have X11-based implementations that support drops across different clients.

Support for feedback during dragging is more difficult, and there are (at least) two ways to accomplish it. A dynamic protocol uses messaging during the drag to communicate with each client whose window is under the pointer [4]. A preregister protocol requires clients to place informatioan about potential dropsites in a database. Messaging is avoided by obtaining information directly from the database. This technique has been used in HP VUE.

The major contribution of our implementation is that it supports both types of protocols, and integrates them cleanly. This allows drag & drop to be used across a wide range of system and network configurations.

Our implementation allows drag & drop to be done between different applications that have no knowledge of one another, and cooperate in no way, beyond support for the drag & drop protocol, and agreement on the target atoms identifying the types of data they can interchange. Because the entire drag & drop protocol is layered on top of the standard X11 protocol [5], it is network transparent, and so drag & drop automatically works between clients who are running on different host machines.

This paper will start out by describing the fundamentals of dragging and dropping from the user's point of view – what does the user expect to happen, and what does the user see.

Next we describe the two protocols used for dragging – the dynamic protocol and the preregister protocol. The actual protocol to be used can change during the drag, and we describe how the protocol is chosen.

Finally, we describe the drop protocol – in particular, how it is completely layered on top of the X11 selection mechanism.

About Dropping

When the user drags a source and drops it at some destination, the user may expect different things to happen depending upon the context. These include:

- Changing Placement – the visual location of the source is changed. For example, drag & drop can simply be used to move graphical objects from one place to another in a drawing program.

  In some cases, the change in placement has no underlying semantic effect, for example, when moving a file icon from one location to another in a directory container. But, whether there is a semantic effect or not can depend upon the destination; dropping the file on a directory icon or container may physically move the file to that directory.

- Data Transfer – the data represented by the source is transferred to the destination, as if Cut (or Copy) and Paste were combined in the single drag & drop gesture. When using drag & drop in this way, moving (i.e. cutting) the data is generally considered the default (so long as the source data can be deleted from its container), but there is usually some way (e.g. by using a modifier key) to force a copy.

- Linking – a link is made between the source and the destination. This may be manifested in a number of ways. Often the result of the linking operation is to place an icon in the destination. From that icon, it may be possible to either traverse back to document containing the source, or to view (and maybe even edit) the source in a separate window. More sophisticated systems will be able to display (and perhaps even allow editing of) the linked data in the destination, and keep the original source, and the displayed view of it in the destination up-to-date. Linking often makes sense in the same situation as outright data transfer does, so there is often a separate way (e.g. some other modifier or combination of modifiers) to invoke it.

- Tool Input – The destination may act as a tool, and the source provides input to the tool. Additional input, if needed, is sometimes provided by popping up a dialogue box. Alternately, different areas of the destination are used to provide different inputs, and the tool isn't activated until all inputs are provided. If the tool produces output (e.g. a compiler), it may be filed in some standard location. Tools that are more tuned in to the direct manipulation metaphor may even place icons for the resulting documents in yet another area of the destination window.

  Sources dropped on tools such as compilers or printers usually are treated as being copied – i.e. the original source is not deleted. In other cases, a move is more appropriate, for example, if the tool is a trashcan or shredder. In yet other cases, the choice between a move or copy best depends upon a user's profile – for example, when dropping a document in a mailbox.

- Tool Application - In this model, the source is the tool; dropping it on a destination applies the tool to the destination. This model has been used in a number of X applications such as xmag [6], and including window managers such as twm [7]. Modifiers are typically used to invoke different actions among those associated with the tool.

Once the drop has been done, either the source client, the destination client, a third party, or some combination, has to decide what is be done, and has to arrange for it to happen.

In our implementation, the destination determines what happens on a drop, albeit based on information it gets from the source. This approach directly supports each of the five situations described above, with the exception of tool application, where the source is the tool. The other four situations can each be modeled by some sort of data transfer or link, possibly followed by some additional action taken by the destination client.

Specifically, the source provides information about the various kinds and formats of data it is willing to provide; the destination decides exactly what to request. The source indicates whether it is willing to copy, move, or link its contents; the destination determines exactly which is to be done.

We leave to the source the interpretation of modifier keys; in our implementation, Ctrl forces a Copy, Shift forces a Move, and Ctrl+Shift forces a Link. If the user has modifiers pressed at the time of the drop, the source only reports the single forced operation (if the source supports it). If the user does not have modifiers pressed, the source reports which of the operations it is willing to support. As we noted above in describing the Tool Input paradigm, the final choice really needs to depend upon the type of the destination; in our model, the destination client chooses, based upon the set of available operations (or the single operation forced by the user) as reported by the source.

Once the user makes the drop, there may be a need for more information before the corresponding action can be performed. For example, the destination client may not be able to understand the preferred data format of the source. The source client may be able to provide the source contents in two other formats the destination does understand, however, both of them lose different kinds of information. The destination client may want to popup a dialogue box or menu so that the user can choose among the alternatives, or cancel the drop.

When drag & drop is being used for Tool Input, a dialogue box may be popped up to provide additional inputs. For example, when a document is dropped into a mail tool, it is likely to post a dialogue box asking to whom the mail should be sent if that cannot be determined from the document contents directly.

Finally, a dialogue box may be posted because the user explicitly requests help. A user may not be sure what will happen if a source is dropped on some destination. In our implementation, if the user presses the Help key while dragging, the destination is notified, and can post a dialogue box explaining the result of a drop at that point, and asking whether the user wants to perform the drop (and possibly whether a Move, Copy, or Link should be done) or cancel it.

Even if the destination client can accept the data formats provided by the source, the drop may fail; once the data is actually processed by the destination client, the actual contents of the data may turn out to be inappropriate. So it is important that feedback be provided indicating whether or not the drop was successful. In fact, since the transfer of data can take some time, feedback is needed simply to indicate when the drop is complete.

As we will describe in more detail below, the pointer cursor used during a drag typically provides feedback about the source and the potential destination under the pointer. When the drop occurs, our implementation turns this cursor into an icon and leaves it where it was dropped. Once the transfer is finished, transition effects are used to show that the drop has completed. If the drop was successful, we show the icon melting into the destination; if the drop failed, we show the icon snapping back to the source.

More interesting cases might arise if the drop were only partially successful. For example, a user may select a number of files and drag them to a directory, but only some of the files may be able to be legally moved to that directory. It is unclear whether just those files should be moved, or whether the entire drop should fail. The best solution might be to move the files that can be moved, and provide appropriate feedback. We do not currently support a partial success model, so at present we recommend that the destination post a dialogue box asking the user what action to take.

About Dragging

In our implementation, dragging is, by default, associated with Btn2. Dragging starts when the user presses Btn2 and moves the mouse, and finishes either when the user releases Btn2 to make the drop, types the Help key to obtain information about what would happen if the drop were done at the present pointer position, or types the Cancel or Escape key to cancel the drag.

In between, various kinds of feedback can provide information about the drag which is in progress, including

- Whether the pointer is over a dropsite or not. Not all applications participate in drag & drop, and not all areas of the windows in applications that do are legal places to make a drop.

- Whether or not the drop would likely succeed at the current pointer position. In particular, does the destination understand any of the data formats the source can provide, and can any of the operations supported by the source (or the single operation specified by the user) be done by the destination. Of course, such feedback might only be a hint, since the drop might still fail based on the appropriateness of the contents of the transferred information.

- The operation that would be performed if the drop were done.

- The type of the source data (e.g. text, graphics, a file, etc.)

- What kind of information would be transferred if the drop were done at the current position. At best, this is the same as the type of the source data, but may be some less desirable format (with some loss of information) if the destination does not understand the source's preferred format.

- The type of the source container (i.e. where does the source data come from) – e.g. in the case of text, from a text document, a label, etc.

The feedback can be provided in a number of different mediums – visual feedback is most common, but there are interesting examples of audio feedback as well. Three types of visual feedback are most common, all of which can be done using our implementation:

- Drag-Over Feedback – in which the shape or color of the pointer's cursor changes. For example, some systems change the shape to a "DO NOT ENTER" symbol when the pointer is not over a dropsite, or when the drop would fail. Our current thinking is that drag-over feedback is best used to show the type of the source data (or possibly the kind of information that would be transferred), and secondarily to show the operation that would be performed. The OPENLOOK(tm) Style Guide [3] makes similar recommendations.

- Drag-Source Feedback – in which the appearance of the source changes. In particular, if a drop at the current pointer position would cause a Move, some systems (such as PM's new Workspace Shell [8]) would hide or grey out some or all of the graphics associated with the source.

- Drag-Under Feedback – in which the dropsite under the pointer is highlighted or animated in some way. Usually the feedback is only provided if the drop would likely succeed. Sometimes more subdued feedback indicates that the pointer is over a dropsite, but that the drop would likely fail.

An additional kind of feedback, Destination Feedback, is worth mentioning, though it is not dependent (or so dependent) upon the pointer position. Destination Feedback highlights all dropsites in some region, or more commonly, all dropsites on which the source could successfully be dropped. It can be evoked by pressing some key, or can be done automatically when the drag starts, or when the pointer enters a particular region (e.g. a top-level window, or graphics drawing area). Destination feedback that is shown for the duration of the drag has been called Duration Highlighting [4]; the cited paper also describes how it can be implemented for X11. In our current implementation, only limited types of destination feedback are available.

Especially on small screens, the source and the destination may not be able to be made visible at the same time. There are a number of ways to deal with this situation:

- Perform the action in some other way. Cut and Paste may done using the clipboard, or a primary transfer may be done. Primary transfer uses Btn2 Click to transfer the current primary selection to the pointer location (however, the default operation for data transfer is a copy, though the same modifiers – Ctrl, Shift, and Ctrl+Shift – force a Copy, Move, and Link, respectively). Primary transfer requires that the source be selectable, and Cut & Paste requires at least that the source be able to take focus. In our implementation, labels meet neither requirement, but Drag & Drop requires neither, and in our implementation, labels can be dragged and dropped.

- Allow side effects during dragging that change visibility. In particular, a technique called Drag Auto-Scroll is useful. If during a drag, the pointer is parked (with Btn2 still pressed) on the edge of a scrollable region, the region automatically scrolls away from that edge. This can be supported in our implementation using the dynamic protocol.

  Another barrier to visibility is window stacking. Drag Auto-Raise (automatically raising a window when the pointer parks, for example, on the window edge) and Auto-Lower (automatically lowering a window when the pointer parks, for example, in the window title) can solve this problem, though we have not yet tried this out in our window manager.

  Parking can be used in many other ways – for example, parking over an icon could open the corresponding window; if the icon represented a different workspace or "room" [9, 10], parking there could switch the display to that workspace. So long as icons can be used to represent navigational choices, parking can be useful. In many cases, though, a user may need to perform a search to find the destination; parking is unlikely to be helpful in this case.

- Temporarily interrupt the drag. This can be done by pressing some special key, or by releasing Btn2 over a special interrupt area, or perhaps anywhere that is not a dropsite, or where a drop would fail. This leaves an icon at the pointer location, which should be identical or similar to the pointer cursor used during the drag.

  The user can then proceed normally to take other actions, in particular, to find the destination, and make it visible. The user can continue the drag at a later point by pressing Btn2 over the interrupt icon. A method similar to this one is used in the PenPoint system [11]. Interrupted drags are not fully supported in our current implementation.

  While a drag is interrupted, there are likely to be limits to the actions allowed at the source. For example, if selected text is being dragged out of a text document, editing the document, or dragging something else out of it, is likely to be disabled until the drag is completed.

  While one drag is interrupted, another drag (probably with a different source) could be started, and also interrupted, though a system might well disallow this for stylistic reasons.

A system that supported interrupts could, optionally, automatically interrupt a drag (rather than complete it) on a drop, particularly if the drop failed. That is, after the drop fails, an interrupted drag icon could remain over the dropsite, to be dropped somewhere else, or to be explicitly canceled.

It could be even more useful to leave an interrupted drag icon around if a drop was partially successful, allowing some components to be dropped in one place, and allowing the rest to be dropped somewhere else. Keeping an interrupted drag icon available could even be useful after a successful drop, if a user wanted to drop something in multiple places.

As we've noted, our current implementation defaults to Btn2 to initiate a drag. Since our implementation is based on Xt, this can be changed simply by changing translations. In systems that use a one-button mouse, we would recommend that dragging be integrated with selection and activation on a single mouse button, as it is on the Mac [1]. This also may be appropriate for those with a two-button mouse who wish to use the second button to pop up menus (although Alt+Btn1 is recommended for popup menus as well, and a number of servers use chording of Btn1+Btn2 to simulate a third button).

However, the use of Btn2 has a number of advantages; it allows unselected objects to be dragged without disturbing the current selection, it enables a user to distinguish between dragging selected text and making a new selection that happens to start within the current selection, and it enables text labels and pixmaps to be dragged out of pushbuttons without activating them.

The Dynamic Drag Protocol

Since each destination client knows where its dropsites are, and how each should respond to pointer motion within it during a drag, the simplest and most natural model for a drag protocol would arrange for the window under the pointer to continuously receive events as the pointer moves within it during a drag.

Similarly, the drag-over and drag-source effects most appropriately are handled by the source. Since the actual effects may depend upon the details of the dropsite underneath the pointer, information needs to be sent from the destination to the source as the pointer moves.

Now, X11's pointer grab model effectively requires that the source client initially get the events generated by the X11 server during the drag. (A third part surrogate client could be used instead; we'll discuss that possibility later). So, each motion event has to first go to the source, which then sends a message (with useful information about the source) to the destination, which then echoes the message (with additional information) back to the source. Since all the messaging in our implementation is based on the X11 protocol, all of the messages go through the server, so the actual flow for each motion event is

```
server -> source -> server -> destination -> server -> source
```

There are ways to potentially reduce and even eliminate some or all of this messaging, which we'll discuss later, but our basic dynamic drag protocol works in exactly this manner.

As the pointer moves within a window that supports dragging, the source client sends the destination client a ClientMessage, from which the destination can determine the x,y position of the pointer, the set of allowable operations (from among Move, Copy, and Link), and the list of targets (i.e. the types and formats of data) the source can provide. The ClientMessage doesn't actually have room for all this information, in particular, for the targets; details about the way it is all transmitted are described later.

When the destination client receives the ClientMessage, it determines which drop site (if any) the pointer is within, and if any of the source's targets and operations are acceptable. The destination client then performs the appropriate drag-under effects.

The destination client can implement other effects as well. It can notice that the pointer has entered a particular region within the window, and provide destination feedback for all the appropriate dropsites in the region. By using timeouts, the destination client can determine whether the pointer is parked at a particular location (e.g. at the edge of a scrollable region) and can perform the corresponding action to change visibility.

The destination then echoes a message back to the source identifying the dropsite (if any), whether the pointer is entering, inside, or leaving it, whether the drop would likely succeed or not, and the operation that the destination would choose on the drop (as well as the set of operations from which the destination chose). It could be useful to return the main target that the destination would choose to transfer on a drop (so that drag-over effects might indicate the target that would be transferred, for example, instead of the source's preferred target); we currently do not do so.

The source then uses this information to perform the appropriate drag-over and drag-source effects.

Our toolkit (both on the source side and on the destination side) can produce most of the common drag-over and drag-under effects automatically based on various client- and user-settable resources. Callbacks allow client code to do anything extra.

A message from the source to the destination and back is also sent when the user presses or releases a modifier key. Changing modifiers changes the set of operations sent from the source to the destination, which may change the information sent back to the source, such as the resulting operation and even whether a drop would likely succeed or not.

Dragging across screens is supported; the source client is notified when the screen changes so that it can, if it chooses, change its drag-over effects so they are suitable to the size and resolution of the screen.

As we noted, a ClientMessage has limited size, and cannot hold all the information the source client might like to send to the destination, in particular, the list of targets. Luckily, this information is unchanged during the drag and can be provided in another way.

When the drag starts, the source client takes ownership of a selection atom that is guaranteed to be unique for the lifetime of the drag and drop transaction [the details are described in the discussion of the drop protocol]. The source puts the static source information in a property on the source window named by the selection atom. When, during a drag, the pointer enters a top-level destination window (and the dynamic drag protocol is in use), a ClientMessage is sent to the destination with the id of the source window and the selection atom. The destination client then retrieves the static information from the property.

In addition to the targets, this information includes a version number, and byte-ordering information. Byte ordering information is needed since the information sent in the ClientMessages associated with the drag have different sizes, and cannot be byte-swapped properly by X11 itself.

The target list is not actually stored directly in the property. Instead, the property contains an index into an array of target lists maintained in a separate per-display property. On starting a drag, the source client checks whether the array already contains an entry containing the list of targets the source can provide. If so, its index is used. Otherwise, the server is grabbed, and the property is reread to check that so such entry has been added in the meantime; if not, a new entry with the source's target list is added, the property is updated, and the server is ungrabbed.

The dynamic drag protocol has the advantage of being both powerful (i.e. allowing almost any drag-over, drag-source, and drag-under effects to be done) and conceptually elegant.

It does have two potential problems however. First, if the destination client and the server communicate over a high-latency connection, the performance of drag and drop will suffer (if the source client and the server communicate over a high-latency connection, performance problems are unavoidable, but the dynamic protocol will make them worse). Second, if the source and destination clients are both running on the same limited memory machine, the dynamic protocol can cause serious thrashing as the two clients swap each other out.

Both of these problems can be avoided completely if a source client can obtain enough information about a destination client to take over all of its responsibilities. The preregister drag protocol, described next, does exactly that.

The Preregister Drag Protocol

To avoid messaging, a potential destination client stores information about its drop-sites in a database. The source client reads the database, and uses the information to determine whether the pointer is in a dropsite, whether a drop would succeed, and what the resulting operation what be – in other words, exactly the information that a destination client would echo back using the dynamic protocol. Moreover, the database indicates the drag-under effect desired for the dropsite, and contains enough additional information to ensure that the source client (or more accurately, the toolkit operating in the source client) can render it accurately.

Each dropsite is specified as a bounding box (x/y/width/height) with an optional shape (currently specifiable only as a list of rectangles), a list of acceptable targets (specified using target list id's, described previously), a set of acceptable operations, and the drag-under effect to be performed when the pointer is in the dropsite and a drop would be likely to succeed.

The drag-under effects currently supported include a border (of a specified color and width) drawn around the dropsite's shape, a shadow border (of a specified width and top-left and bottom-right colors), and a specified pixmap to be rendered over the dropsite. The latter is quite powerful, allowing, for example, a folder to appear to open when a suitable source is dragged over it.

Support for other drag-under effects could be added quite easily. Even animation could be supported if a standard format were to be used to describe it in the database.

Dropsites may overlap, which requires that drag-under effects be clipped properly – i.e. by other dropsites which obscure it. Since dropsites need not be windowed objects, stacking information must be provided in the dropsite database (even if dropsites were all windowed, this information probably needs to be included in the database considering the cost of obtaining it from the server) based on stacking declarations made by the destination client.

Dropsites can be nested within other dropsites, and these relationships are also stored in the database. Dropsites can be clipped by their ancestors (especially dropsites in a scrolled window), whether or not those ancestors are dropsites themselves. The geometry of such ancestors are also stored in the database. In our implementation, they are computed automatically by the toolkit.

As the pointer moves within a window, the source client knows the x,y, and the set of available targets and operations. But when the preregister drag protocol is used, this information is not sent to the destination client. Instead, the source client looks at the destination client's database to determine which drop site the pointer is in (by using the bounding box, shape, stacking, and nesting information), and whether any of the available targets and operations are acceptable (by matching the source's set of available targets and operations respectively against the dropsite's set of acceptable targets and operations).

If a drop at the current position would likely succeed, the source client's toolkit does the specified drag-under effect (using the stacking and nesting information) by rendering directly into the destination client's window. This does require that the server be grabbed so that the pixels beneath the drag-under graphics can be saved and restored correctly, and also requires that the source and destination have the same visual type and depth.

Grabbing the server has its benefits, however. The X11 cursor is limited to two colors. Worse, its maximum size is implementation-dependent, and many servers limit the size to 32x32, which is generally too small for a popular style in which the cursor consists of an outline of the source. If the server is grabbed though, the cursor can be made invisible, and replaced by a pixmap of arbitrary size and depth which is rendered directly by the source client onto the root window. And indeed, our implementation supports this cursor style when the preregister protocol is used. [Note that if X11 had supported output-only windows, then in conjunction with the shape extension, this approach could be used to support arbitrary cursors without grabbing the server.]

There are some problems associated with the preregister protocol specific to our current implementation.

The set of acceptable operations really needs to be an ordered list. In the dynamic protocol, when the source allows multiple operations, it is the destination that decides among them; as we've noted, for pure data transfer, the destination usually prefers a move, but for destinations that represent tools like compilers, the preferred operation is a move. Our current implementation only supports passing an unordered set of acceptable operations. When Move and Copy are both specified, Move is assumed to take priority; destinations that prefer Copy need to leave Move out of the set. The worst this can do is provide incorrect operation-specific feedback during dragging; if a user tries to force a Move operation, it will appear to be disallowed; but if the user persists in doing the drop anyway, while forcing a Move, the destination will have a chance to accept it.

Another potential problem is that the dropsite database for a destination top-level window is stored as a property of that window. This property is read by the source client during dragging when the pointer enters the destination window. If the server has limited memory, applications with a large number of dropsites could eat up a significant amounts of server memory. Also, if a source client is connected by a moderately low-bandwidth line to the server, reading the property from the server could take a noticeable amount of time. Both of these situations are characteristic of low-end X terminals connected over serial lines.

The server memory problem could be attacked by storing the dropsite databases in a separate off-server dropsite database client. Going outside of X11 to transfer the dropsite data to the source client (i.e. using a separate transport mechanism) could solve the problem of bandwidth to the server (then again, by bypassing the server, it could also solve the problem of high-latency server connections, which would allow dynamic messaging to work).

To work correctly, the preregister protocol does require that all dropsites be declared. The database (that is, the destination window's property) can be updated, but this can be problematic if it needs to be updated frequently. In addition, the current implementation of our toolkit requires that an Xt object be associated with each dropsite, which can be quite expensive if there are a large number of dropsites.

Even with these limitations, the preregister approach has proven to be useful. Most importantly, of course, it supports a wide range of reasonably sophisticated dragging effects in situations in which the dynamic protocol would exhibit unacceptable performance.

Moreover, if all dropsites are predeclared, the dropsite database is useful even when the dynamic protocol is used. The toolkit on the destination side uses the dropsite database (stored internally) to automatically provide the common drag-under effects and echo messages back to the client. Client code only needs to be provided to handle drag-effects more sophisticated than those which can be implemented automatically.

Such clients work well using either the preregister or the dynamic protocol. If the preregister protocol is used, the worst that will happen is that the less sophisticated drag-under effects which are automatically supported will be used in place of more exciting effects implemented by the destination client.

Even when dropsites are not predeclared, the preregister protocol can be useful. Consider a file manager application in which a directory contains a large number of files and other directories, many of which are potential dropsites. The client could preregister a dropsite only for the outer directory. Its allowable targets and operations would be the union of the targets and operations of the nested dropsites.

If the dynamic protocol were used, this client would explicitly track the position of the pointer, and explicitly provide drag-under effects for the (non-predeclared) dropsite under the pointer. If the preregister protocol were in use, these individual drag-under effects would not be available; in fact, all the feedback effects would be the same wherever the pointer was in the outer dropsite. Still, the feedback would indicate that the drop would fail if it would not succeed in any of the nested dropsites. In any case, this feedback is merely a hint. Once the drop is done, a drop message will be sent to the destination, who will determine definitively whether or not the drop can be done.

The dynamic and the preregister protocols are really two ends of a continuum. There may be various interesting hybrid solutions worth exploring, especially in environments in which the dynamic protocol is usable, but still slower than one might like.

For example, the source client might read the dropsite database to limit messaging. It would still send messages to the destination client, but only if the pointer was in a dropsite. The destination client would perform drag-under effects, but it would not need to echo the messages back to the source, unless perhaps the dropsite contained nested undeclared dropsites.

It may also be useful to consider using a separate client rather than the source to drive the dragging. If this client read not only the dropsite databases, but also obtained enough details from the source client to implement common drag-over and drag-source effects, then neither the source nor the destination client would need to be involved during dragging. Such a client could run locally on an X terminal and perform well during dragging independent of the bandwidth of the server connections to the source and destination clients. It should be noted that without extending the X11 protocol to transfer a grab from one client to another, there are potential timing problems in implementing this approach [4].

Choosing the Drag Protocol and the Drag-Over Visual Style

The choice of protocol in our implementation is made dynamically. Each time during the drag that the pointer enters a different top-level window, the protocol to be used is recalculated by the source client, based on the wishes of both the source and the destination client (both of which may be controllable by user settings).

There are actually two additional protocols available in addition to the Dynamic and the Preregister protocol.

With the DropOnly protocol, the source client neither reads the destination's drop-site database, nor messages with the destination. However, the default drag-over feedback indicates that a drop is possible somewhere within the destination window. The DropOnly protocol acts as if a single dropsite were associated with a top-level window accepting all possible targets and operations.

A protocol value of "None" indicates that drops are not allowed within the destination window, and will automatically fail. Drag-over feedback indicates that no drop is possible.

The wishes of both the source and destination client are specified through resources that can be set by either the client or the user [both the names and values of the actual resources differ, for the sake of simplicity, from those given in the paper].

The resource sourceProtocol specifies the protocol desired by a client when it contains the source; the resource destinationProtocol specifies the protocol desired by a client during a drag when it is a potential destination (i.e. when the pointer is in its window).

These resources can take on the values: None (N), DropOnly (DO), RequireDynamic (D), RequirePreregister (P), PreferDynamic (PD), and PreferPreregister (PP). In addition, sourceProtocol can take on the value PreferDestination (PX).

The actual protocol to be used is based on the source's sourceProtocol and the destination's destinationProtocol in the following way:

```
If either resource is None => None is used
  (actually, if the source specifies None,
    dragging is simply disabled)
Else if either is DropOnly => DropOnly is used
Else if the resources have conflicting requirements,
  (that is, one is RequirePreregister, and the
    other is RequireDynamic) => DropOnly is used
Else if either requires Dynamic or Preregister =>
  the required protocol is used
Else take the source's preference (though if the
  source specifies PreferDestination, this takes
  the destination's preference)
```

Figure 1: Drag & Drop matrix.

The matrix (column header "Destination", row label "Source"):

Source \ Destination	D	PD	PP	P	DO	N
D	D	D	D	DO	DO	N
PD	D	D	D	P	DO	N
PX	D	D	P	P	DO	N
PP	D	P	P	P	DO	N
P	DO	P	P	P	DO	N
DO	DO	DO	DO	DO	DO	N
N	N	N	N	N	N	N

A matrix (as shown in figure 1) expresses this more clearly.

By default, sourceProtocol is set to PreferDestination, and destinationProtocol defaults to PreferPreregister. Clients that prefer the dynamic protocol (e.g. for sophisticated drag-under effects, or to support non-declared dropsites) are told to set destinationProtocol to PreferDynamic in their app-defaults file.

The user can override the default and app-defaults settings to handle various common situations.

- If the server has too little space to hold the dropsite database, the defaults file can include

    ```
    *sourceProtocol: RequireDynamic
    *destinationProtocol: RequireDynamic
    ```

- If clients are connected to the server over connections that do not support messaging well, the defaults file can include

    ```
    *sourceProtocol: RequirePreregister
    *destinationProtocol: RequirePreregister
    ```

- If both conditions above hold (as with low-end X terminals connected over serial lines), the defaults file can include

```
*sourceProtocol: DropOnly
*destinationProtocol: DropOnly
```

- If some clients run on the server machine, with adequate memory, while others run remotely, communicating with the server over high-latency connections, we want to disallow dynamic protocols when remote clients are involved. Although the server's per-host defaults file is not changed, the per-host defaults files of the remote machines can include

```
*sourceProtocol: RequirePreregister
*destinationProtocol: RequirePreregister
```

We have discovered that these resources alone are not adequate for specifying all common situations. In particular, suppose that a machine has somewhat limited memory, and thrashing occurs if dynamic messaging is used between two clients that both run on that machine. At the same time, a dynamic protocol can be used perfectly well between one of the clients, and a client on another machine. We'd like to say that the sourceProtocol of clients on the thrashing machine should be RequirePreregister, but only if the destination client is on the same machine. We expect that adding some source-side resources to specify requirements in the face of various relationships between the source and destination machine (e.g. whether or not they are the same) can handle almost all useful situations.

We've noted previously that only the pointer can be grabbed when using a dynamic protocol, so that the drag-over effects are limited to that provided by X11's cursors – i.e. two color and limited size. We call this the dynamic visual style.

When the preregister protocol is used, the server must be grabbed, and a preregister visual style is used in which the drag-over effects may use a pixmap of any size and depth that the server supports.

Clients may wish to use the same drag-over effects in both the dynamic and preregister visual style, except in environments in which one style heavily predominates. Otherwise, the switch from one visual style to another, as the pointer is moved from one top-level window to another, can possibly be disconcerting to some users, though this has not been shown to be a problem is practice.

A user who finds the differences between a particular client's preregister and dynamic visual styles to be bothersome can set sourceProtocol to PreferDynamic for that client. Assuming that no destination has RequirePreregister set, all interactions will use the dynamic protocol, and there will be no switch to the preregister visual style. This is the best way to limit changes in visual style when some destinations request PreferDynamic (e.g. for whizzy drag-under effects) while others do not.

The user can instead set sourceProtocol to PreferPreregister if the user wants visual consistency, and the whizzy preregister drag-over effects are more desirable than the drag-under effects that would be lost.

In either case, a user can set the destinationProtocol of a particular client to RequirePreregister or RequireDynamic to override the source's preference.

When the protocol in use is DropOnly or None (or when the pointer is not in a top-level window), the value of the source's sourceProtocol determines which visual style to use. If sourceProtocol is RequireDynamic or PreferDynamic, the dynamic visual style is used, otherwise the preregister visual style is used. This serves to limit the change in visual style.

A client's destinationProtocol is stored in the same property as the dropsite database. If the destinationProtocol is None, the property is actually not stored at all. If the destinationProtocol is DropOnly or RequireDynamic, only the value of destinationProtocol is stored in the property; there is no need to store the database, since neither of those values would allow a Preregister protocol to be used.

When the pointer enters a new top-level window, only the style is read from the dropsite database property. The rest of the property (i.e. the dropsite database) is only read if the resulting protocol is Preregister.

Finding Top-Level Windows

When the pointer enters a different top-level window, the dropsite database property needs to be read to determine the destinationProtocol, and, if necessary, to load the dropsite database.

But, how does the source client determine which windows are the top-level windows, so that it can arrange to be notified when the pointer enters or leaves one during a drag? We'll describe a number of possibilities we've considered.

First of all, remember that when the user initially maps a top-level window, the request is redirected to the window manager, who usually reparents the window one or two levels deep inside a frame window that provides various window-specific decorations and controls. The frame windows are typically all placed in a single window, which we'll call the frame parent. The frame parent is often the root window, though a number of window managers, including dxwm [12] and tvtwm [13], for a variety of reasons, use a descendant of the root window instead.

The ICCCM [14] could (but doesn't currently) require that window managers provide a standard way of making the identity of the frame parent window known. If the ICCCM then required that each frame window had a WM_TOP_LEVEL property containing the id of the top-level window it contained, finding the top level windows would be relatively easy. It would also be easy to determine when a new top-level window was mapped.

At present, there is only one foolproof technique the ICCCM provides for identifying a client top-level window. It must have a WM_STATE property, which must be placed on it by the window manager. To find the frame parent, you need to search the window hierarchy to find two windows with WM_STATE, and the frame parent is then their nearest common ancestor. Once the frame parent is known, the frame windows are found among its children, but finding top-level windows is still none too easy. There is no guarantee that a child of the frame parent is a frame window (as opposed to some other window mapped by the window manager). Even if it is, it is necessary to search for the descendant of the frame window with the WM_STATE property.

Another technique for locating the top-level windows is selection-based. The window manager (or perhaps some other manager) for screen i would take ownership of a screen-specific property, say WM_QUERY_i. The owner would respond to an appropriate request with a list of the top-level windows. A straightforward extension could be used to arrange for the requester to be notified of any newly mapped top-level windows, until another request disabled further notification. See [4] for additional discussion of this issue.

The Drop Protocol

When a drop begins (in our implementation, by releasing Btn2) over a destination window that supports dropping, the source ends its pointer or server grab (if a dynamic or preregister protocol is in use), and places an image identical to the current drag-over visual in an override-redirect window at the location of the drop.

The source client then sends a drop message to the destination. Using the techniques described for the dynamic drag protocol, the destination client can obtain the x,y position of the pointer, the set of allowable operations, and the lists of targets the source can provide.

The destination then determines which drop site (if any) contains the pointer, and if any of the source's targets and operations are acceptable. The destination client then echoes the drop message back to the source indicating the drop site, the destination's best guess about whether or not the drop will succeed, and the operation (from among Move, Copy and Link) to be done, and then starts requesting information to be transferred from the source.

Once the drop echo is sent, the remainder of the drop protocol is layered entirely on top of the X11 selection mechanism, with the destination client in control.

As we noted previously, when a drag is started, the source client takes ownership of a selection atom. It uses this atom to name the static information property stored on the source window for the duration of the drag. When the drop occurs, this atom is passed to the destination in the drop message. The destination client uses this selection atom for making standard X11 conversion requests. Since our implementation is built on top of Xt, this approach allows us to use the existing Xt functionality which deals with selections.

The destination may request conversion to targets that are not included in the source's target list (but which will be returned if a TARGETS request is made). The source's target list describes the data that the source represents, both in its preferred format, as well as some other targets that are less desirable, either because they require computation or because they lose information. Nonetheless, the source is certain to be able to provide additional auxiliary information. If this information does not reflect the essence of the source, the target may not belong in the target list.

Data transfer may take some time, especially in a networked environment; the user may wish to start another drag while an outstanding transfer is still in progress, with the same or a different source. Consequently, each drag cannot simply reuse the same selection atom.

Instead, we maintain a pool of selection atoms on a display-wide property, obtaining one from the pool when the drag starts, and returning it to the pool when the drop completes. If the pool is empty, we create a new selection, incrementing a count in the property used to generate a unique name. Naturally, interactions with this property are done within a server grab to ensure atomicity.

Once a transfer is complete, the destination client sends a message to the source indicating whether the drop was successful or not. As we mentioned previously, this may not be definitively known until the transfer is done, since it may depend upon the contents of the transferred data. This completion message is actually sent as a conversion request with a target of DROP_SUCCESS or DROP_FAILURE.

When the source receives the drop completion message, it unmaps the override-redirect window, and performs the appropriate visual transition effect (i.e. melting or snapback).

A destination client implements a Move operation just like a Copy, except that, if the transfer has been successful, a DELETE request is made of the selection atom. This is a standard ICCCM request for the selection owner to delete the source.

As in other transfer situations, not just drag & drop, the destination owner needs to be cautious about including the DELETE request as part of a MULTIPLE request that includes data transfer requests, unless the destination can be certain that the data is acceptable and can be stored successfully. Otherwise, the data can be lost. Some destination clients may even find it prudent to backup the transferred data before requesting the DELETE, just in case the destination crashes before it can be explicitly saved. The alternative is to depend on the ability of the source to undo the deletion, however, there is currently no standard way to determine if the source can do so.

If the data transfers are all successful, but the DELETE request fails, it is not clear what the destination should do. One possibility is to report success on drop completion anyway; at worst, an extra copy of the data is maintained at the source. The other possibility is to undo the effects of the transfer (in the destination) and report failure. Support for partial success feedback could be helpful here as well.

If a dropped source acts as an input to a tool (e.g. a compiler), the destination needs to decide whether to signal completion of the drop immediately after the transfer is done, or wait for the results of the tool's action (e.g. compilation). If the operation is a Copy or Link, and especially if the tool action can take some time, we recommend that the destination signal completion on transfer, and use some other visual cue to indicate the result of the tool action. Even if the operation is a Move, the destination can signal completion on transfer if the original source can still be obtained from the destination if the tool action fails. For example, if dropping a document on a mailbox deletes the source document, the drop can complete immediately, so long as the mail tool reliably allows the user to subsequently retrieve undeliverable mail.

When the user presses the Help key during a drag, the drag completes, and a drop message is sent to the destination, exactly as if a regular drop were done, with the exception that the message indicates that Help was requested. The destination echoes the drop help message back to the source, who may wish to change the drag-over and drag-source effects back to something suitable.

The destination then typically posts a dialogue box, providing information about the drop site at the pointer position where the Help key was pressed, indicating why a drop would fail, or what would happen if it would succeed, and if appropriate, asking the user whether to perform the drop (using which operation) or to cancel it. If the user selects Cancel, a drop completion message indicating failure is sent to the source. Otherwise, the destination proceeds with the transfer. It could be useful to send another message to the source at this point indicating the operation chosen, but we have not found it particularly important to do so.

If the Help key is pressed while the pointer is not in a window that supports drops, only the source client is notified, who can choose to provide a Help dialogue describing the source data, and the available targets and operations.

Conclusions

This paper has described our goals for implementing drag and drop in the X11 environment, the issues we addressed during design and implementation, and the protocols we developed. Some of our goals were generic to drag and drop support irrespective of the underlying system. Others were specific to the X11 environment and our desire to support the widest possible range of X11-based system configurations. We ended up with an architecture which provides the following features:

- dynamically scalable in both the performance and visual domains

- configurable based on the run-time environment

- supports a wide range of visual styles that includes all of the prevalent implementations

- layered solely on top of the standard X11 protocol, with the drop protocol layered solely on top of the standard X11 selection mechanism.

- provides full support for the Motif Style Guide and the Common User Access Style Design Guide

Time will tell how much use the various configuration options will receive and how well we foresaw the feature set of the eventual X11 standard for drag and drop.

The design described in this paper is currently implemented as a prototype system integrated with the Motif toolkit. It has been tested on a variety of vendor platforms that provide a range of performance profiles including everything from the HP9000/700 series workstations (50-70 mips) down to low-end HP9000/320 (5 mips) systems with various memory configurations. Further testing on low-bandwidth transports is still needed. Still, since the protocol supports the DropOnly mode, there is always a fallback that will provide adequate performance.

Acknowledgements

Much of the work described in this paper is an outgrowth of proposals presented to the wmtalk working group of the X consortium by a joint HP/Sun team, with contributions from Brian Cripe and Dongman Lee of HP, and Stuart Marks and Tom Wood from Sun Microsystems. Various participants of the wmtalk working group also provided valuable input, including Bob Scheifler of the X Consortium, Phil Karlton from Silicon Graphics, and Mark Manasse, of Digital's Systems Research Center.

The extended Motif design, development and documentation team was instrumental in helping us to arrive at the final architecture described in the paper. Special thanks go to Bob May, Joe Whitty, and Ellen McDonald of HP, Leo Treggiari of DEC, and Vania Joloboff, Robert Mattews, and Mavinakayinahalli Ramesh of OSF, and most of all to Ben Ellsworth and Paul McClellan of HP for their part in the design and implementation of the Motif prototype. The drag preregister implementation is based on donated HP VUE code which was implemented by Rick McKay and Fred Taft of HP.

Finally, we would also like to thank the HP management team headed by Ted Wilson and the OSF management team headed by Jeanette Horan for their support of this work.

References

[1]   *Macintosh^{TM} System Software User's Guide*, Version 6.0, Apple Computer, Inc., 1988

[2]   *Friendly Desktops*, Alan Southerton, Steve Mikes, UnixWorld, Vol 8, #9, November 1991.

[3]   *OPENLOOK^{TM} Graphical User Interface Functional Specification*, Sun Microsystems, Inc., Addison-Wesley, Reading MA, 1989

[4]   *Implementing Drag and Drop in X11*, Stuart W. Marks, X Technical Conference, 1991

[5]   *X Window System*, 2nd Edition, Robert Scheifler, James Gettys, Digital Press, Bedford MA, 1990

[6]   *xmag*, Dave Sternlicht, Davor Matic, X11R5 Documentation, MIT, 1991

[7]   *twm*, Tom LaStrange, et.al., X11R5 Documentation, MIT, 1991

[8]   *OS/2 2.0: A Pilgrim's Journey*, John Udell, Byte Magazine, Dec 1991

[9]   *xrooms*, Erik Fortune, Terry Weissman, Mike Yang, MIT X11R4 /contrib Documentation, MIT, 1990

[10]   *Rooms: The Use of Multiple Virtual Workspaces to Reduce Space Contention in a Window-based Graphical User Interface*, Austin Henderson, Stuart Card, ACM Transactions on Graphics, V5 #3, 1986

[11]   *The Power of Penpoint*, Robert Carr, Dan Shafer, Addison-Wesley, Reading, MA, 1991

[12]   *dxwm*, Ultrix DECWindows User's Guide, Digital Equipmemt Corporation, 1991

[13]   *tvtwm*, Tom LaStrange, X11R4 /contrib Documentation, MIT, 1990

[14]   *Inter-Client Communications Conventions Manual*, David S.H. Rosenthal, X11R4 Documentation, MIT, 1989. Reprinted in [3]

Virtual Screen: A Framework for Task Management

Jin-Kun Lin

Abstract

Virtual Screen is an X window tool that extends a physical screen into multiple virtual screens. Virtual Screen enhances the capability of window management by expanding the workspace and providing task-level management. A virtual screen has dual identities. On one hand, it is a common window which users can open, close, move, resize, iconify, and deiconify. On the other hand, a virtual screen, like a real screen, is used as a container for a group of windows and when accompanying with a window manager, it allows users to manipulate individual windows in it.

Unlike the other multiple workspace systems, it allows users to display more than one virtual screen at the same time so that they don't need to switch between workspaces. Virtual Screen is open to any client and window manager. When applying Virtual Screen, users can keep using their window managers. A virtual screen is usually used to contain windows for a task. Virtual Screen allows nested virtual screens which could be used to define nested subtasks. Since a virtual screen is a separate environment, we also use it in implementing constraint-based systems.

Introduction

Since window systems became popular, users have been able to interact with quite a number of objects when dealing with daily work and the used windows frequently fill up the whole screen. The small size of a display screen became a serious problem. Icons and window overlapping are the most commonly used method to alleviate the problem. Some window managers, like tvtwm and swm [LaStrange 1990], provide a virtual desktop which extends the workspace to be much larger than a screen. By zooming around, users

Jin-Kun Lin is a graduate student at the Department of Computer Science of the University of North Carolina at Chapel Hill.

locate a screen-size scope on the virtual desktop and work in the scope. Some other window managers, like Rooms [Henderson 1986; Card 1987], provide multiple virtual workspaces so that users can switch between workspaces.

Although some window managers have handled size limitations (e.g. virtual desktops), they have not addressed task-level management. By observing users' behaviors in front of workstations, we found that people quite often work on more than one window in handling a task and they tend to switch back and forth between tasks. A window is used to accomplish only a subtask, not a whole task. Switching between window-level subtasks is achieved by moving focus from a window to another and it is supported by almost all window managers. However, there is no generally accepted method for task-level window management. Most window managers help users only in window-level management and it is the user's responsibility to arrange windows on the plain display screen and associate windows with tasks. For window managers like tvtwm that support an enlarged virtual desktop, users may be able to define tasks by areas of the virtual desktop and it is quite simple to switch from one area to the other. However, there is often inter-task relationship that requires users to bring together two or more pieces of information from separated tasks. If the related tasks were not located as neighbors, windows containing the related information must be moved together. This movement inevitably destroys the original association between the windows and their tasks. In addition, nested subtasks can not be conceived and are difficult to use because the relationships are not clearly represented. Focusing in management at the task level, some systems use the metaphor of rooms. A room is usually used to handle a task. Since a person can be in a room at a time, switching from room to room is necessary. Xerox's Rooms [Henderson 1986; Card 1987] allows a user to specify the windows he/she intends to bring along from one room to the other when there is some inter-task work. Supported by the working set model, Rooms provides facility to allow associating rooms with windows so that a window may be in more than one room. Building window working-sets for tasks is performed manually and we suspect that the complexity may discourage users from using it. Hierarchical subtasks are simulated by "a door in a room leading to a sub-room" which is awkward because all rooms occupy the whole screen and the concept of sub-rooms is not straightforward. Rooms is a window manager which, like other window managers, provides users no other options but to adapt to it. Not only task switching is controlled by Rooms, all rooms are dominated by it and there is no way to provide other window management policy in the other rooms. Unfortunately, in some cases, different window managers are needed to handle separated tasks. For example, X-conference or HyperText systems require different window managers to meet their special needs. And when a workstation is time-shared by people, it is very likely that they have quite different window management policies for their tasks. It is almost impossible that a single window manager, like Rooms, will ever meet everyone's demands.

In the Artifact-Based Collaboration (ABC) Project [Smith&Smith 1991] at UNC, we need a system to provide task-based and constraint-based management. This requirement inspired the idea of Virtual Screen. Thus, to provide X-conference in the ABC Project, we intend to provide a white board with a consistent view for all participants. The white board should function as a screen shared by all participants and should be controlled by a single window manager. It should also be operated as a typical window which can be iconified, deiconified, moved, lowered, or raised. The system should also allow conference participants to work on their private workspace while the conference is in process. Sometimes there may be some inter-task relationship between the white board and the private workspace so that both should be at least partially visible at the same time. The system should also be conference transparent so that users can keep using all their programs, including window managers. These requirements led us to discard our idea of implementing a task-management system by writing a window manager. Instead, we implement a system, Virtual Screen, which emulates a physical screen with a window which is called a virtual screen. The system provides multiple independent virtual screens while there is only one physical display screen. A virtual screen has dual identities. On one hand, it is a common window which users can open, close, move, resize, lower, raise, iconify, and deiconify. On the other hand a virtual screen, like a real screen, is used as a container for a group of windows and it is policy-free to window managers so that when accompanied with any selected window manager, it allows users to manipulate windows on it.

Virtual Screen is implemented based on X window systems [Scheifler86]. X is designed as a network-transparent graphics system which splits the job of drawing windows into two parts with client/server model. One or more clients communicate with the server by sending and receiving packets of instructions, data and replies conforming to X protocol [Nye 89]. Since the communication between clients and the server depends on X protocol which is simply in the form of byte streams, some process may be inserted between the X clients and the X server to relay and modify protocols. To meet specific needs, systems, like XTV [Abdel-Wahab 91], are able to use the inserted process to change the behavior between the client/server pair. The primary concept of Virtual Screen is to intercept and modify X protocols so that a group of clients, including window managers, could be mapped onto a regular window instead of the screen's root window.

Implementation

In an X window system, one or more displays are allowed. For each display, the X server accepts connections from clients by listening to a TCP/IP socket at a well-known port. Users are free to map clients to a selected display by connecting clients to the X server at port X_TCP_PORT + DisplayNumber where X_TCP_PORT is the designated port number for the first display whose DisplayNumber is zero. Clients are mapped to a display by the DISPLAY environmental variable which includes a machine name and DisplayNumber.

To intercept and modify X protocols, Virtual Screen, at first, needs to find and listen to a port with an unused number of X_TCP_PORT + DisplayNumber. This means that Virtual Screen creates a fake X server with a non-existing display for clients. For clients that contact this port, Virtual Screen will receive, modify (if necessary) and send protocols between them and the real X server. A window, called a virtual root, is created as the root window for the non-existing display. The purpose of X protocol modification is to make adjustments so that the virtual root would work as a real root window.

There are three classes of processes serving for a virtual screen. The first is a console process which starts the session, finds a free port which maps to a non-existing display, listens to this port, and forks other processes. The second is a root-window monitor. It monitors the location of the root window (virtual root) of the virtual screen. The third class is protocol filters which relay X protocols after some modification. For each client, there is a protocol filter accompanying it. Most of X protocols are not modified except those involved with the real and virtual root windows.

The console process is invoked when a virtual screen is to start. It serves through the whole session of the virtual screen. First, it finds a suitable free port for an unused display number at the local machine so that X clients with the DISPLAY variable, including the local machine name and the display number, will be mapped onto the virtual screen. A window, which is called a virtual root, is then created to serve as the root window of the virtual screen. Soon after that, the console process forks a root-window monitor to monitor the location of the virtual root. To facilitate the session of a virtual screen, an X client is invoked by the console process. This client, with its environment variable DISPLAY set for this virtual screen, is registered as the console client. When finished, the console client tells the console process to terminate the session. The console client provides a convenient way to invoke the other clients since all its child processes inherit its DISPLAY variable. After the console client is created, the console process enters a wait-and-fork service loop. It waits on the port until some clients request to map onto the virtual screen. When a request comes, the console process forks a filter process responsible to receive, modify, and send X protocols between the requesting client and the X server. After forking a filter process, the console process waits again. The console process may be interrupted when the console client finishes. In this case, it terminates all forked processes and cleans the system resource used for inter-process communication.

A protocol filter stands between the X server and a client. Its jobs is to manipulate X protocols between the X server and the client. In the X server's side, a protocol filter acts like a usual client. And in the client's side, it works just like the X server. It receives, modifies, and sends X protocols between the X server and a client. Most protocols are relayed unchanged. The only modified protocols are events and replies which are related to the real root window and are sent from the X server. Whenever an ID of the real root window is found, the protocol filter substitutes it with that of the virtual root window. And when a coordination value is relative to the real root, it will be substituted with the one relative to the virtual root.

Coordination substitution requires protocol filters to calculate the coordination relative to the virtual root from that relative to the real root window. One way is to use XTranslateCoordinate to request the X server to translate the coordination from the real root to the virtual root. This method creates a lot of request and reply protocols and seriously deteriorates the performance. Our way is to maintain the relative location from the real root to the virtual root. Because a virtual screen is not moved very often (compared with the frequency of protocols sent between the X server and clients), this value is usually unchanged. The virtual screen designates a process, root-window monitor, to keep this value correct. It monitors the location of the virtual root. When the virtual root is moved, root-window monitor updates the location to shared memory so that all filter processes can have access to it. With this value, filter processes can easily translate coordinations.

Virtual Screen is transparent to all X clients so that there is no need to modify any X programs, including window managers. Figure 1 and figure 2 illustrate the usage of Virtual Screen.

Task Management

Virtual Screen extends the screen from two dimensional to two-and-half dimensional. It provides users with the feelings that they have more than one screen at hand. Because a virtual screen can be manipulated as a usual window, users can group windows in a virtual screen and manipulate them all together. When used homogeneously, Virtual Screen provides users the capability of grouping windows. And virtual screens, like folders to papers, can be used to the tasks categorized by projects, applications, owners, etc. Cognitively, the boundary of virtual screens helps users to identify which task they are in. The size of a virtual screen can be adjusted to meet users' needs. When the needed information is contained in more than one virtual screen, users can open all of them.

Hierarchical virtual screens are permitted since a virtual screen is indeed a group of X clients that we can invoke in the other virtual screen. The physical containment of layered virtual screens is straightforward for the concept of "subtasks".

At first look, it seems redundant to have a separate window manager for each virtual screen. However, we found it desirable especially when tasks are categorized by persons. When a workstation is time-shared, users are very likely to have different window management configuration for their tasks. This allows users to share a machine without the overhead of login and logout. (Security function is yet to be done, but it should be quite simple.)

Except for the simple homogeneous usage mentioned above, Virtual Screen is now being developed in heterogeneous usage. For example, a virtual screen may be the white board of a conference and some additional functions must be added. A virtual screen can also provide some constraint checking so that displayed clients must have conformed to some necessary constraints.

Evaluation

Virtual Screen was developed, tested, and refined in approximately two man-months. It is written in C and requires understanding of low-level X protocols. We have tested many X clients at hands and have not found any failed clients. When considering the possible performance deterioration due to protocol relaying, we found that users did not feel any delay even in nested virtual screens. (On DEC 5000.)

In heterogeneous usages, we have already implemented prototypes of X Conference and record/replaying. The concept of Virtual Screen helps and simplifies the work in defining task boundary among conference-mode, recording-mode, and usual mode. Since task boundary is well-defined, implementing these prototypes was quite straightforward.

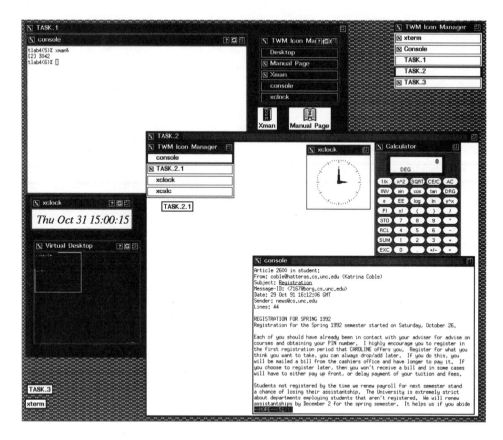

Figure 1 : A screen dump when Virtual Screen is used.
There are four virtual screens shown on the real screen and they are labeled as TASK.1,
TASK.2, TASK.2.1, and TASK.3.   The virtual screens of TASK.2.1 and TASK.3 are
iconified. Note that the real screen and the virtual screen of TASK.2 are managed by
twm; while that of TASK.1 is controlled by another window manager, that is, tvtwm.
Virtual screen of TASK.2.1 is a child virtual screen for TASK2.

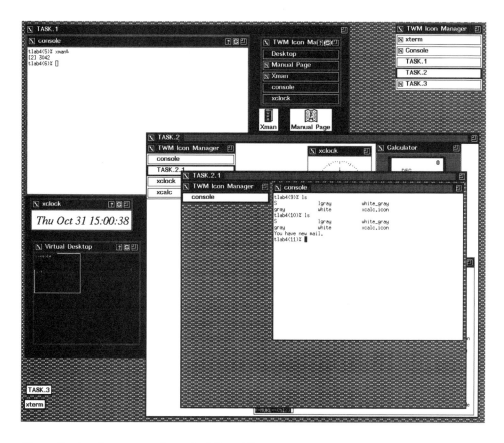

Figure 2. Another screen dump for Virtual Screen.
The layout of this screen is almost the same as the previous one except that the child virtual screen, labeled as TASK.2.1, is deiconified. In this case, a virtual screen is contained and opened in another virtual screen.

The flexibility in the size of virtual screens runs counter to all available window managers' assumption. Since window managers adjust the location of their pop-up menus to make them shown fully on the screen, they use the real screen's size which is always a constant during a session. Unfortunately, this assumption is incorrect to Virtual Screen. For these window managers, the adjustment of pop-up menus, therefore, does not function well. From real experience, we do not sense it as a problem to users. However, we think that the model of window management should include the possibility of updating screen sizes in a session.

Conclusions and Future Goals

This paper has presented a framework, Virtual Screen, for task management. It is simple, yet powerful in defining and managing tasks. Since there is no limitation to clients, including window managers, users do not need to adapt themselves for this tool. The independence among virtual screens provides much more freedom in task management than the other existing tools do.

There is still some possible refinement to Virtual Screen. For example, it should allow windows to be moved from a virtual screen to another like moving a paper from a folder to another.

Based on the success in implementing basic virtual screen, we are also developing constraint-based system to enforce constraints in accessing programs and databases.

References

[Abdel-Wahab 1988] Abdel-Wahab, H. M. and Feit, Mark A., [1991] *XTV:A Framework for Sharing X Window Clients in Remote Synchronous Collaboration*, Proceedings of TriComm '91 (April 1991) pp. 159-167

[Card 1987] Card, S. K., and Henderson, D. A., Jr., [1987] *A Multiple, Virtual Workspace Interface to Support User Task Switching*, CHI+GI 1987 Conference Proceedings on Human Factors in Computing Systems and Graphics Interface, (April, 1987) pp. 53-59

[Henderson 1986] Henderson, D. A., Jr and Card, S. K., [1986] *Rooms: The Use of Multiple Virtual Workspaces to Reduce Space Contention in a Window-Based Graphical User Interface*, ACM Transactions on Computer Graphics, Vol. 5, No. 3, (July 1986) pp. 210 - 243

[LaStrange 1990] LaStrange, Tomas, [1990] *swm: An X Window Manager Shell*, Proceedings of 1990 USENIX Summer Conference (June 1990) pp. 299 - 306

[Nye 1989] Nye, Adrian, [1989] *X Protocol Reference Manual for Version 11*, Volume 0, O'Reilly & Associates, Inc., Sebastopol, CA (1989).

[Scheifler 1986] Scheifler, R. W. and Gettys, J., [1986] *The X Window System*, ACM Transactions on Computer Graphics, Vol. 5, No. 3, (April 1986) pp. 79-109

[Smith&Smith 1991] Smith, John B. and Smith, F. Donelson, [1991] *ABC: A Hypermedia System for Artifact-Based Collaboration*, University of North Carolina at Chapel Hill, Department of Computer Science, Technical Report TR91-021

Using XTrap to Help People with Manual Disabilities

Keith Packard

Abstract

The XTrap extension provides a mechanism to interpose a complicated application between the X input devices (pointer and keyboard) and the X server. Using this mechanism, an interesting system for reducing the amount of manual ability required to operate X clients is investigated and compared with other systems.

X requires a high degree of manual ability

The X Window System is designed to provide the basic window system on which applications using a graphical user interface can be built. As a general system, it has the responsibility of providing the interface between the user and all applications. In addition to the standards which have been agreed upon by the industry, there are some unwritten, but nontheless strong, assumptions:

- The user can operate a two dimensional pointing device, such as a mouse.

- The user can hold down multiple keys at once, such as Shift and Control while performing some other operation.

- The user can hold down multiple keys, a mouse button and operate the mouse with a high degree of precision simultaneously.

One operation which is particularly difficult is the "drag" operation, where the mouse buttons (possibly in combination with some modifier keys) are held down while the mouse is moved. Even those of us who use a mouse every day are frequently frustrated by the coordination required in this operation.

Keith Packard is a member of the research staff at the MIT X Consortium.

There are several cases where these assumptions cannot be met; two of these are the most common: physical disability and environmental constraints. A person with limited manual ability may not be able to operate the mouse at all and may not be able to depress more than one key or button at a time. In the other case, the environment in which the system is used may not be conducive to the operation of a pointer device: either the mouse could not survive in the environment, or the user could be unable to use the mouse in the environment.

The general problem then, is emulation of the expected modes of interaction with other modes. One common mechanism is to provide keyboard accelerators, or "hot" keys, which activate menu entries or other mouse-selected actions, without the complications of the normal mouse interaction. This has been included in many systems as experienced users complain about the inconvenience of driving with the mouse. The X Toolkit translation and accelerator mechanisms even make this technique user customizable.

However, there are many interaction modes which do not fit into this model. Direct manipulation schemes such as "drag and drop" use the mouse to position objects directly. Graphical drawing editors are unusable without the mouse to select the appropriate positions on the screen. And, I have yet to meet an X window manager which does not require using the mouse to position and resize applications. Additionally, the hot keys discussed above frequently require the user to depress more than one key at a time.

While X applications are frequently customizable in this manner, a system which expects to work for any application must work with even the most intransigent of clients.

Why mouse emulation is difficult

The operations related to the mouse are the most varied, largely because the mouse has come to be used as the instantiation of the users hand in the world of the computer. It grasps, depresses and moves, performing tasks which are nearly as diverse as the operations manually abled persons perform daily in the physical world. Because of this metaphorical usage, providing a suitable replacement for the mouse is complex. While a straightforward emulation is easy, all but the most infrequent operations quickly become cumbersome. For a person to be able to use the machine in an intensive manner, a better scheme is necessary.

Such a scheme would attempt to isolate the various tasks that the mouse is used to perform, and instead of emulating the mouse emulating the human hand, the scheme would instead provide a way of replacing the entire task with a different paradigm. For example, I often use my mouse to simply select another window on the screen to which I would like the keyboard input to be directed. A scheme which simply moved the keyboard input from window to window using a single button press would be much more efficient. Many window managers provide this particular replacement action.

While an exhaustive list of the interaction paradigms would be difficult to list, a short list of common activities will be useful:

- Selecting where keyboard focus should be directed both among applications and within an application.

- Operating push buttons, check boxes and radio groups.

- Operating scroll bars and panners.

- Performing window geometry manipulation, such as move and resize.

- Selecting large objects, such as window icons.

- Selecting and editing text.

- Operating menus.

- Graphical editing.

As should be obvious by the above list, most of the operations using the mouse do not require pixel-level positioning. However, most of the operations do require the identification of regions of interest on the screen, regions within which the position is not important, and regions to which the pointer should be moved without stopping in intervening space.

Requirements of the solution

Given the problem as stated above, the first task is to set down the requirements of a solution:

- Any proposed system must be operatable with only one button/key depressed at any time.

- Any proposed solution must provide a means to eliminate the mouse and emulated it with key strokes.

- Any proposed solution must be able to be transparent to applications; a solution which also allowed cooperation by applications to enhance the system would be acceptable, but that should not restrict the set of applications which could be used.

- An solution should provide a way to get at the semantic structure of the system to reduce the dependence on pixel-level positioning and improve the performance and usability of the system.

- The scope of changes inside the X server should be minimal so that different mechanisms to be tried without a large amount of difficulty.

Existing systems

I have looked at two existing systems, one which is very similar to the system described here, and one which allows for hands-free operation.

EasyAccess

In 1987 Apple included handicapped support into their Macintosh line of computers with System 4.1. This system, called EasyAccess, was designed to provide access to all Macintosh applications to manually disabled persons. It has largely met this goal, but some people I know using the system find it cumbersome at times.

EasyAccess provides three essential aids:

- Locking modifier keys (Shift, Command and Option).

- Emulation of the mouse button with the keyboard, both locking and momentary.

- Pointer positioning using the keyboard.

To enter the system, depress the Shift key four times in a row; after that, when a modifier key (Shift, Command and Option) is pressed, it remains logically down until after the next non-modifier key is pressed, at which time the modifier key is logically released. The keypad drives the mouse, the numeric keys act like a joystick; depressing the 7 key moves the mouse northwest etc. The 5 key is used to click the mouse button, while another key is used to lock the mouse button down for drag operations. Depressing the Shift key four times again disables EasyAccess.

A major advantage of EasyAccess is that it is transparent to applications; they see the simulated devices as real, making them fully functional. A major disadvantage of Easy-Access is that the event mapping is static; the mouse motion is always controlled in the same way. Because of the acceleration characteristics of the motion generation, quickly picking diverse objects on the screen is very difficult. I was unable to perform the simplest Macintosh actions, such as pull down menus without feeling a sense of frustration.

DragonDictate

DragonDictate is a voice recognition system coupled with sophisticated software which enables a PC to be completely controlled using only the voice. Each phrase spoken by the user can be mapped to an arbitrary sequence of keystrokes. This means that any application which can be driven from the keyboard can be driven with this system. However, the restriction to keyboard input is not severe in this environment, as most PC applications are happy enough without a mouse.

A large feature of this system is that it is speaker independent. After training with the machine for a few short hours, the entire existing dictionary is accessible to the user, unlike older systems in which the entire dictionary needed to be repeated by each new speaker. This means that it is feasible to provide a very large dictionary of phrases with the system. Additional phrases can be added to the dictionary by either spelling them out with the phonetic alphabet or by typing them.

This does provide a workable system for hands-free usage, but has the disadvantage of being expensive, not replacing the mouse and being limited to PC class machines. One additional disadvantage is that speaking to a machine is uncomfortable for many people.

Parameters for the implementation

The implementation should be constrained to work with the existing hardware, expecting additional hardware to be available will reduce the accessibility of the system to potential users. So, we've got only the existing mouse and keyboard to work from.

To eliminate using the mouse directly, it can be be emulated with keys on the keyboard. By making the mouse buttons and modifier keys locking by having modes where they are held down (logically) while other actions are performed, only one key at a time needs to be held down. To completely eliminate the mouse, the only additional requirement is that the mouse buttons be emulated with keys on the keyboard.

All of this emulation takes the form of a simple mapping of events; incoming event sequence A should be replaced by event sequence B. This remapping must occur before any X event processing inside the server, as keyboard and pointer grabs must operate as expected. In addition, this application must be immune to server grabs, otherwise it would stop functioning at such times.

Context-sensitive event mapping allows the user to provide less input to manipulate the system. The window structure of most applications provides clues as to the internal structure of the interface. The ICCCM provides information on each top-level window about what application controls it. Another useful system is the EditRes protocol which provides detailed information about the internals of Xt based applications. A combination of these three systems provides substantial semantic knowledge about each application in the system.

Because of device and server grabs, an X application which simply selected for all input and used the SendEvent protocol request will not solve the problem, even given a sufficiently complex application. The interdependencies between the window hierarchy, the registration of grabs, and the workings of keyboard focus are just a few of the problems to be encountered. And, there isn't any way to make this transparent to clients which attempt to perform device grabs; either they receive all events from those devices, or the grab fails. Therefore, some extension to the existing X protocol is required to solve the entire problem.

How XTrap fits in

The XTrap extension developed by Digital Equipment Corporation was designed to provide a mechanism for monitoring both the X server and clients connected to it. The original architecture talks about trapping the interactions between the client and server. It provides mechanisms for detecting the invocation of each protocol request and monitoring the generation of each X event. It includes counters which measure the number requests/events of each type, and it provides a means for generating synthetic events.

The original design (fortunately) suffered a bit from the existing sample X server interfaces. It was originally specified to trap events as they were being sent to clients. However, inside the server there is no central place through which events are passed. Instead, a collection of different functions, some of which are also used to perform other tasks, is used. Because of this, XTrap provides a way to trap the device events before they were processed by the server; this redirection is simple, function pointers inside the device structure are "wrapped" redirecting the event delivery.

While the original design would not have been much better for this application than simply using SendEvent, the existing code provides exactly what was needed. By placing itself between the input devices and the input-management code of the server, XTrap provides a mechanism for interposing a separate application at this point. Only by operating at this level will device grabs perform as if the synthesized events were real while the real events have no effect on the server state.

In addition, XTrap provides a mechanism for disabling the effect of a server grab, allowing the XTrap client to continue executing requests. However, a client using XTrap must be very careful when operating under this situation; any core requests which occur while the server grab is in progress will potentially conflict with and confuse the client which holds the server grab. For example, a common usage of server grabs is when the window manager is painting lines on the screen in xor mode for window geometry manipulation; any rendering to the screen which occurs while this is happening will cause stray bits to be left on the screen.

While this extension was originally developed to monitor X client operations within the server, it has performed well in its new role. Some slight modifications in the sample implementation were required to make it work for this new task. The original implementation had the synthesized input events re-redirected back into the extension. I have changed this so that synthesized events are delivered directly into the event provessing code.

The event filter: hand

I've developed an application called *hand* using XTrap. This application has an embedded configuration language called *Handcraft* which provides control over the mapping of input events to actions.

The *hand* application sits (logically) between the X input devices and the X server. Events received from the devices pass into this application and, under the control of the configuration script, may generate a sequence of events to be interpreted as if they were real device events by the X server. The dynamic structure of *hand* is a simple event loop; for each event received from XTrap, *hand* executes the configuration script, performing tasks described therein.

The hand configuration language: Handcraft

Handcraft is a fairly straightforward language. It supports typed variables, functions and Algol-like control structures. The implementation uses a simple interpretive scheme to evaluate it. The basic format of a program is

$$Handcraft ::= Declarations\ Predicates$$
$$Declaration ::= Function$$
$$::= Variable$$
$$Function ::= \text{type } \mathbf{function} \text{ name } (Args)\ Locals\ Statement$$
$$Predicate ::= \mathbf{when}\ Expression\ Predicate$$
$$::= \mathbf{receive}\ MatchingEvent\ Statement$$

All of the declarations are interpreted, and the list of predicates saved away when the configuration file (`~/.handcraft`) is read.

Events in Handcraft

In X, input events are pretty straightforward; each has a type, timestamp and position. Keyboard events have, in addition, the effected key, while mouse buttons contain the button. However, this simple description of events is not sufficient for the task at hand. For instance, this geometric notion of position does not encapsulate all of the information which would be nice to have. To solve problems related to the window (or widget) hierarchy, each event must mirror this structure. To solve problems related to the geometry of related windows in the screen, the event must mirror this layout.

Because the types of information needed for different tasks is different, *Handcraft* events are specified as dynamic association lists. Each event contains a list of name/value pairs called *fields* which are referred to using the name. This allows each event to contain as many (or as few) values as needed. Additionally, this system allows fields to be lazily evaluated, delaying the actual computation of the value until it is requested.

Some fields have a conventional meaning (such as x and y) while others can be created as necessary by the user. When an X event is translated to a *Handcraft* event, the position, time and other information are translated into the appropriate field specification; the reverse translation occurs when an event is sent from *hand* to the X server. The event fields which are built into the existing implementation are

x, y The position where the event occurred, in absolute screen coordinates

type The type of the event. *Hand* predefines numeric variables with the values of each event, allowing them to be referred to symbolically.

time The time at which the event occurred. Because of the way XTrap is implemented, sending a time value to the server is ignored, so this field is useful only in received events.

button
    The button which was operated.

key, keycode, keysym
> These three fields give different ways to refer to the same object: which key was pressed. Any one of them can be stored or fetched; conversion between them happens automatically.

win The target window of this event.

Event matching

When an X event is received, the list of predicates which was read from the configuration file is executed. One of the predicates available is **receive**. This predicate takes an event and *matches* it against the X event. This match is performed by testing each field in the events for equality. Fields not specified in one or the other event are skipped. This means that a partial event specification can be given which matches a wide variety of X events. The event

```
event { type = ButtonPress }
```

matches any ButtonPress event, regardless of which button was pressed. The event

```
event {
        type = KeyPress
        key = "Shift_L"
}
```

would only match key press events for the Shift_L key. This is another advantage of the association list used to specify events: the same mechanism used to extend the values associated with an event can be used to restrict which values are significant when matching events.

Event generation

One of the statement types is the **send** statement. This takes the specified event and sends it to the X server. The fields in the event are mapped into an X event and then sent along. A potential problem is that the event may not have enough information to build a complete event. *Hand* is pretty lenient about which fields are required to be set:

- MotionNotify events require some indication of screen position; either an absolute position or a window specification.

- ButtonPress and ButtonRelease events need only the button number.

- KeyPress and KeyRelease events need some indication of which key: either a keysym, a key name or a keycode.

The **send** statement takes an event as its argument:

```
send event {
type = KeyPress
key = "Return"
}
```

This example synthesizes a KeyPress event from the return key.

Windows in Handcraft

Much as events require a flexible description to load additional semantics onto them, windows also require more information to provide enough information to navigate the hierarchy in a useful way. Windows are similar to events, in that they are implemented as dynamic association table. However, quite a bit of the information stored in a window refers to other windows. The builtin window fields are

x, y, width, height, borderWidth
> The geometry of the window.

parent
> The parent window. The root window has no parent, which is indicated by a value of zero.

applicationClass, applicationName
> The application to which this window belongs.

widgetClass, widgetName
> For Xt applications which speak the EditRes protocol, this field gives a symbolic representation for the window in terms of the widget hierarchy.

north, northNorthEast, northEast, eastNorthEast, etc.
> The next window (geometrically) in the indicated direction.

firstChild, lastChild, nextSibling, prevSibling
> These allow the hierarchy to be walked.

While the fields inside events are relatively isolated, the fields inside windows interact in strong ways; resetting any field can potentially change which window is indicated by the values. *Hand* dynamically invalidates fields in a window which become incorrect as a result of new information. The lazy evaluation of these fields means that this invalidation should be transparent to the user.

Window matching

Just as events can be matched using a partially specified event, windows can be matched in a similar way. Unlike events which are matched against input events, windows are matched against the entire window hierarchy. Thus, the value of any automatically computed field in the window can change over time, as the window system changes configuration.

```
window {
        applicationClass = "Xmh"
        widgetClass = "Text"
}
```

This matches any Text window which is inside of an Xmh application.

Combining event matching and window matching allows *hand* to be sensitive to both the user input and the context of that input. Combining the event and window examples together we get

```
event {
        type = KeyPress
        key = "Shift_L"
        win = window {
                applicationClass = "Xmh"
                widgetClass = "Text"
        }
}
```

This example now matches F1 key presses, but only when inside a Text widget inside an Xmh application. Context sensitive event mapping is only a small additional step.

Putting it together: matching and sending events

The examples above are not complete; they don't show how the language is expressing event mapping, only how it expresses event matching and sending. Here is a self-contained part of a *Handcraft* program which demonstrates both halves in concert.

```
event e
window w

receive event {
                type = KeyPress
                key = "F1"
                win = window {
                        applicationClass = "Xmh"
                }
        }
{
        e = event { type = MotionNotify }
        w = window { widgetName = "inbox" }
        w.applicationName = currentEvent.win.applicationName
        e.win = w
        send e
```

```
send event {
        type = ButtonPress
        button = 2
}
send event {
        type = ButtonRelease
        button = 2
}
}
```

In this example, the F1 key is being used to automatically select the *inbox* folder inside xmh. This interaction is done without modifying xmh, and without touching the mouse. The syntax in the existing language should be considered experimental as it has not been used enough yet.

Why build another language

I considered whether I should adapt some existing language to this role and have instead opted to design a new language. The advantage is that no old baggage from an old system has crept into *Handcraft*, and the language is tailored quite closely to the needs of the system. However, there are a few disadvantages as well. The most obvious is that users need to learn a new language to configure the system, another is that the language has not had extensive use which would uncover its failings.

How XTrap could be improved

The existing XTrap extension has proven quite capable in developing this sample system. However, as with any new use of an existing system, I have some suggestions for changes which would make the system more usable.

Device events vs. X events

XTrap has only one notion of events: that of X events. The original intention of the extension was to trap the delivery of events to X clients. This is a useful function, but the X server has another notion of events as well, the raw events as delivered by the input devices. *Hand* needs this later form, which is what is provided by the existing XTrap implementation. Both forms are useful; XTrap should be extended to recognize the difference between them.

Finer-grain input selection

With the existing XTrap specification, *hand* is required to receive all device input events, filter them and forward them back to the X server unchanged in many cases. This is inefficient. A better mechanism would be to allow the extension to specify which keys and buttons and whether motion events should be redirected.

Also, the existing gating mechanism whereby the delivery of events to the event processing code is very crude; usurping a key on the keyboard and requiring the user to toggle it on and off. The same effect could be gotten by using a synchronous grab, a request which forwarded the contents of the event queue on to the client and an explicit request to control the gating. Placing the gating under the control of the application would make it much more flexible.

Event filtering

XTrap is not carefully designed to work in an environment where multiple clients are performing different tasks with it. For example, an event recording client which wishes to save an event stream to be played back at a later date will get the raw X device events, and (with my modified implementation) not get the filtered output of *hand*. While this seems like it would work, the modified XTrap also prevents the playback program from directing its events back to *hand*, preventing the events from being filtered. Thus the application will not work as expected when driven from the playback.

A better scheme would be to treat each XTrap client as a filter, receiving events from the previous client and sending them on to the next. This would allow the playback client to deliver events to *hand*, and to have them work correctly. I don't know how the system would be configured as to which client was first in the chain, additional requests may be necessary. Clearly the event gating should be per-client as well.

Trap contexts

Each XTrap client has a single server context to work with. The XTrap toolkit covers this up and provides multiple trap contexts. This is a good abstraction, and I believe that it should be pushed down into the server. This provides a way of implementing multi-threaded clients with reasonable client-side data hiding.

It would also provide a mechanism for XTrap clients to receive its own events so that a single client could generate and monitor those generated events. Simply create two trap contexts, monitor events from one and generate them with the other. By replacing the notion of per-client in the extension with per trap-context, the extension would become more flexible.

In addition, the events delivered to the XTrap client should be tagged with the trap context which was used to select the event. This would give the client the ability of dispatching the events in an easy fashion.

Future work

While the existing system has proven a useful testing ground for developing context-sensitive event mapping systems, there are still many ways in which the X environment could be made more accessible. This system does not address working without either keyboard or mouse, and instead receiving input through some non-X mechanism. It is also currently limited to using the existing X input devices.

Voice input

While emulating the mouse with the keyboard is useful, voice recognition is slowly becoming more available in the commercial market. By connecting a PC with Dragon-Dictate running kermit to the workstation, and modifying *hand* to read from a serial port, it should be possible to get easy access to voice input in the X environment. The event matching scheme should extend easily to support this new form of input.

Alternative input devices

The XInput extension provides a way to add new input devices to the X server; it seems natural that *hand* should be extended to take advantage of the additional input modes available from some of these devices.

Conclusions

The XTrap extension has proven to be a useful tool in experimenting with complex new systems for improving the accessibility of the X Window System. Because the extension provided the essential hooks into the X server, the interesting development could take place on the client side. This work has also shown how the XTrap extension could be improved to allow it to be used in more applications.

Hand and *Handcraft* together provide a solution which enables the X Window System to be operated without using the mouse and by pressing only one key at a time. By using the XTrap extension, the operation of *hand* is made transparent to other clients. This highly contextual and configurable system significantly enhances the accessibility to and performance of the X Window System for users with manual disabilities.

Author Information

Keith Packard has been part of the research staff of the X Consortium at the MIT Laboratory for Computer Science since 1988. He is the author of several X Consortium standards and has written large parts of the MIT sample X server while participating in the development of the last three MIT releases of the X Window System.

MuX: An X Co-Existent, Time-Based Multimedia I/O Server

Earl Rennison, Rusti Baker, Doohyun David Kim,
Young–Hwan Lim*

Abstract

A multimedia input/output (I/O) server, MuX, is being jointly developed by SRI International and the Electronics and Telecommunications Research Institute (ETRI), Korea. Currently, the MuX server is a co–existent server to the X Window System server that provides support for integration and synchronization of time–based media. The MuX server is based on the abstract concept of a media multiplexer or mixer. Key features of the MuX include a well–developed media integration model; a scripting capability to specify time, space, and relationships among the media relative to a logical time system (LTS) for media integration; abstractions for multimedia operations; and fine–grained media synchronization.

This paper presents an overview of the MuX and is primarily focused on describing the concepts and models upon which the MuX is based. It does not address MuX implementation issues. It also includes a brief discussion of the design goals and functionality of the MuX server. The media integration model and the synchronization mechanism employed by the MuX server are described. The concept of network–transparent access to multimedia data is introduced. A simple ASCII–based scripting language, MuXScript, is introduced and described. The grammar of the script language and an example script are provided. A brief description of the client–server interface is also provided. This paper concludes with a discussion of related work, a summary of the current status, and future research directions.

*Earl Rennison and Rusti Baker are software engineers at SRI International. Doohyun David Kim is an International Fellow at SRI International visiting from ETRI. Young–Hwan Lim is a section manager at ETRI.
This project was sponsored by Electronics and Telecommunications Research Institute, Korea.

Introduction

The X Window System* [1] provides network–transparent access to display resources based upon an abstraction of event–oriented management of a bit–mapped graphics display. While the X environment is appropriate for the presentation of non–time–based multimedia, such as 2–D graphics, font–based text, and images, it is inadequate for time–based media, such as video and audio. Extensions have been proposed for the X server to handle time–based media such as Xv [2] and MVEX [3], but these extensions do not adequately address the problems of synchronization of related media, and more importantly, media integration. Other proposed extension and co–resident server models provide mechanisms for synchronization at the X event level; however, they do not explicitly address the problem of media synchronization that is based on media integration. Media integration is key to the development of useful multimedia applications; while putting video in a window is a good technological advance, its use in applications in a single media form is limited. Hence, there is a need for a multimedia server that supports the integration of multimedia information from diverse and distributed sources (e.g., devices, files, network), as well as services for synchronization of various media. Based on this need, window systems must depart from only being event–based display systems, to being both event–based and time–based systems. More specifically, window systems in the future will be thought of as media multiplexers.

Until recently, much of the work by multimedia vendors has been focused on attaching various media devices, such as a VCR, to a computer. This has enabled the integration of canned presentations into applications such as on–line help documents or educational presentation systems. However, this approach is not useful for media producers who are creating multimedia products such as business presentations, multimedia mail, and training documents. To make multimedia technology more useful for information producers and consumers, a video production model is needed for multimedia information systems.

In a video production environment, audio visual (AV) systems provide users with the the necessary tools to help them compose presentations. AV systems allow users to record, process, mix, and integrate media from a variety of different sources and store and play the resulting composition. With these tools, a media producer can extract important information from stored media and compose a presentation that conveys a message concisely. An environment based on these tools should facilitate human–computer interactions that support the accelerated pace of information and knowledge workers to better communicate and visualize results.

The video production model (in a limited form) has been employed with success in applications such as MacroMind's Director. To facilitate a more conducive environment for multimedia integration and interaction for all applications, we have chosen this model as the basis for MuX. The MuX server is a co–existent server to the X server and provides support for integrated and synchronized multimedia I/O. It has been designed** to provide:

---

*All product names used in this document are the trademarks of their respective holders.
**The MuX was jointly developed by SRI International and the Electronics and Telecommunications Research Institute (ETRI), Korea.

- Client–server model to facilitate distributed computing
- Well–developed media integration model based on the video production model
- Fine–grained synchronization and integration, i.e., frame–level synchronization
- Network–transparent access to multimedia data, including abstractions for sources and destinations
- A scripting language to specify the time, space, and intermedia relationships for media integration
- Abstractions for multimedia operations (play, stop, pause, reverse)
- Frame–level composition.

This paper provides an overview of the X co–existent, time–based multimedia I/O server, MuX. It is primarily focused on describing the concepts and models upon which the MuX is based. It is important to note that not all of the concepts discussed in this paper have not all been fully implemented in the current server implementation; however, they are currently under development.

The remaining sections of this paper are broken down as follows. Section Two describes the design goals of the MuX server. Section Three describes the high–level concepts of the MuX and its co–existence with X. Section Four describes the media integration and synchronization model. Section Five describes the concept of network–transparent access to multimedia data that is employed in the MuX. Section Six describes the MuX scripting capabilities. Section Seven describes the current client–server interface. Section Eight provides a discussion of related work. Section Nine discusses implementation status and future research directions. And, section Ten provides some concluding remarks.

Design Goals

To meet the objective of providing a conducive environment for multimedia integration and interaction, the architecture and design of the MuX server is based on the following design goals:

- **Single Interface:** The MuX server should have a single interface for interacting with all media I/O in order to provide both control and convenience.

- **Parallel Multimodal I/O Channels:** The MuX server should support multiple, parallel I/O channels with powerful multimedia processing to provide more effective communication between computers and humans, and between humans and humans.

- **Coherent Presentation:** To ensure that the meaning of presented information is not lost or distorted, the MuX server must provide adaptive, fine–grained synchronized presentation of multiple streams of continuous–media data across multiple I/O channels.

- **Contextual Representation:** The server should provide support for expressing contextual relationships among related pieces of multimedia information, including time and space relationships. In addition, the MuX server should provide the ability to access and gather data and integrate the data into a logical presentation.

- **Network Transparency:** To achieve efficient use of computing resources, applications should be able to run on separate machines while still being able to use the capabilities of the MuX server.

- **Transparent Access to Multimedia Data:** Access to multimedia data should be transparent to both the client application and the server to allow media producers latitude in creating media products and to allow the collection of media resources to be configurable.

- **Extensible Interface:** An interface should provide the flexibility, extensibility, and portability needed by the MuX server to allow for growth and change.

- **Presentation Editing:** The MuX should provide support for editing multimedia presentations.

- **Tailorability:** The server must be tailorable to accommodate user or application presentation preferences. Users should be able to specify what type of media is preferred, and, in the case of limited resources, users should be able to specify how a presentation should be degraded in order to meet time requirements or presentation quality.

- **Adaptability:** The server should provide mechanisms to adapt to changing resource availability and application demands.

- **Performance:** Fast performance is critical, since a slow multimedia user interface will be unusable.

We feel that meeting these goals is essential in providing an effective multimedia user interface and we have taken them into consideration in all phases of the MuX development, including conceptualization, design, and implementation.

MuX Server Concepts

Media Multiplexer

To address many of the forementioned goals, we have based the MuX on the fundamental concept of a programmable media multiplexer or media mixer as illustrated in Figure 1. This concept is a direct correlation to that of an audio mixer used in concert productions. The video extension is derived from that of a switch or video editor used in a video production studio. In the media multiplexer concept, the multiplexer takes input from a variety of sources, mixes them based on controllable parameters (such as a slide bar on an audio mixer) and directs the result to an output port or destination. Example sources include devices such

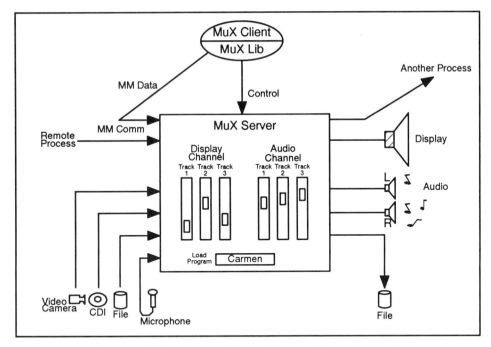

Figure 1: Programmable media multiplexer concept.

as microphones, musical instruments, and video cameras, files, or, ideally, remote processes including its clients. Example destinations include devices such as audio speakers and a display, files, and, ideally, remote processes, such as other MuX servers.

Another important concept is programmability. A media mixer should be interactively programmable (this is analogous to a video editor interactively defining cuts from one or more media into another medium) and have the ability to store the resulting programs for retrieval at a later time. Stored programs should also be editable. The concept of stored programs has significant implications, namely these stored programs allow the control of the mixer without human interaction. A set of stored programs can be thought of as a script. In addition, programs can be thought of as sequences of actions or simply sequences.

To provide a better understanding of the implications of stored programs and sets of stored programs, consider the analogy of an opera. In this analogy a script is equivalent to the opera's score and a sequence is equivalent to an act. The script language allows an editor to define the cast and orchestra (inputs or sources) and define when and how each member of the cast performs during each act. This concept is illustrated in Figure 2.

The MuX provides support facilities for achieving this concept. They are described in subsequent sections.

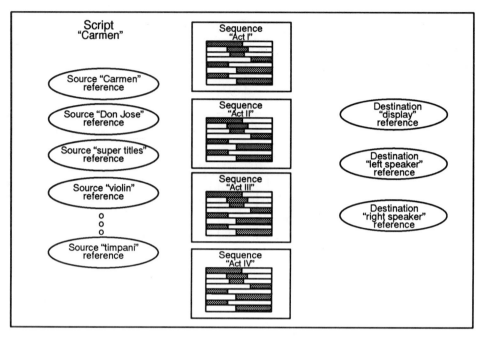

Figure 2: Script concept.

Co–Existent Server

The MuX server is a co–existent server with the X server as illustrated in Figure 3. The main reason for having a co–existent server is to develop an environment that focused on supporting time–based media. The MuX server provides support for access and integration of time–based media. The server provides support for presentation of multimedia data according to a script. The source of multimedia data may include devices, files, or remote processes.

The X server provides support for standard non–time based media and events, such as mouse and keyboard interaction, and display of window–based graphics and text.

The concept of a co–existent server does have significant implications—especially concerning shared resources, such as the display, the window hierarchy, and the colormap. Because the management of these resources is not a primary objective of MuX, these services remain provisions of the X server. However, coordination of these resources must be provided. For this purpose, communication between the MuX server and the X server is needed. For performance reasons, MuX directly accesses the display frame buffer. The communication between the two servers is used for control only.

In addition to communications with the client and the X server, MuX must also communicate with the sources of multimedia data (which may include the client).

At this point one important distinction should be made about the MuX server. Once a script is loaded into the MuX server and a sequence defined, it is the responsibility of the server to open access to files, devices, and remote processes, and to control the flow of data. This

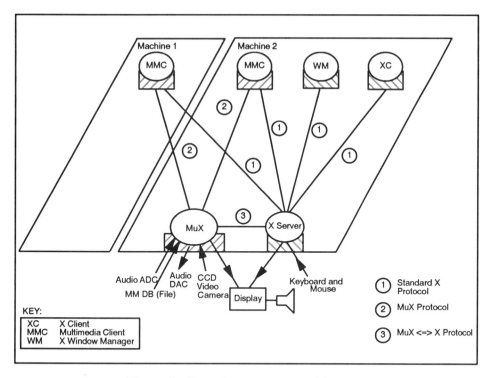

Figure 3: Co–existent server architecture.

action is transparent to a MuX client. A MuX client gives complete control of the presentation over to the server. Thus, a client application need not know the contents of a script. This greatly simplifies the task of an application. This differs from the ACME [4] approach where by a client must specify connections to the server and must notify the source processes when to start sending data to the server. This aspect is covered in more detail in the section on network–transparent access to multimedia data.

Model for Multimedia Integration and Synchronization

To facilitate multimedia integration and the synchronized presentation of multiple streams of digital continuous media (DCM), a model for multimedia integration was developed. The primary objective of this abstract model is to facilitate media integration and synchronization across multiple, parallel I/O channels. The model is a derivative of the video production model and employs many similar concepts. These concepts are also used in MacroMind's Director [5] and Apple's QuickTime [6]; however, there are some important differences that are discussed in the related work section. This section provides an overview of the media integration model and describes the synchronization mechanisms associated with the model. The model is built on object–oriented principles, hence each object is described by its data and its methods.

Media Integration

The basis elements for the media integration model are summarized in the following table:

Element	Function
Source	A origin of medium data
Destination	A recipient of integrated media data
Presentation Context	A state in which a medium is presented
Compositor	A mixer of multimedia data
Medium	A representation of a physical medium object
Clip	A cut from a medium
Track	A medium I/O path specification
Channel	A logical construct that integrates a group of media into one logical I/O stream
LTS Clock	The basic synchronization mechanism
Sequence	An abstraction for a multimedia presentation
Script	A collection of sequences

The relationships among each of these elements are given in Figure 4. A description of each of these components is provided below.

A *source* is the origin of medium data. A source of medium data may be either a file, device, or a remote process accessed through an IPC mechanism. A source typically contains a single medium.

A *destination* is the recipient of processed multimedia data that can be presented or stored. A destination may be either a file, device, or a remote process accessed through an IPC mechanism. Media directed to a destination can be an integration of multiple forms of media, but is represented as a single medium. Multiple forms of media are composed into a single stream prior to being sent to a destination. Destinations are logical entities, thus it is possible to have multiple references to the same physical destination.

A *presentation context* defines how media are composed and sent to a destination. This definition consists of a set of state variables. A presentation context can contain state variables such as priority, weight, group, mapped, and speed. The presentation context contains a set of variables that are applicable to all multimedia data, but given that the model is based on object–oriented principles, a presentation context can be subclassed to support medium specific state variables such as transformation matrices for graphics, or gain or volume for audio. Presentation contexts are hierarchical and inherit the state of a parent context. As illustrated in Figure 4, presentation contexts exist at multiple levels in the model. A track inherits the presentation context from a channel; likewise, a channel inherits the presentation context from the sequence.

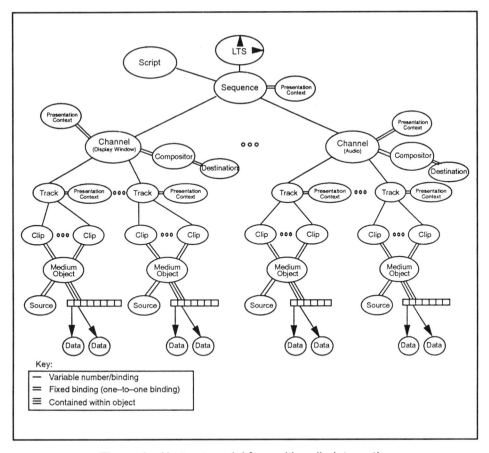

Figure 4: Abstract model for multimedia integration.

A *medium* is an abstract representation of a physical medium such as a video segment or an audio stream. A medium essentially facilitates access to data and provides mechanisms to convert between sample rates that are different from the frame rate of a sequence presentation (this is described in more detail below).

A *compositor* is a mixer of multimedia data. It performs frame–level composition operations. Composition operations could include image composition as defined by Porter and Duff [7] or texture mapping [8,9,10]. These operations are specified by the presentation context.

A *clip* is a cut from a medium's data stream. A clip defines a sequential segment within a medium object's continuous data steam and is specified by a "cut–in" or start frame, and a "cut–out" or end frame. A series of clips effectively takes a set of non–sequential segments of the medium and sequentially serializes them into a new continuous data stream.

A *track* defines a path for media to follow from the source to the destination and specifies how and when to follow that path. To facilitate this, a track essentially serializes a set of clips from a medium and directs it to an I/O channel at the appropriate time. A track has a start time that defines when the series of clips are directed to the destination. This timing mechanism is described in more detail in the following section on timing and synchronization. A track also has a presentation context associated with it. This presentation context defines how the medium should be composed and presented to the destination. This presentation context can vary over time, thus allowing for such effects as fade–in or fade–out. Though not depicted in Figure 4, tracks can be hierarchical. Hierarchical tracks facilitate the specification of inter-media relationships. Example intermedia relationships include such effects as rotoscopy or texture mapping using a video stream as the texture. (Note that while it is possible to specify this operation, few systems can support this type of operation in real time).

A *channel* is a logical construct that integrates a group of media into one logical I/O stream such as left audio channel (left ear) and right audio channel (right ear). To facilitate this, a channel bundles together a group of tracks that contain a series of clips from a medium object. A channel integrates and synchronizes the composition and presentation of each of the tracks to a destination via the compositor. A channel also has a presentation context associated with it. This presentation context specifies state variables that apply across all tracks associated with the channel. An example for an audio channel is a master channel volume.

The *logical time system (LTS) clock* is the basic synchronization mechanism for the MuX. It provides a logical abstraction of a clock that "ticks" at a constant rate with a predefined interval between ticks. These ticks are used as the primary synchronization mechanism. The basic operations supported by an LTS clock include start, stop, pause, reset, move time, and set time. The duration of an LTS clock may be fixed or endless (for real–time media). If the duration is fixed, an LTS clock can also move backwards in time, thus allowing a sequence to be presented backwards. The LTS clock is discussed in more detail in the next section.

A *sequence* is the primary element of the media integration model. It provides the basis for media integration and synchronization. A sequence is the glue that holds the multimedia presentation together. A sequence interfaces between an LTS clock and channels associated with the sequence. A sequence provides synchronization mechanisms for each channel associated with the sequence. A sequence manages time in a presentation, including setting the duration and speed of a presentation, and playing, stopping, pausing, recording, fast forwarding, and rewinding a presentation. A sequence also facilitates and controls the access of media data via the channels. A sequence also contains a presentation context. The state variables contained in its presentation context are general and apply to the presentation as a whole. Examples include mapping and speed.

An example of a multimedia sequence is given in Figure 5. This example illustrates several important concepts. First, there is the notion of parallel channels, in this case three: display, left audio, and right audio. Second, the sequence may specify multiple audio tracks that can be selected according to the user's preference (e.g., the Korean tracks may be played for native Koreans, whereas the English track can be selected for native English speakers). This capability is controlled via the presentation contexts.

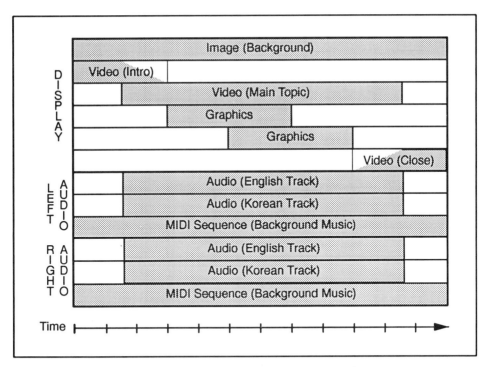

Figure 5: Multimedia sequence example.

A *script* is a container for sequences. It also contains references to media sources and destinations. A script provides the mechanisms to dynamically define sequences that integrate media from a set of sources and presents or stores them to or in a destination. Currently, the mechanism for defining sequences is loading scripts that are based on a scripting language. These scripting capabilities are described in further detail in a later section.

Timing and Synchronization

As described in the previous section, a sequence is the central element for providing synchronization in a presentation. It interfaces between the timing mechanisms and the media integration mechanisms. The timing and synchronization mechanisms in the MuX server are based on the logical time system (LTS). The logical time system is a relative time system and consists of two major components: one, a start time, and two, an inner tick time where the inner tick time is the time between ticks on the clock and is specified in a real–time measure, such as milliseconds. Given these two quantities, it is possible to transform between logical time and real time (i.e., absolute time) interchangeably. An advantage of the logical time system is that time can be scaled simply by scaling the inner tick time. Since it is easier to work with a logical time system, we have adopted it for the MuX server.

Another important aspect of the LTS is that it is possible to have different time domains for different elements. This allows significant flexibility. We utilized this aspect to define the timing mechanisms for the MuX server based on the media integration concepts described in the previous section, namely sequences, channels, tracks, clips, and the underlying media. The timing relationship between each of these components is illustrated in Figure 6. The sequence time domain is the master time domain. Channels inherit the time domain from the sequence. A track has a separate time domain that is entered by translating from the channel domain using the track start time. To get from the track domain to the medium time domain, both a translation and a scale must be performed. The translation is based on the cut–in time of the appropriate clip, and the scaling factor is a ratio of the established frame interval (i.e., the inner tick time of the master LTS) and the frame interval of the underlying medium. The scaling factor eliminates the problem of media with different frame rates. Note also that by tying each of the channels to the master LTS time, synchronization between tracks can be achieved by simply specifying the track start time (in the sequence master LTS time domain) appropriately.

Synchronization is done on a frame basis. In the MuX, a frame is considered to be a slice of time, from time t_i to t_i+Dt, where Dt is the interframe time. Associated with each frame duration is a quantity of data. Within each frame there may be one or many samples of data that are dependent upon the physical medium.

The presentation of a sequence is initiated by retrieving and composing the first frame of data. Then upon receiving each time "tick" from the LTS clock, the sequence instructs the associated channels to present the composed frame. After presenting the frame, the data for

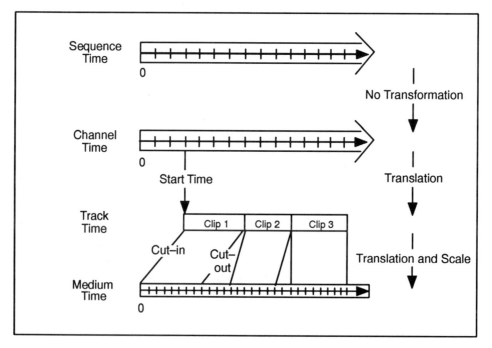

Figure 6: Timing relationship between MuX components.

the next frame is read and the frame is composed. This process is similar to double buffering. The end result of this process is fine–grained synchronization.

Adjustable speed is supported, by first establishing the master frame rate or an interframe time. When the master frame rate is established, the mapping from the LTS time domain to the intrinsic time domain of the medium is calculated and the quantity of data associated with the specified frame rate is also determined. Once the frame rate and frame data have been established, the master interframe time can be varied, thus changing the speed of the presentation. Note, however, that when each frame is presented all of the data are presented. In the case of audio, this may mean that data samples are expanded or subsampled to fill the frame duration.

Network–Transparent Access to Multimedia Data

As noted in the concepts sections, the MuX server takes complete control of a presentation once a sequence has been defined. This includes opening up access to sources and destinations and controlling the transfer of data from a source to the MuX. This a necessary aspect of achieving fine–grained synchronization. This model differs from ACME where a client must specify the connection and instruct the data originating process to begin flow of data.

To facilitate this model for the server, network–transparent access to multimedia data is needed. To achieve this, our goal is to provide a uniform interface to the various different sources of multimedia data. The sources of multimedia data include the following:

- A file or database (DB) that is accessed through the UNIX file system. This may include files that are accessed over the network via NFS or another network file system.

- A remote "generator" process that may be another MuX server (an example generator process may interface with physical devices on another machine such as a video camera or video deck, or a generator process may be a multimedia database process).

- A physical device on the local machine such as a video camera or a microphone.

Additionally, our goal is to provide a uniform interface to the various different destinations of multimedia data. The destinations of data include the following:

- A file or DB that is accessed through the UNIX file system. This may include files that are accessed over the network via NFS or another network file system.

- A remote process that may be another MuX server.

- A physical device on the local machine. It includes an audio digital to analog converter (DAC) device of a local SPARCstation, providing an interface to the audio. The audio DAC may be a mono channel such as the speaker or headphones on the SPARCstation, or may be a left channel or right channel of a high–fidelity sound system.

To provide more flexibility for the MuX and remote processes, our goal is to support both a "push" and a "pull" model for sources and destinations. In the "push" model a source sends data to the client of the source at a periodic rate. To support the "push" model for a device, the source must have an LTS clock associated with it. Upon each tick of the LTS clock, the source sends data to the client. In the "pull" model, a client reads from the source at a rate convenience for the client.

The implications of the network–transparent access to data are far reaching. For access to data across the network, the MuX essentially becomes a client to the originating source. Since it is quite likely that the process representing the source will also be a server (possibly another MuX server), this clearly indicates the need to deviate from our standard client–server model and adopt a client–server peer–peer model. This model is illustrated in Figure 7. Support for this environment would dramatically simplify applications.

Furthermore, by adopting a network–transparent data access, a MuX need not run on a machine that has any devices attached to it. In this light, a MuX server could be used as a back–end multimedia I/O processor.

The MuX server has been designed to meet the goal of network–transparent data access, though it has not been fully implemented. This work is discussed in more detail in the implementation status section.

Scripting Capabilities

In the video production model, AV systems provide users with the the necessary tools to help them compose presentations. Those systems, however, are special–purpose systems that have dedicated functions that are not accessible to an open desktop system. In addition, these

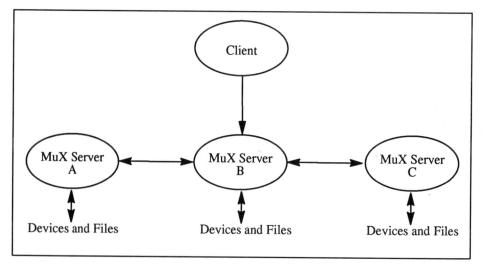

Figure 7: Client–server, peer–peer model.

systems generally are not interactively programmable (although parameters such as cut–in and cut–out points are adjustable, it is not possible to programmatically compose a sequence).

In contrast to special dedicated systems, multimedia computer systems should provide users programmable ways to specify information sources such as video camera, microphone, networks, or files, and more importantly, to compose sequences that build time–based presentations.

One of the primary objectives of the MuX server is to provide media integration capabilities. For this purpose, we have defined an ASCII–based high–level script language, MuXScript, to allow applications or users to specify how media should be integrated and presented. The MuXScript language expresses the media integration concepts of the MuX. Thus, the scripting language allows users to define source references, destination references, and sequences based on the concepts of channels, tracks, and clips described above.

A MuXScript file contains three parts: source definition, destination definition, and sequence definition. The source definition specifies which sources are going to be used in the sequence. The destination definition specifies where the mixed multimedia output should be sent. The sequence definition section specifies how sources should be arranged in both time and space, mixed, and presented to the output destinations. Both sources and destinations are logically named for use in defining sequences. Separating the script file into these three sections allows the named source and destination definitions to be used multiple times in the sequence definition. Sequence definitions are also given a logical name so they can be reference by an application.

A script can be defined by auxiliary applications and loaded into the MuX, or can be defined by a MuX client interactively. Though the MuX server provides support for interactive definition of scripts, the current client–server interface does not support these interactions.

Appendix A contains a description of the MuXScript language grammar and Appendix B provides an example of a script file.

Client–Server Interface

Currently, the client–server interface focuses on presentation control of a sequence, including script control, sequence control, and context control. The interface also provides presentation feedback. The protocol allows the client to load and unload scripts; play, stop, pause, and rewind sequences; and control the presentation attributes such as volume and speed.

In addition, the MuX interface allows an application to define an X window as a multimedia window. When an X window is defined as a multimedia window, the MuX takes control of the display region occupied by the window. However, since the MuX server is co–existent to the X server, this does impose limitations on what can be done with the multimedia window because the window hierarchy is not known by the MuX server. As a result, multimedia windows must be forced to the front. This is a significant drawback of the co–existent server architecture, but one that would be rectified by merging the two servers. Once a multimedia window has been defined, sequences can be assigned to be presented in the multimedia window.

The client–server interface also allows a client to instruct a MuX server to load and eject script files. Once the script has been loaded, an application can query the server to find out the logical names of the sequences defined in the script file. Once a script is loaded, the interface supports standard operations such as play, stop, pause, and rewind a sequence. MuX also provides an interface for setting presentation context parameters, such as speed and volume.

The MuX also provides an interface for receiving feedback from the server. Currently, presentation feedback consists of periodic progress updates as to where the presentation is with respect to the master LTS clock. The MuX interface provides two mechanisms for receiving presentation feedback from the MuX: notification and polling. For notification, a callback function is registered with the MuX specifying the tick interval between callbacks. With the polling mechanism, feedback events are queued up in an event queue. Either the notification or the event–based interface could be used to implement time–based actions by clients to be synchronized with sequence presentations.

Related Work

ACME [4], a multimedia I/O server developed at the University of California at Berkeley, is a set of abstractions intended to extend a network window system to use continuous media such as video and audio. Most continuous media is not handled by the actual window system, but rather by a separate ACME kernel that is implemented as another thread or process. In the ACME design, continuous media is not mixed with graphics or window requests. This work is very similar to our MuX work; there are differences in data access control, the model for media integration, and scripting capabilities.

DEC and MIT have developed an audio server for the integration of audio and telephony into a graphics workstation environment [11]. Their server allows shared access to audio hardware; provides synchronization primitives and presents a device–independent abstraction to the application programmer.

In addition to research projects, there are a couple of noteworthy commercial products that relate to the MuX. MacroMind Director (MacroMind, Inc.) is an application that runs on Macintosh computers that allows a user to create and display animated multimedia presentations [5]. Although it is an example of a successful multimedia animation and presentation tool, it is an application only and therefore does not support general multimedia input and output requirements.

QuickTime* is a product from Apple Computer, Inc. that is an extension to the System 7 operating system. It supports the integration of time–based data into mainstream Macintosh applications [6] and addresses many of the problems associated with the presentation of prerecorded time–based media. QuickTime is based on a video production model similar to that employed by the MuX; however, the QuickTime media integration model is based on the abstract concept of a movie rather than the more general concept of a sequence, and MuX has an additional abstraction of a channel. Though the MuX model is less concrete, it does allow

---

*At the time of this publication QuickTime is an announced, but not yet released product.

for diverse multimedia I/O environments. In addition, QuickTime does not integrate with distributed window systems or provide a model for integrating media input from networked data sources.

Implementation Status and Future Research Directions

At the time of this publication a prototype MuX server has been implemented in C on the Sun SPARCstation running the SunOS 4.1, and supports both audio and video. The sequences are defined using the script language described in Appendix A. Network transparency through access to remote devices and files has not been fully implemented at this point. Although a client–server interface has been implemented, it is a subset of that defined in the design section. A client is able to perform a limited number of operations, and the sequence information is loaded statically from a script file. Interactive control by the client has not been fully implemented in the MuX library interface, but hooks exist in the server to support these capabilities when the libraries are completed. Additionally the X–MuX protocol has not yet been implemented, instead the MuX server is passed information about window properties from the client which is also a client of the X server.

We have implemented enough of the functionality of the server to understand it's performance parameters and constraints given the architecture, operating system scheduler and the IPC mechanisms utilized in our current implementation. As anticipated, we are able to achieve real–time or near real–time performance for small (256x256 pixels) full motion video clips combined with multiple mixed audio streams. We have been successful in providing synchronization mechanisms that adapt well in a non–real–time OS and within an environment that does not provide preemptive scheduling. In order to provide better synchronization, a modified kernel is needed.

We realized at the onset of this project the importance of providing a single unified multimedia user interface. However, because of the disparities between the objectives of MuX and X, we adopted the approach of co–existent servers. In the future we plan to address how time–based and non–time based environments should be combined to provide an effective integrated interface that supports both types of media. At that stage we plan to merge the functionality of the X and MuX servers to provide a single unified multimedia user interface. Whether is is implemented as a single or multiple server will be defined at a later time.

In addition, we plan to extend the MuXScript language to support more interactive capabilities that are non–deterministic in nature. For example, adding a when statement to the language would allow us to play a sequence to a predefined location and then paused to await some action or event. When the event occurred, the sequence would continue to play. Or, if MuXScript supported a conditional statement, the MuX could decide to continue playing the script or play another script based on the event received. The future extensions to the language will continue to focus on the time aspects of media integration and interaction.

It is important to note that not all of the aspects of network–transparent access to multimedia data have been fully implemented at the time of this publication, though they are under development. More specifically, not all of the network components have been integrated into the network–transparent data access model, and larger system–wide issues such as standard protocols and delay need to be addressed. However, SRI has conducted research in this area and has developed IPC software to support multimedia communications. In the future, we plan to integrate this software into the MuX server.

Conclusions

MuX is a multimedia I/O server that provides support for time–based media. It is based on several important concepts, namely those of a programmable media multiplexer and co–existence with the X window system. These concepts are embodied in the media integration and synchronization model, the scripting capabilities, and the notion of network–transparent access to multimedia data.

The MuX design fulfills several important goals. It provides support for fine–grained synchronization for multiple, parallel I/O channels through its timing and synchronization mechanism. It is based on a media integration that supports specification of time space and intermedia relationships and a scripting language that allows expression of the contextual relationships among related pieces of multimedia information to be programmable. These features facilitate coherent presentation of multimedia information.

Currently, the MuX does not provide a single multimedia interface, we are planning on addressing this issue in future research. In addition, although multimedia presentation editing is supported in a limited fashion, we also plan to improve these capabilities in the future.

As a final note, it is important to highlight that the MuX server is only one component in a larger system. This larger system consists of a presentation manager, the client–side API, and a communications toolkit that provides support for sources and destinations. Discussion of these components is beyond the scope of this paper.

Acknowledgements

This work was conducted with the cooperation and support of the Electronics and Telecommunications Research Institute, Korea who is sponsoring the "Integrated Multimedia User Interface for Intelligent Computing" project. The authors wish to acknowledge the efforts of other SRI staff who contributed to the ETRI project. Ruth Lang and Martin Fong were instrumental in developing the MuX and provided valuable feedback when preparing this paper. Jose Garcia–Luna and Earl Craighill contributed substantially to the development of the project's vision. Len Schlegel was instrumental in developing the event management and IPC software upon which the MuX system is built.

References

1. Scheifler, R.W., and J. Gettys, "The X Window System," *ACM Transactions on Graphics*, Vol. 5, No. 2, April 1986, pp. 79–109.

2. Carver, D., *X Video Extension Protocol Description, Version 2*, Digital Equipment Corporation, 1991.

3. Brunhoff, T, *MVEX: Minimal Video Extension to X, Version 6.0*, Tektronix, Inc., 1991.

4. Homsy, G., R. Govindan, and D.P. Anderson, "Implementation Issues for a Network Continuous–Media I/O Server," TR No. UCB/CSD90/597, Computer Science Division, EECS Department, University of California at Berkeley, September 1990.

5. MacroMind Inc., *MacroMind Version 2.0 Product Brochure*, MacroMind Inc., San Francisco, CA, 1990.

6. Poole, L., "QuickTime in Motion," *MacWorld*, pp. 154–159 (September 1991).

7. Porter, T., T. Duff, "Compositing Digital Images," *Computer Graphics*, Vol. 18, No. 3, July 1984.

8. Catmull, E.E., "A Subdivision Algorithm for Computer Display of Curved Surfaces," Ph.D. dissertation, University of Utah, Salt Lake City, UT, 1974.

9. Catmull, E., and A.R. Smith, "3–D Transformation of Images in Scan Line Order," *Computer Graphics*, Vol. 14, No. 3, July 1980.

10. Blinn, J.F., and M.E. Newell, "Texture and Reflection in Computer Generated Images," *Communications of the ACM*, Vol. 19, No. 10, pp. 542–547, October 1979.

11. Angebranndt, S., R. Hyde, D.H. Luong, N. Siravara, and C. Schmandt, "Integrating Audio and Telephony in a Distributed Workstation Environment," in *USENIX–Summer'91*, pp. 419–435, Nashville, TN, 10–14 June 1991.

Author Information

Earl Rennison is a software engineer at SRI and is the project leader for the Integrated Multimedia User Interface for Intelligent Computing project. His areas of interest include applied research and development in the following areas: computer graphics systems; multimedia information systems; advanced man–machine interfaces; object–oriented programming; and systems analysis, design, and optimization.

Rusti Baker is a software engineer at SRI working on the Integrated Multimedia User Interface for Intelligent Computing project. Her areas of interest include distributed systems and protocols; simulation, and analytic performance evaluation; high–performance graphics, and modeling tools; multimedia user interfaces; distributed, interactive applications and environments.

Doohyun David Kim is an International Fellow at SRI International visiting from ETRI. He is working on the Integrated Multimedia User Interface for Intelligent Computing project. His areas of interest include interactive multimedia environments, multimedia operating systems, and application of neural networks for multimedia user interfaces.

Young–Hwan Lim is a section manager at ETRI. He is the ETRI program director for the Integrated Multimedia User Interface for Intelligent Computing project.

Appendix A: MuXScript Language Grammar

\<script\> ::=	\<source-list\>
	\<destination-list\>
	[\<timedomain-statement\>]
	\<sequence-list\>
\<at-statement-list\> ::=	\<at-statement\>
	[\<at-statement-list\>]
\<channel-list\> ::=	\<channel\>
	[\<channel-list\>]
\<clip-list\> ::=	\<track\>
	[\<track-list\>]
\<destination-list\> ::=	\<destination\>
	[\<destination-list\>]
\<during-statement-list\> ::=	\<during-statement\>
	[\<during-statement-list\>]
\<source-list\> ::=	\<source\>
	[\<source-list\>]
\<sequence-list\> ::=	\<sequence\>
	[\<sequence-list\>]
\<set-statement-list\> ::=	\<set-statement\>
	[\<set-statement-list\>]
\<track-list\> ::=	\<track\>
	[\<track-list\>]
\<channel\> ::=	(CHANNEL \<destination name\> [\<set-statement-list\>]
	[\<at-statement-list\>] [\<during-statement-list\>]
	\<track-list\>)
\<clip\> ::=	(CLIP \<time\> \<time\>)
\<destination\> ::=	(DESTINATION \<destination name\> \<medium type\> \<io type\>
	\<format\> \<physical name\>[\<port\>])
\<sequence\> ::=	(SEQUENCE \<name\> [\<set-statement-list\>] [\<at-statement-list\>]
	[\<during-statement-list\>] \<channel-list\>)
\<source\> ::=	(SOURCE \<source name\> \<medium type\> \<io type\> \<format\>
	\<physical name\> [\<port\>])
\<track\> ::=	(TRACK \<source name\> [\<set-statement-list\>]
	[\<at-statement-list\>] [\<during-statement-list\>]
	\<clip-list\>)
\<at-statement\> ::=	(AT \<time\> \<set-statement\> | \<changeby-statement\>)
\<changeby-statement\> ::=	(CHANGEBY \<value-pair\>)
\<during-statement\> ::=	(DURING \<time\> TO \<time\> [STEP \<time\>] \<changeby-statement\>)
\<set-statement\> ::=	(SET \<value-pair\>)
\<timedomain-statement\> ::=	(TIMEDOMAIN \<time domain\>)
\<value-pair\> ::=	\<value type\> \<value\>
\<destination name\> ::=	\<string\>
\<device name\> ::=	\<string\>
\<file name\> ::=	\<string\>
\<host name\> ::=	\<string\>
\<io type\> ::=	DEVICE | FILE | NETWORK
\<logical time\> ::=	\<integer\>
\<source name\> ::=	\<string\>
\<physical name\> ::=	\<device name\> | \<file name\> | \<host name\>
\<port\> ::=	\<integer\>
\<real time\> ::=	\<integer\>:\<integer\>:\<integer\>[.\<integer\>]
\<time domain\> ::=	LOGICAL | REAL
\<time\> ::=	\<logical time\> | \<real time\>
\<value\> ::=	\<integer\> | \<real\> | \<string\>

Appendix B: Example MuXScript

(TIMEDOMAIN LOGICAL)

(SOURCE background AUDIO FILE AU_ALAW /data/audio/background.au 0)
(SOURCE lead_au AUDIO FILE AU_ALAW /data/audio/intro.au 0)
(SOURCE talk_au AUDIO FILE AU_ALAW /data/audio/talk.au 0)

(SOURCE backdrop IMAGE FILE IM_XWD /data/images/backdrop.xwd 0)

(SOURCE lead_vd VIDEO FILE VD_DVI /data/video/lead.dvi 0)
(SOURCE talk_vd VIDEO FILE VD_DVI /data/video/lead.dvi 0)

(DESTINATION disp_dev VIDEO DEVICE ALAW /dev/audio 0)
(DESTINATION au_dev AUDIO DEVICE ALAW /dev/audio 0)

(SEQUENCE a_presentation
            (SET FRAMERATE 25)
            (SET DURATION 600)
            (SET SPEED 1.0)
            (CHANNEL au_dev
                    (TRACK lead_au
                            (SET STARTTIME 0)
                            (DURING 100 TO 120 (CHANGEBY VOLUME –0.05))
                            (CLIP 0 120)
)
                    (TRACK background
                            (SET STARTTIME 100)
                            (SET VOLUME 0.0)
                            (DURING 0 TO 20 (CHANGEBY VOLUME 0.01))
                            (DURING 480 TO 500 (CHANGEBY VOLUME –0.01))
                            (CLIP 0 500)
)
                    (TRACK talk
                            (SET STARTTIME 120)
                            (CLIP 0 240)
                            (CLIP 500 620)
                            (CLIP 1000 1140)
)
                    (TRACK lead_au
                            (SET STARTTIME 480)
                            (DURING 0 TO 20 (CHANGEBY VOLUME 0.05))
                            (CLIP 0 120)
)
)
            (CHANNEL disp_dev
                    (TRACK lead_vd
                            (SET STARTTIME 0)
                            (CLIP 0 120)
)
                    (TRACK backdrop
                            (SET STARTTIME 0)
                            (SET ENDTIME 600)
)
                    (TRACK talk
                            (SET STARTTIME 120)
                            (CLIP 0 240)
                            (CLIP 500 620)
                            (CLIP 1000 1140)
)
                    (TRACK lead_vd
                            (SET STARTTIME 480)
                            (CLIP 0 120)
)
)
)

How to Publish in The X Resource

There are seven steps that normally occur in the process of publishing in the X Resource. Note that this applies only to the three regular issues each year—the MIT X Consortium Technical Conference Proceedings issue is prepared differently.

Step One: Select an Appropriate Topic
Step Two: Send Proposal
Step Three: Write
Step Four: Submit First Draft
Step Five: Rewrite Based on Review Comments
Step Six: Submit Final Draft
Step Seven: Compensation

These steps are described in detail in the next few pages.

One: Select an Appropriate Topic

We are interested in a wide range of topics, but we may not publish everything sent to us. Unlike many journals, which serve as organs of record for academic research, this is a journal for people who are writing software. The key characteristics of an article topic we are likely to accept include:

- will it be of practical use to a significant number of people in the X community? The answer should be yes.

- has it already been covered elsewhere with wide readership (such as in books)? The answer should be no.

We seek articles that help people understand X better and write better X software. The journal tends to concentrate on the lesser known programming tools, techniques, and concepts that haven't received coverage in books. For example, we will publish papers about Motif, but they will not cover the same aspects of Motif that have been covered in the many books available. We will also cover useful free software tools, which may be changing too fast to be covered in any book. The journal will also cover commercial programming products, but will demand fairness and completeness and cannot accept articles that sound like marketing literature.

The journal focuses on information for programmers, but this includes coverage of administration and advanced use of the X Window System. Most X programmers use X, and they often administer their own workstation. Furthermore, they need to understand administration issues in order to understand the environment in which their application will be installed. Similarly, they need to know about the user environment in which their application will operate.

Contributions to the journal might fall into one or more of the following categories:

- Descriptions of new features in X releases and how to use them.

- Reviews and guides to programming with freely available and commercial software development tools and free-software applications.

- Descriptions of how to use existing X features efficiently.

- Experiences and strategies for application software development or porting.

- System administration of X and X terminals.

- User configuration and customization of X applications.

- Illumination of difficult concepts, or of simple concepts that are hidden behind details.

- Server implementation details that impact application writing.

- Interoperability.

Submissions are not limited to traditional papers in length or content. We make a strong effort to publish documentation (tutorial and reference material) in every issue; this can be of virtually any length. This documentation should be about software tools that have not received coverage in books, and whose supplied documentation is poor or nonexistent. In some cases some version of this documentation may already be available on the network, but has never been in print. We pay for documentation in accordance with its length and quality, usually more than for papers.

TWO: SEND PROPOSAL

Potential contributors should submit (by email if possible) a brief proposal and/or outline before writing a complete paper. This allows the editor to find out what you have in mind, guide you in the right direction, make plans for related articles, and avoid duplication of effort.

Complete papers that arrive uninvited will be considered, but the author takes an unnecessary risk.

The editor's email address is *adrian@ora.com* or *uunet!ora!adrian.*

THREE: WRITE

Once your proposal has been accepted, the editor will send you the deadline for the next issue, and send you the author's guidelines (similar to this document), and the publishing agreement. The publishing agreement must be signed and returned when you submit your paper for consideration.

You should select a word processor or formatter that can generate the formats required for drafts and final copy. For drafts, we prefer email in PostScript plus a troff -ms or Ascii format. For final manuscript formats, you should contact the editor as we are still experimenting with different production techniques.

For the January MIT X Conference issue, we require camera-ready copy—get a separate document from us that specifies the required appearance.

Many authors ask what writing style is preferred, academic or informal. Either is OK, although we prefer informal writing. First person writing (using I or we) is acceptable and even preferred since it often leads to less passive writing.

Be sure to use figures, tables, and examples wherever they help. Each should have a number, and should be referenced by number in the text. For example, use "As shown in Table 1, . . ." not "As shown in the table above . . .".

The journal is normally black and white. Unless it is impossible to understand the point being made in the paper without the use of color, we won't print color plates.

Probably the most important thing to keep in mind is that the reader must be able to use the information you are giving them in some practical way. Write as if you were explaining the material to someone you know, and give enough detail so that someone can actually do something with the information. If you are writing about your experiences in a particular project, concentrate on what is generally applicable about that experience.

The audience for the journal should be assumed to be primarily programmers, most of them C programmers, and most of whom understand the basic concepts of X. If your article requires any other expertise or knowledge, be sure to say that early in the article, or better, provide an introduction that gives readers the required knowledge. Since most of the basic concepts of X have been covered in many books, and most readers know them, there is no need to rehash this material in articles. For example, there is no need to say "X is a device-independent, network-based window system."

One note on terminology. Don't use the term "user" to refer to a programmer, even if the programmer uses the item in question. A "user" in this journal is an end user—the person who will use an application. A "programmer" is the person who writes applications using a software tool. When the application is question is also a software tool, use the term programmer.

Since this is a software journal, the handling of code is crucial. As a general rule, authors should excerpt useful sections of code instead of including the entire source; comments can describe the code not shown. Pages and pages of continuous code are discouraged. When large sections of code are necessary, they should be heavily commented, and should be broken up into sections and described piece by piece.

Whenever possible and with the author's approval, the journal would like to arrange to place the code described in the manuscript on the network for public ftp and uucp access. This reduces the need to print the entire code in the journal.

There is no limit on length of manuscripts, although space should not be wasted.

Footnotes should be kept to a minimum. Footnotes that acknowledge trademarks (such as UNIX) are not necessary, because the journal includes a generic acknowledgement on the copyright page. Instead, all trademarks should be in caps or initial caps as the trademark is claimed by its owner.

FOUR: SUBMIT FIRST DRAFT

When your paper is complete, submit it to the editor. This is done preferably by email (PostScript, plus Ascii or troff -ms) or on paper. The editor will read the paper, and will decide whether it is ready to send to the editorial advisory board for review. You may be asked to make some changes based on comments by the editor.

Once you have cleared this hurdle, the paper is sent out to several members of the editorial advisory board. These people will read and comment on your paper, and may make suggestions for changes. At the very least they will recommend whether the paper should be published as is, with changes, or not at all. In most cases the comments will be forwarded to the author for revision of the manuscript.

The criteria used to determine publication will be those described above in Section 1 (topic) and Section 3 (writing).

FIVE: REWRITE BASED ON REVIEW COMMENTS

The review period is usually the two weeks after the deadline you were given for submitting your first draft. In many cases you will be asked to make changes on short notice toward the end of this period. This tight schedule is necessary in order to publish the journal while the information is still timely.

SIX: SUBMIT FINAL MANUSCRIPT

Final manuscripts must be submitted in both electronic and hardcopy form (one copy) whenever possible. However, you should contact the editor for current requirements for format of final electronic submissions.

At present, most graphics are being redone by our in-house graphics staff. This imparts a consistent appearance to all the figures in the journal.

However, any unique or difficult-to-reproduce graphics should be submitted in Encapsulated PostScript (EPS) format.

These files can be emailed or (preferably) submitted on a Macintosh diskette (carefully labeled). (Avoid making the figures with Cricket Draw, since it declares an incorrect bounding box.) Manuscripts should clearly reference each figure, table, and example by number and each figure, table, and example should have a matching number.

The title of the paper, the name, affiliation, address, phone number, and email address of the author, a ~100 word abstract should appear at the beginning of the manuscript. The abstract should not be a mere duplication of the introduction or conclusion of the article. Please also send a short (< 50) word biography which will appear as a footnote on the abstract page.

Intext references should refer to a numbered list at the end of the submission.

Please address manuscripts, correspondence, and any questions to:

The X Resource
c/o Adrian Nye
4466 West Pine Blvd. 20-G
St. Louis MO 63108
(314) 531-1231
adrian@ora.com or *uunet!ora!adrian*

SEVEN: COMPENSATION

Authors of accepted papers will be sent a small honorarium, between $100 and $1,000, depending on the length and quality of the submission. Documentation is eligible for higher rates. The amount will be decided after the final draft of the paper has been received and after the crush of preparing the issue for typesetting is over. Normally this will be around the date of publication.

The authors will also receive five free copies of the journal issue containing their article.

YES, send me a subscription to *The X Resource*. I understand that I will receive timely, in-depth, practical articles and documentation. (If I'm not completely satisfied, I can cancel my subscription at any time.)

❏ $65 Quarterly issues. *(Extra shipping for foreign orders: Canada/Mexico—$5; Europe/Africa—$25; Asia/Australia—$30. All foreign shipping by air.)*

❏ $90 Quarterly issues PLUS supplements: Public Review Specifications for proposed X Consortium standards and introductory explanations of the issues involved. *(Extra shipping for foreign orders: Canada/Mexico—$10; Europe/Africa—$50; Asia/Australia—$60. All foreign shipping by air.)*

Note: Foreign orders must be by credit card or in U.S. dollars drawn on a U.S. bank.
To subscribe, call (800) 338-6887 (US/Canada) or mail in this card.

NAME

ADDRESS

CITY/STATE/ZIP

COUNTRY
BILL TO MY CREDIT CARD:

❏ MASTERCARD   ❏ VISA   ❏ AMERICAN EXPRESS

ACCT. #   EXP. DATE

NAME AS IT APPEARS ON CARD

SIGNATURE

J21R

YES, send me a subscription to *The X Resource*. I understand that I will receive timely, in-depth, practical articles and documentation. (If I'm not completely satisfied, I can cancel my subscription at any time.)

❏ $65 Quarterly issues. *(Extra shipping for foreign orders: Canada/Mexico—$5; Europe/Africa—$25; Asia/Australia—$30. All foreign shipping by air.)*

❏ $90 Quarterly issues PLUS supplements: Public Review Specifications for proposed X Consortium standards and introductory explanations of the issues involved. *(Extra shipping for foreign orders: Canada/Mexico—$10; Europe/Africa—$50; Asia/Australia—$60. All foreign shipping by air.)*

Note: Foreign orders must be by credit card or in U.S. dollars drawn on a U.S. bank.
To subscribe, call (800) 338-6887 (US/Canada) or mail in this card.

NAME

ADDRESS

CITY/STATE/ZIP

COUNTRY
BILL TO MY CREDIT CARD:

❏ MASTERCARD   ❏ VISA   ❏ AMERICAN EXPRESS

ACCT. #   EXP. DATE

NAME AS IT APPEARS ON CARD

SIGNATURE

J21R

NAME _____

COMPANY_____

ADDRESS_____

CITY_____ STATE_____ ZIP _____

BUSINESS REPLY MAIL

FIRST CLASS MAIL PERMIT NO. 80 SEBASTOPOL, CA

POSTAGE WILL BE PAID BY ADDRESSEE

O'Reilly & Associates, Inc.

103 Morris Street
Sebastopol, CA 95472-9902

IIıIıııIıIıIıIıIIııIıIıIıIIIıIıIıIııIIııııIıIıııIII

NAME _____

COMPANY_____

ADDRESS_____

CITY_____ STATE_____ ZIP _____

BUSINESS REPLY MAIL

FIRST CLASS MAIL PERMIT NO. 80 SEBASTOPOL, CA

POSTAGE WILL BE PAID BY ADDRESSEE

O'Reilly & Associates, Inc.

103 Morris Street
Sebastopol, CA 95472-9902

IIıIıııIıIıIıIıIIııIıIıIıIIIıIıIıIııIIııııIıIıııIII